LOUIS VAN GAAL

LOUIS VAN GAAL

THE BIOGRAPHY

MAARTEN MEIJER

EBURY
PRESS

1 3 5 7 9 10 8 6 4 2

This edition published 2014
First published in 2014 by Ebury Press, an imprint of Ebury Publishing
A Random House Group company

The Random House Group Limited Reg. No. 954009

Addresses for companies within the Random House Group can be found at
www.randomhouse.co.uk

A CIP catalogue record for this book is available from the British Library

The Random House Group Limited supports the Forest Stewardship
Council® (FSC®), the leading international forest-certification organisation.
Our books carrying the FSC label are printed on FSC®-certified paper. FSC is
the only forest-certification scheme supported by the leading environmental
organisations, including Greenpeace. Our paper procurement policy can be
found at www.randomhouse.co.uk/environment

Designed and typeset by seagulls.net

Printed and bound in Great Britain by Clays Ltd, St Ives PLC

HB ISBN 9780091960148
TPB ISBN 9780091960162

To buy books by your favourite authors and register for offers visit
www.randomhouse.co.uk

CONTENTS

MARCH TO THE BEAT OF A DIFFERENT DRUM

'I am a very consistent, honest and direct person.
And sometimes that strikes people as being hard.'

Louis van Gaal

The story goes that the Dutch club SC Telstar asked the KNVB (the Dutch FA) if its team could start playing on a blue pitch. The KNVB turned to FIFA to settle this bewildering question. Why blue, when everyone has been so happy, for so long, with playing on a green field? It would be unfair to lay the blame for causing such confusion in the sacred halls of the highest football authorities at the feet of Louis van Gaal, but one cannot help but wonder if, somehow, this persistent troublemaker is not the engine generating such unorthodox ideas. Van Gaal has been proven to champion innovations that others would hesitate to endorse. Although he agreed that nothing beats the smell of freshly sprayed grass pitches in the early morning sun, he has also embraced artificial turf: 'Then every ground in the world would be the same, which I prefer over the extreme differences in quality of grass pitches.' The current match schedule indeed leaves little time for a pitch to recover, which can be detrimental to the quality of the football on display. The development of artificial turf has reached its 'third generation' which constitutes a mix of synthetics and grass. Most professional teams have at least one training ground equipped with it.

After falling from the managerial heights of his golden 1990s, perhaps van Gaal, like all wise men, has realised that the highs and the lows in football are married to each other. His rehabilitation began at AZ Alkmaar and was completed at Bayern Munich in 2010. He is never one to rest on his laurels though, and football has long been on the alert for relentless van Gaal activity – be it verbal, tactical or ideological. Long before the start of the 2010 World Cup in South Africa, for example, van Gaal was already offering his forthright opinions: 'Little boys all over the world saw that one of the biggest stars of today's football cheated. [Thierry] Henry used his hands to shoot France to the World Cup. Over the last few decades, football as a sport is enormously on the rise. You can tell at all levels: the money stream, the number of viewers, the development of nations like Australia and the USA, which normally have lots of other sports to engage in. We need to embrace that global interest. The World Cup is the platform for all that is football. There's lots at stake, so I say, let's use technology where we can.'

On the eve of Bayern Munich's 2010 Champions League last-16 clash with Fiorentina, van Gaal suggested making radical changes to football rules. In an article entitled 'Van Gaal's Revolution' in the German magazine *Kicker*, the Bayern boss revealed his vision for the football of the future. He argued that deciding a game through penalties was too random: 'Penalties are a lottery. I'm for the gladiatorial game! If extra time is required following a draw, it should consist of two 15-minute periods, with each team losing a man every 5 minutes. After 95 minutes 10 would play against 10, after 100 minutes 9 on 9. From the 115th minute it would only be 6 on 6. Then only the best team would secure the win – and not just a single player through a penalty. If there is still no result after 120 minutes, a golden goal would decide the game.'

Computer technology, he argued, should decide important situations: 'The speed of the game has increased dramatically in the last 10 years, and viewing figures have grown. We must protect this interest. It is important that things are no longer decided by people. I want only technology to decide. Technology is impartial and objective.' Van Gaal would like an electronic chip to be placed in the ball to register whether or not it crossed the line. That FIFA earlier had rejected this technical innovation was an incomprehensible decision for van Gaal: 'It is nonsense that we don't use that.' He also proposed to abolish the throw-in: 'A throw-in should be a positive thing for a team, but with more than half of the throw-ins the ball ends up with the opponent. It's easy to defend a thrown ball. And it's a bit weird too. It's *foot*ball, so why would we suddenly use our hands for a throw-in? It has to be a "kick-in". That is better because then the defending team won't simply kick the ball out. With a "kick-in" we can change the game – it is also more attractive.'

Furthermore, according to van Gaal, a game needs two referees and a TV official instead of linesmen: 'The job of linesmen is to determine who gets the throw-in and when a player is offside. They also tend to put their flag up when they spot a foul, but 9 out of 10 times they wait for the referee's whistle until they start flagging. In today's football, offside is extremely hard to determine. The game is quicker now and to be able to view the moment a ball is played and to check at the same time where the forwards are is basically an impossibility. No one can see those moments at the same time.

We need two referees, as in basketball or ice hockey, one in each half, positioned diagonally. They would then be directly by the ball and be able to see the backs of the players. They would be joined by a third referee, who would watch the game on computer. They would all have those headsets with mikes. It doesn't matter where the computer expert would sit, whether at the edge of the field or up in the stands. I believe we should use as much technology as possible. Technology is always neutral and doesn't make the mistakes human beings make.'

Van Gaal realised that his ideas might be chucked straight into the rubbish bin at the FIFA offices: 'I know. That's a bunch of old men up there. They don't seem to care about the game; they care about keeping their jobs and offices and expense budgets. This is the biggest sport in the world and it's governed by the most conservative people, who are willing to gamble the future of our sport for personal reasons. But they can't stop me from thinking.' That is one thing that is certain. And neither can they stop van Gaal from speaking his mind.

Following his appointment as Dutch national coach in 2012, Louis van Gaal went on to select six different goalkeepers. Every game it seemed to be a toss-up who would be in goal. Maarten Stekelenburg, Tim Krul, Michel Vorm, Kenneth Vermeer, Jasper Cillessen and Jeroen Zoet were all selected, some of them making their international début, all of them failing at times. There was no clearly designated first keeper. The battle was open, as for most other positions. Under van Gaal the keeper lost his protected status in the team: even someone who is a reserve at his club – Cillessen – got playing time. Stekelenburg confessed that he had difficulty with van Gaal's management, after he had been dropped at the first qualification game. The Fulham keeper had for many years been the undisputed first choice. But suddenly he found himself on the bench, with Tim Krul preferred. Michel Vorm commented, 'No, I don't know of any example of a club or country where it works this way. In Spain, Iker Casillas always was first choice, even when he did not play at Real. This is a different, more unconventional approach.'

When selecting the goalie, van Gaal is assisted by Frans Hoek, his goalkeeper coach, who also worked with him at Barcelona. Hoek is known to be obsessed with his trade; he endlessly analyses and scrutinises new training methods. Hoek has a peculiar view on the art of stopping the ball, often at odds with the accepted norms. Van Gaal had met his match.

Van Gaal set about reducing the team's age, paying particular attention to the back four, where he favoured Daryl Janmaat, Stefan de Vrij, Bruno Martins Indi and Jetro Willems, with an average age of 21. He also handed PSV prodigy Adam Maher an international début. On the rationale for his selection procedure van Gaal said, 'When there isn't any stimulation by a young group that stirs things up, you get stuck. That is why I am always attracted to young players, who automatically provide such stimulation. The old players have seen it all. It kills a group if you have too much of that. I continually play players who are most fit; never those who are just big names. Names matter to the media, but not to me. The previous federation coach Louis van Gaal did give credit to, and had faith in, recognised players. That was something I shouldn't have done. Now I do exactly the opposite, and that works quite well. It also keeps everybody on their toes. At this time too, though, there are a few key players who – if they are playing with their club – in principle will always be selected. Because they perform at a level above the team's average.'

What then is the secret recipe behind good coaching? The masterful tactical plan? The exhilarating pre-game motivational speech? Journalists and coaches are often on common ground when it comes to looking for fitting explanations of team success or failure, ending up with vague concepts such as 'the conditions of the day' or a 'winner's feeling'. Absolute truth does not exist in football: that is one of the reasons that makes it so unpredictable and fascinating, though at the same time it also makes the coach's task a difficult one. It is hard to gauge the exact influence that the coach has on the course of a game, but somehow one coach does much better than another under similar circumstances. Though football is not an exact science, it is clear that some coaches understand what makes the game work and the players tick better than others. Louis van Gaal is one of these gifted individuals. Patrick Kluivert, match-winner against AC Milan in the Champions League final of 1995, has called van Gaal 'the most important man in my career' and a 'master at building a team'. Bayern captain Mark van Bommel insists he is 'a joy to work with'. The 32-year-old midfielder said, 'He's very clear, very demanding and always puts the team first. He has exactly what a coach needs to win trophies.'

At the same time, van Gaal has had his share of criticism. Simon Kuper once wrote, 'Everything about the Dutch coach is ungainly. He is flat-faced, pot-bellied, and brandishes a notebook at the unlikeliest moments. Being a football manager is mostly a presentational job, and van Gaal does that terribly.' If his reception in Germany was bad, in the Netherlands it was worse. The Dutch, after all, more or less feel that they invented the game of football, probably because, truth be told, they are quite good at it. And because they think they are the ultimate connoisseurs of the game, they also feel they are entitled to condemn anyone – player or coach – who does not match their precise expectations. Fortunately, van Gaal is sufficiently thick-skinned to hold on to his convictions. Indeed, it is very difficult to change his mind, and this is one of the coach's greatest strengths. To protect himself and his players from the distractions of the circus surrounding professional football, he aggressively guards his sphere of influence.

Getting close to Louis van Gaal is not an easy thing to do. Like others with a certain celebrity status, he is protective of his privacy. By any standard, van Gaal's hard shell and his toughness in the public arena are quite extraordinary. This has not endeared him to a lot of people, and, were it not for his quite extraordinary track record, his detractors might be more numerous. He reserves his warmth and kindness for those closest to him – his family, friends, and the players on his team. But even in those close quarters, van Gaal's standards arc cxacting. Hc is famous for running a tight ship – even his daughters have to address him using the polite form, in Dutch (*u* not *jij*), just as he was accustomed to addressing his own mother formally: 'That was normal in Holland then, and I expect it from my own daughters now. I am friends with my children and they love me, but I am from a different generation and they have to realise that. My youngest daughter has never had a problem addressing me formally. My older one did, but she is now 33 and is doing it herself. I think it's good. My players also address me formally of course.'

This hard exterior and tough-guy attitude do not make the biographer's task an easy one, and it really does take some digging to uncover the sources of van Gaal's energy, vision and leadership excellence. But it is worth the trouble because there really is more quality and depth here than meets the eye. Certainly, the Dutch often have difficulty with recognising or at least acknowledging *excellence*. The national psychology follows the local geography: in the classless Dutch ideal, everyone is on level ground, in emulation of the defining geographic feature of the country. A leader can never be more than a *primus inter pares*, a first among equals. On the one hand, such a philosophy guarantees fair opportunity to all and it helps to keep the haughty humbled. But it can also turn into an assurance that mediocrity will prevail because true leadership is not naturally allowed to make its full impact. In footballing terms, this can mean that teamwork may be sabotaged since the views of neither the coach nor of any one team member are regarded as inherently better than those of anyone else. The result is that the Dutch are good at chasing their most talented individuals abroad and at limiting or even undermining their own co-operative efforts, and not only on the football field.

Professional football, more so than the manufacturing and service industries, is a heavily internationalised enterprise. This is the result of the nature of the game. Whereas companies only take on their competitors indirectly in the free market, direct engagement of foreign competitors at international tournaments is part and parcel of the football business. This exposes both players and coaches to intensive interaction with foreign 'products' – footballing cultures, strategies and personalities. Hence, importing new styles and ways comes relatively more easily to football organisations than their corporate equivalents. A good example is the 'Dutch school' of football, better known as 'total football', which really is no longer Dutch but has become the collective property of the footballing fraternity. Within the football world, as elsewhere, reliance on convention and self-preservation persist only among the mediocre, and at their own peril.

Barcelona, Bayern Munich and Manchester United fans may resent and even reject the idea that outside talent was needed to upgrade their favourite team's performance. Still, there was room for improvement in Catalonia in 1997, in Bavaria in 2009 and in Manchester in 2014. Barcelona have had probably the world's best football team in recent years. Without wanting to take away anything from the accomplishments of the team Josep Guardiola created, it should be noted that over the two decades prior to his appointment the Catalan club was coached by Dutch managers for the best part of 17 years – Johan Cruyff, Louis van Gaal and Frank Rijkaard. These extraordinary coaches are all Ajax veterans in the total football tradition created by Rinus Michels (who also managed Barcelona back in the late 1970s). Barcelona has an unshakeable identity that runs right through the club, and it is one whose roots are firmly in the Ajax school of Dutch pressing football.

The ancient Greeks understood the power of sports; hence, they created the Olympic Games as a venue to help keep the appetites of the ambitious and often warring city-states of their loose federation in some sort of unified coexistence. The stated goal of the modern Olympic Movement is to 'contribute to building a peaceful and better world by educating youth through sport practised without discrimination of any kind and in the Olympic spirit, which requires mutual understanding with a spirit of friendship, solidarity and fair play'. The football governing body, FIFA, has similarly lofty aims: 'The world is a place rich in natural beauty and cultural diversity, but also one where many are still deprived of their basic rights. FIFA now has an even greater responsibility to reach out and touch the world, using football as a symbol of hope and integration. We see it as our mission to contribute towards building a better future for the world by using the power and popularity of football. This mission gives meaning and direction to each and every activity that FIFA is involved in – football being an integrated part of our society.' Van Gaal is a coach who understands both the relativity of football and its potential impact. Football is a game that has the power to change lives forever.

Most toddlers learn in nursery that 'charity begins at home'. Bringing 'friendship, solidarity, hope and integration' to the world requires imposing high standards of personal conduct, especially in the age of the Internet where every move of public figures is scrutinised and broadcast around the world within minutes. Today's celebrities are trendsetters and opinion-leaders, affecting the way of thinking and behaviour of millions of people the world over, particularly the young. This is why in this book Louis van Gaal's life and football career have been placed in a larger social and cultural context. He is a serious man – serious about football, about management, about life. He is a man others can learn from.

I wrote this book with the desire to make Louis van Gaal – the man, the football coach, the manager – more familiar to international football aficionados and to help them understand in what way he is a 'typically Dutch' coach and in what way he is not. But I also wrote it for people who ordinarily do not pay much attention to 'the beautiful game', but nevertheless are curious why this tall and rather outspoken fellow seems to cause such a stir wherever he goes. Why does he get the job done where others fail? Can something indeed be learned from his management and leadership style that has applications beyond the sports world, as some hopeful business school operators and starry-eyed social and political reformers insist? Certainly van Gaal seems to think so himself, as he accepts invitations to address audiences of managers and CEOs about how to make their organisations more efficient and their businesses more profitable.

Sportsspeakers, an agency with a variety of accomplished sportsmen and sportswomen on offer, represents van Gaal. They describe their client as follows: 'Controversial, conspicuous, but always with integrity – former football player and current trainer Louis van Gaal is outspoken. By now, he has more than earned his silver spurs. In the past he received many titles and reached many championships, both domestically and internationally. His secret? He will gladly share that with you – Louis van Gaal is a born leader. He takes initiative, defends the group-interest, and tries to professionalise and optimise an organisation. Louis van Gaal is a perfectionist and expects that all trainers and players he works with are 100 per cent motivated. He has a clear, personal vision, which he openly shares. During his presentations he speaks about leadership, development of talent, co-operation and achievement.'

Back home in the Netherlands, I mined football club archives, wading through piles of dull football statistics from yesteryear until happening upon some gems of rare biographical beauty. I went to towns where Louis van Gaal once lived or worked to meet friendly old neighbours, former classmates and colleagues. The resulting book is a portrayal of van Gaal's life, from his boyhood in Amsterdam to his latest role at Manchester United. It follows him through school, his own football education, his experiences as a teacher of physical education, his career as a professional football player and his rise to his current state as a world-class coach. It is a generally sympathetic account written by a compatriot, a fellow Dutchman, who stood on the sidelines of van Gaal's rapidly ascending career and found himself transformed into a van Gaal admirer in the process. It is a review of the life and times of one of football's most gifted architects and a record of his ongoing adventures. I hope that this book will shed some natural light on an intriguing and inspiring person, one working in a public environment that commonly provides more heat than illumination.

Louis van Gaal was appointed Manchester United manager on a three-year deal and is scheduled to start work at Old Trafford in July 2014, immediately after the completion of his World Cup duties with the Netherlands. For the first time since its founding in 1878, Manchester United has a manager who is not from England, Scotland, Wales or Ireland. It certainly is a time of dramatic change at the club. In 2013, after 26 years in charge, manager and revered club icon Sir Alex Ferguson retired. The subsequent appointment of David Moyes to succeed him proved a dismal failure: in the 2013–14 season the club finished a distant seventh and failed to qualify for Europe for the first time since the end of the 1989–90 season.

If the club was preparing for a period of transition when Moyes came on, a year later it feels more like a total makeover is needed. Van Gaal inherits a squad both short of confidence and bereft of that will to win that was the backbone of many triumphs. Fortunately for Manchester United, van Gaal thrives in such conditions. If proof were needed, his recent restoration of the collapsed Dutch national team is a vivid illustration that he is a team builder from scratch. In this respect he is the right man for the club at this point in their history.

Van Gaal said of the appointment, 'I always have the ambition to become number one. I am not going to the World Cup to participate with the Dutch national team; I am going there to win. That should be clear from everything I am investing. I am trying to find the system that will make us invincible. The same will apply at Manchester United. I have always had the mentality of a winner, maybe not so much as a player, but certainly as a coach. That is why I have won much. […] It was always a wish for me to work in the Premier League. To work as a manager for Manchester United, the biggest club in the world, makes me very proud. I have managed in games at Old Trafford before and know what an incredible arena Old Trafford is and how passionate and knowledgeable the fans are. This club has big ambitions; I too have big ambitions. Together I'm sure we will make history.'

YOUNG LOUIS, THE FOOTBALL PLAYER

'A sound mind in a sound body is a short,
but full, description of a happy state in this World.'

John Locke

His full name gives it away: Aloysius Paulus Maria was born into a Roman Catholic family, and not just any, but one staunchly devoted to the teachings of the Church. Every Sunday, his parents made sure that the whole family went to the neighbourhood church at the Linnaeushof, in the Amsterdam suburb of Watergraafsmeer. He was born on 8 August 1951 as the youngest child in a family of 11 – a complete team. Some of his four brothers and four sisters suggest that Louis as 'the baby' of the family was spoiled by the loving affections of his parents and older siblings. Van Gaal himself disagrees. Though love and warmth seem to have been in ready supply in the van Gaal home, his parents had things clearly organised. All the children had a designated household chore: one set the table; another did the dishes; Louis himself had to go shopping and peel the potatoes. 'Just think of that. Peeling potatoes,' he later observed.

Louis has said that he resembles his father in some important ways. Van Gaal senior had a management function at what today is SHV Holdings. The company came into being in 1896 after a merger between a number of large coal trading companies. After the decline of coal as the primary source of energy, SHV moved into other business areas, most notably oil and natural gas. Louis' father seemed to have a knack for leadership and quickly rose up the corporate ladder, affording the family a comfortable standard of living when others had difficulty making ends meet. To match his firm work ethic, Louis' father also had a firm sense of discipline, which he instilled in Louis' older siblings.

'I think that my father had the same character as I have,' van Gaal has said. 'He had an open mind towards his fellow man: he listened and had the courage to make decisions that were difficult to accept for some, but that were necessary for the company. He was a leading figure.' Other than this terse observation, Louis' memories of his father are limited. Van Gaal senior suffered a severe heart attack which largely incapacitated him when Louis was only 6 years old and passed away when his son was 11. As a consequence, Louis was raised mostly by his mother. Whenever van Gaal speaks of her, his love and respect for her are evident: 'My mother probably will have inherited something from her husband. By word of mouth – I barely experienced it consciously – I heard that my father was quite strict and disciplined.' He adored his mother. From her he inherited a sense of direction in life and values such as honesty, respect, faithfulness and discipline, together with a strong sense of responsibility. These were the values that he passed on to his children and that he used when training his players, with varying success.

Van Gaal's kinship with Dutch football culture was established at a very early age. The legendary Johan Cruyff grew up in a neighbouring suburb, poetically named Betondorp or 'Concrete Village' for its distinguishing architectural feature. Watergraafsmeer, meanwhile, was the location of the De Meer, for more than six decades the home of AFC Ajax. (Ajax's move to the Amsterdam ArenA in 1996 coincided with the final months of van Gaal's reign at Ajax.)

Louis came of age when there were few cars around – his father owning one of them – which meant there was plenty of space for children to play football on the street. Louis and his friends would gather on the roller-skating rink at the Galileiplantsoen, across from the van Gaal home. Even as a child, Louis was outspoken and was quick to assert himself if a goal was in dispute. He'd brag about his qualities as a football player, and not entirely without reason: among his peers he was one of the best. These were the days of Ajax stars such as Sjaak Swart, Piet Keizer, and of course Johan Cruyff. But van Gaal's favourite among the 'sons of the gods' was Henk Groot. Groot was very strong in the air and van Gaal, too, had a knack for heading in crosses. Whenever he scored, he'd shout 'Henkie, Henkie, Henkie!' after his hero.

In a way, Louis grew up at the right time. The games he and his friends played on that roller-skating rink were rough – tackles and bruised knees were part of the experience. According to his peers Louis did not mind giving someone a little shove that caused the person to lose his balance, though he was less tolerant if this happened to himself! He wanted to be the best, to always win, and it was there on those Amsterdam streets that the seeds for van Gaal's future mastery of the game were sown. He learned through trial and error and built up the resourcefulness that would serve him so well as a coach later on.

The swinging sixties were more or less lost on Louis. While others grew their hair long, he kept his relatively well trimmed.

When others flaunted faded, tight-fitting jeans, he wore a pair of pants made of *terlenka*, a type of polyester commonly used in Dutch clothing of the time. He wasn't particularly a partygoer, and the Catholic youth society underneath the church at the Linnaeushof did not have a strong attraction for him. Yet it was there in 1969 that he got to know Fernanda Obbes. He was 18, she was 16, and it was love at first sight. They would marry in 1973, when he was just 21.

The one fad Louis did permit himself was a *brommer*. He fell in love with the Puch, an Austrian moped that was incredibly popular with the Dutch youth of the day. To supplement his allowance, Louis distributed newspapers in the neighbourhood. On his shining red Puch he was able to do this in no time.

The De Meer and its adjacent training complex were within walking distance of van Gaal's home. It was clear that Louis has his sights set on Voorland, the club's youth setup, but for the Catholic van Gaals, the conversion to a secular football club did not come that easily. Division along religious, sociopolitical lines – *verzuiling* – is one of the idiosyncrasies of the presumably liberal Netherlands. In 1961, Louis started playing at Rooms Katholieke Sportvereniging De Meer (the Roman Catholic Sports Association, known as RKSV). Besides football, children could play baseball, handball, tennis and gymnastics. The entire van Gaal family were involved: the boys played football at the club and the girls did gymnastics.

In the 1960s, baseball was an upcoming sport in the Netherlands, and a good number of future football greats, such as Johan Cruyff and Guus Hiddink, were attracted to the sport. So was Louis van Gaal. He enjoyed being a pitcher: on that mound he stood a little higher than his teammates and could put his personal stamp on the way the game was played. Apparently, he wasn't a bad catcher either. Because of his dedication and concentration he did as well in baseball as he did in football.

Louis was also good at playing cards. Because he was a student and did not have much money, he placed his bets carefully. One of the board members at RKSV De Meer decided to 'finance' Louis a little. With this new sugar-daddy and a modest supply of cash, van Gaal became more audacious. He always exactly remembered which cards had already gone out of the round of the Dutch game they most commonly played, *klaverjassen*. Soon he was earning some money for both himself and his benefactor.

Van Gaal was a gifted midfielder, a central position which enabled him to display his natural talent for leadership. He spoke a lot on the pitch and gestured to his teammates, directing them where they should position themselves. Some of his elder teammates got irritated by his incessant comments and directions. To shut him up they would sometimes push him a little hard on the pitch to get him back in line, which on a few occasions brought young Louis to tears. His coach, Rob Nieuwenhuis, was not particularly charmed by Louis' constant verbal input but nevertheless was sufficiently convinced of the young man's football qualities to allow him to make his début in the first team. In his first game at De Meer he made four of his team's seven goals.

Football intelligence and regular intelligence might have little in common with each other, but van Gaal possesses both. Under those circumstances someone can succeed in the coaching business. A coach experiences pressure from many quarters: supporters, sponsors, the club board, colleagues and the media. To be able to handle that stress and still be successful you need to be smart and have a stable personality. Often, this is even more important than possessing all kinds of tactical skills. The bravado on the surface does not mask that van Gaal is a well-rounded and steady person. This basis for this was set in these formative years. Young Louis attended the Hogere Burger School. The HBS was a fairly prestigious establishment, and students who completed their education at the institution were allowed to enter university. His football prowess made him a likely target for Ajax scouts, but even if there was such early interest, his brothers and sisters, who adored their smart youngest sibling, protected him from overly intrusive inquiries. They wanted to make sure he finished his school education and encouraged him to just keep playing for De Meer for a while. He was a good student and managed to graduate from high school at 16.

Van Gaal wanted to become a teacher of physical education and enrolled in the Academy of Physical Education (ALO) in the Amsterdam suburb of Geuzenveld. At ALO van Gaal 'learned what makes people tick. I was as green as grass. I barely knew what a woman looked like and I was always playing football. That changed at the academy, which was co-educational. You learned how to interact with women, and even more, how to interact with people. What mattered at the ALO was not just learning how to do a certain exercise but also what the underlying psychology was. Everything I learned I learned at the Academy for Physical Education.'

Louis was only 17 years old when he enrolled. 'I grew wiser at the academy because I learned to think abstractly. Not so many people are learning that at such a young age. I had subjects like pedagogy, psychology and philosophy, and I was interacting with boys 23 years old. So I think that because of that I matured a little faster than my brothers. I had a fantastic teacher, Max Koops. He was able to bring structure into everything he did. I got my motto from the philosopher John Locke: "The spirit is stronger than the body." And from John Rijsman, the psychology teacher of the trainer's course, I learned that it is better to deal with people in a positive than in a negative way. I am the harmony-type. Rinus Michels and Johan Cruyff were the war-type.' These lessons proved to have a lasting beneficial impact on his future coaching career.

One of van Gaal's role models was the Ajax and Dutch manager Rinus Michels. 'He was a PE teacher first as well. Players are just like big children. So there really is a resemblance between being a teacher and being a coach. The difference is in the objective. At school you have educational objectives, but I am a performance-animal and that is why I wanted to work in sports. As a PE teacher I was too focused on performance. That is not a dirty word – I think it is actually good – but you should not lose sight of the educational aspects. I didn't. For me performance was a means to convey the educational aspects to the children. Other than that, everything is the same. You approach students in a certain way, based on a particular philosophy; you do so with football players in exactly the same manner. And both at school and in a football team you encounter a pecking order and different cultures.'

At the end of the 1970–71 season De Meer played a few practice games against the lower Ajax teams. Van Gaal's qualities particularly shone at these matches and Ajax again expressed interest in the talented and domineering midfielder. Now almost 20, van Gaal did not pass up the opportunity this time. He was contracted and started playing in the second team. He received 750 guilders a month (about £250), quite a good sum of money for a new professional in those days. Ajax was protective of its players and forbade them to play street games to prevent injuries. Van Gaal's moped was out of the question too – much too risky, according to the club management. Instead, he received a Fiat 127 to transport himself in; his Puch was passed on to his friends so that they could come and watch his games.

In *The Undutchables* (1991), the author Colin White colourfully described his personal impressions of getting to the Dutch capital by train: 'Upon arrival at the glorious Amsterdam Centraal Station, don't look anyone in the eye or you'll be hustled – for hashish, heroin, cocaine, a cheap hotel or botel (boat-hotel behind the station), sleep-in, left-wing newspaper, right-wing newspaper, non-affiliated newspaper, shoe shine, petition signing, joining a demonstration or a riot, recruiting squatters (*krakers*), women's liberation or gay liberation movement. In any case, staring at the floor is good practice for the moment you exit the station and encounter the heaps of dog shit which decorate the streets of Amsterdam.' This is of course the cynic's take on Amsterdam, and things may not yet have been as bad two decades earlier when Louis van Gaal started playing at Ajax. But the city and its inhabitants are undoubtedly one of a kind, not only in the world, but also in the Netherlands itself.

Troublesome Amsterdam – the only crowned city in the world. The crown, bestowed upon the Dutch capital by the Austrian Emperor Maximilian I, can still be seen on the Westertoren. Is this perhaps the reason why Amsterdammers feel that they are slightly superior to other Dutchmen? And that many of these other Dutchmen are a little intimidated by and critical of the nation's capital? Van Gaal does not come from downtown 'Mokum', as the city is tenderly called by the locals, and he does not speak with the peculiar twang that distinguishes the Dutch language of many Amsterdammers from that of their countrymen. But he does have the somewhat belligerent, in-your-face attitude that characterises many inhabitants of this town. People from Amsterdam are not always easy to get along with and, indeed, van Gaal has rarely been recognised for an excess of congeniality. But his hard-nosed attitude, his unshakeable conviction of being right, combined with his undeniable expertise in his field, usually got him where he wanted to go. This was definitely the case at Ajax, in a field where competition was tight.

At 20, van Gaal was comparatively old when he arrived. Most of his colleagues in the second team were 18 or 19 years old. Additionally, most had played for the Ajax youth teams and knew all the ins and outs of the club. Van Gaal, by contrast, was an outsider. He was placed as a striker and, even though this was not the place best suited for him, he did well due to his developed technique and understanding of the game. His greatest handicap was that he was heavily built and his movements were sluggish. He did not run and turn well. His acceleration was particularly slow and he got tired more easily than most of his teammates. Running practice did not seem to help much and so was discontinued. Van Gaal later observed, 'I lack the ability to continue for the full 90 minutes. I am no running wonder. If I were, then, with my technical and tactical qualities, I would not have ended up at Sparta [in Rotterdam, a little later in his career]. I would have been able to earn gold. I would have liked to be a great runner, but I am not depressed that I am not. I learned to live with it. I had to.'

These were the years of Ajax's golden generation: players like Johan Cruyff, Piet Keizer, Sjaak Swart, Gerrie Mühren, Ruud Krol and Johan Neeskens dominated Ajax's first team. Van Gaal could not compete with such talent and remained firmly in the second team. During the 1971–72 season his team landed in third place; in 1972–73 in second place behind Den Haag: 'These were two heavy, hard years,' van Gaal said, 'because I simultaneously played football and studied to become a PE teacher. They really did not take that into account at Ajax. I was busy with sports the whole day long, and I got wiped out. I was given no reprieve by the Ajax coaches, Han Grijzenhout and Bobby Haarms. But my game mentality took shape in those years and that still benefits me. You see, playing football well is not enough; you have to want to win. In those days, you were sometimes tortured at trainings and sometimes you received a pat on the back. That way, the Ajax management made sure it prepared football players who were ready to perform at the highest level.' Espousing a little Buddhist philosophy, the Lotus Sutra, van Gaal concluded, 'A beautiful flower has his roots in dirty soil. Young people have to remember that well.'

The schedule at the Academy of Physical Education was tough enough. Classes lasted from eight in the morning until six in the evening. Louis' mother expected him to have dinner at home and then he was off to De Meer for training. Grijzenhout observed, 'I was one of the people who brought Louis to Ajax. He stood out because of his height, his ball control, and his survey of the game. I remember him as a tall, lanky forward, who also had something of a playmaker in him. And he was definitely not a timid guy.' In June 1973, van Gaal graduated from the academy and received his certificate to teach at secondary school level.

Even today there are some 'van Gaal experts' who believe the former second-team player suffers from an inferiority complex incurred at that time. Despite his talent, he permanently stood in the shadow of the stars of his day: so close to the stage of world football and yet so far. During his time as an Ajax player there was always a giant playing in van Gaal's position in the first team: Johan Cruyff. Having hindered van Gaal's breakthrough as a player, Cruyff would continue to feature significantly in van Gaal's professional career.

Whether in Amsterdam or Barcelona, van Gaal had his successes measured by the Cruyff standard.

At Ajax, Louis grew weary of waiting for his chance in the first team. Van Gaal's qualities were acknowledged elsewhere, however, and he was approached by the Belgian club AS Oostende and the French side Valenciennes. When FC Antwerp made him an appealing offer, he accepted. He and Fernanda moved into an apartment in Deurne, a suburb of Antwerp, where the club's stadium was located. Ironically, a few months after van Gaal went to Belgium, Johan Cruyff left Ajax to join Barcelona. Van Gaal observed with some regret, 'I could have become the successor to Cruyff. That would have made sense. I definitely would have been given the chance.' Whether he really would have is open to question – he certainly never came close to Cruyff's level as a player. But with regard to character, the two are similar: both men have opinions about everything and generously share them with everyone in earshot.

The move proved to be a mixed experience for van Gaal. FC Antwerp had the ambition to challenge the supremacy of rivals RSC Anderlecht and for that purpose had imported four foreign players. However, according to Belgium Football Federation rules of the time, only three foreigners were allowed to play at once. Unfortunately for van Gaal, Antwerp coach Guy Thys preferred the other three non-Belgian players, and the Dutchman never got a regular place in the team. Thys was respected in the Belgian football world from delivering results, but his strategy was very defensive, with at least seven players behind the ball, attacking only on the counter. According to team captain Robert Geens there was 'a penalty on crossing the halfway line. Thys never stopped complaining about the "slow van Gaal". He only allowed him on as a substitute when we were ahead. Then Louis was tasked with holding on to the ball and slowing the game down. And that was not the Dutchman's style. Louis always shouted that he was the best, but still I did not find him arrogant because he was also polite and pleasant. But inside the lines or even around the pitch he changed into a different person. Then he could be really fanatical. When Louis played, and he played well, he felt the urge to tell everyone that he had been the star of the show. At those moments he was a very happy man.'

Thys explained, 'I had to choose between four foreigners – Flemming Lund, Karl Kodat, Alfred Riedl and Louis van Gaal. Often, I selected the first three and then Louis was kept off the team. He did not appreciate that. Because Louis could talk very well even in those days, we had some lively conversations. That went something like, "Trainer, I do not understand you. I am the best, am I not?" And then I would say, "No, my boy, you aren't." He just could not understand that. I thought he was a boy with a tremendous personality for his age. But I also thought that he had a body that was out-and-out slow. Against Aston Villa, Louis once played like royalty. We won 1–0; in those days that was a sensation. At home we had already won with three goals from Kodat; at the away game we had to freeze the play. That was Louis' job. I still remember our conversation before the game. He asked me, "Well, trainer, how should I play?" I said, "As usual: as slowly as possible." He did not like that, but he played very well.'

Van Gaal once remarked to Thys, 'I can do everything with a ball,' to which the coach responded, 'The problem is that you never have it.' Decades later, having reached a level of professional coaching that Thys never achieved, van Gaal could still not appreciate that these comments were widely publicised. 'I would never say such things about a player to the media. I protect my players; he did not do that. Self-deprecating humour? If people only knew with how much self-deprecating humour I speak to my players about my own career as a player. About my slowness, for example. But of course I take myself very seriously. I have built up a philosophy and a vision through knowledge and experience. That is the most important thing about a person: that you know who you are and what you want. That is dealing with yourself in a serious manner; you should be capable of introspection and evaluate yourself. If someone blames me for taking myself too seriously, that says more about him than about me.'

Van Gaal could never quite understand that Thys did not appreciate him as much as his other foreign colleagues: 'I don't know what was up with that man, but for some reason he was not particularly fond of me. In Belgium they were only allowed to field a limited number of foreigners, and for that reason he always kept me out of the starting line-up. Technical or tactical reasons he could not have had, because even when I played well he still put me on the bench.' Thys acknowledged that van Gaal was a technically skilled and intelligent player: 'I have said to the media that the midfield with the technically gifted van Gaal was covered well. But for a top player he was much too slow for my taste. That was probably due to his physique: with that big and tall body he waddled over the field. And he did everything at the same speed. So I selected players who were fast because I needed them [for the counter-attacks]. If it had been up to me, I would not have brought in van Gaal – not because I did not like him, as Louis thinks himself, but because he did not fit with the concept of FC Antwerp.'

Van Gaal's teammate and friend, striker Roger van Gool, believed that it was Louis' big mouth that cost him his place in the team. 'There were four foreigners, so one had to be dropped. But I did not think that Louis was the least of the four, and there were others on the team who agreed with me. But Louis was always keen on giving his opinion. Consequently, after a game, he constantly argued about the football with Thys. Thys thought van Gaal was a know-it-all, although he did not say that openly. But it played a role in the coach's player selection. [Thys] really understood football. He proved that he could build a team – first with Antwerp and later with the Belgium national team. All the players were quite satisfied with the trainer, except Louis of course. He was the victim, probably, of his own big mouth.'

Life in Belgium was comfortable for van Gaal, but after four years on the bench he had had enough. In spring 1977 he wrote several dozen job application letters to schools in the Netherlands, looking for a position as a PE teacher. He was accepted at the Don Bosco LTS, a 'Lower Technical School' in Amsterdam, and was given a full teaching load of 29 hours a week. The van Gaal family, which by that time included daughter Brenda, with Fernanda pregnant with Renate, moved to the small town of Avenhorn, 20 miles north of Amsterdam. Football was popular among the male students at the school and van Gaal soon enjoyed a certain celebrity status as a semi-professional footballer who could frequently be seen in TV sports broadcasts.

Van Gaal's career followed the two-track approach of player-cum-teacher that has been taken by other Dutch coaching greats, most notably Rinus Michels and Guus Hiddink. The experience of working with often unmotivated or emotionally troubled youths at school has given these trainers a cutting edge, a degree of psychological insight some of their colleagues lack. This skill can be recognised in the way they deal with their adult charges, who can be just as testy and demanding as high school boys, and who intermittently require patient understanding and tough discipline.

Van Gaal maxims such as 'All people have talent – but they often do not know which' and 'I can be a medium to help the player manifest his talent' originated in his 12-year experience as a teacher. Van Gaal's critics are often perturbed by what they consider the coach's schoolmasterly style and tone. In their view he is still the schoolteacher. Whether this interpretation merits serious consideration is questionable. Neither Michels nor Hiddink ever lacked bold self-confidence. Indeed, in Korea Hiddink published a much-acclaimed Korean-language account of his exploits with the national team, modestly entitled *My Way*. Yet few have ever accused either Michels or Hiddink of having schoolmasterly tendencies. This dubious honour has been bestowed only on van Gaal. Certainly, he taught with much conviction and proved very effective in front of school classes. The day job taught him how to explain things. If the kids couldn't hit a baseball, van Gaal would talk until they could. He was equipping himself for his future career as a coach.

Former Telstar and HFC Haarlem player, Mike Helenklaken, was one of van Gaal's pupils: 'We all thought he was a great teacher. He was straightforward, enthusiastic, even fanatical. You really have to be a little insane to teach at a school like that because there were some difficult characters around. Van Gaal was realistic. Boys who were stiff and a little stout would receive an "eight" ["good" in the Dutch one-to-ten grading system] if they made real effort, while boys who were agile and slim would get a "three" ["very unsatisfactory"] if they did not apply themselves. He was very blunt with kids who got on his wrong side. I remember one incident in particular. A boy just did not try his best. We were doing exercises on the rings and at one point this guy had to do a turn as well. Forwards, it worked, but backwards, it didn't. So he ended up hanging there quite awkwardly. But van Gaal didn't lift a finger, thinking, "You can figure it out yourself." Everyone was in stitches laughing, until the boy let go and crashed to the floor. "You deserved that," van Gaal said. But he did keep his eyes open at all times, and I am certain he would have intervened if it really had become a dangerous situation.'

The school was a tough place. There were problem students, among them a good number of diehard Ajax supporters from the notorious F-side (their equivalent to Chelsea's Headhunters or West Ham's Inter City Firm). There were also a lot of non-native students, immigrant children from Moroccan, Turkish and Surinamese backgrounds, who had difficulties fitting into Dutch society. Fights among these student groups were part of daily life at the school. Van Gaal had to deal with kids from tough social backgrounds, yet he enjoyed working there for many years and learned an enormous amount in the process. Under those conditions a person's capacity to empathise grows almost daily. It is possible, as van Gaal did, to translate that kind of work into working with professional footballers. He could appeal to their sense of responsibility, reminding them of the privileged situation in which they live and work. Van Gaal works with his players not just on ordinary football issues, but also on mental conditioning and a continued growth towards maturity.

The self-disciplined and punctual van Gaal quickly understood that there had to be clear rules in such an environment: rules which had to be strictly and uncompromisingly enforced. In all, he worked for 12 years at Don Bosco until he made a full-time commitment to professional football as the co-ordinator of the Ajax youth department. To van Gaal connoisseurs, this move did not come as a surprise. He had on more than one occasion expressed the desire to either continue as a football coach or fulfil a managerial role in the business world. He had always considered himself to be a born leader and believed that as a schoolteacher he would not be able to manifest his full potential.

While he was teaching, van Gaal also played as a semi-professional, originally for Telstar in the coastal town of Velsen. Because the club could not afford the exorbitant transfer fee demanded by Antwerp, van Gaal went to Telstar on loan. The club had had good times during the early 1970s, but by the time Louis arrived it was teetering on the bottom rungs of the *Eredivisie*, the Dutch equivalent of the Premier League. Romanian trainer Mircea Petescu hoped that the talented new player could help prevent relegation. To that end he positioned van Gaal as striker, a position the tall and sluggish player was ill-suited for. Because Telstar had grown accustomed to losing games, it played defensively. This made matters worse for van Gaal, leaving him isolated up front.

Unlike at Antwerp, van Gaal got along well with his coach. He, Petescu and team captain Fred Bischot could sit at a table discussing football strategies for hours, drawing diagrams and charts in the process. Van Gaal saw eye to eye with the Romanian, and when Telstar were finally relegated in 1978 it was no great surprise that he decided to follow the coach to Sparta Rotterdam. Neither one had much interest in working for a club in the *Eerste Divisie* (First Division), the second tier of Dutch football. Sparta bought Louis van Gaal for 175,000 guilders (about £60,000), and this was the beginning of a fruitful, eight-year period in Rotterdam.

HIGHS AND LOWS AT SPARTA AND AZ

'My friends watched football players and I
watched Rinus Michels. Even then I knew
I wanted to become a coach.'

Louis van Gaal

Sparta and Ajax have a rich past in common. The names of both clubs come from Greek mythology and both names are symbolic of physical over-achievement. Until 1911 both clubs even wore the same shirt colours. Sparta was established in 1888, making it the oldest professional football club in the Netherlands. Although the club had some successes in the 1960s, its glory days were mostly in the first half of the twentieth century. Later, the club usually found itself competing for what is sometimes referred to as the 'championship of the rest of Holland' – the fourth place of the *Eredivisie* after Ajax, Feyenoord and PSV Eindhoven. Sparta is also a club with a somewhat British flavour: a number of English coaches and players have spent time at Sparta's almost century-old stadium Het Kasteel ('The Castle') and the club even boasts its own cricket team.

When van Gaal followed Petescu to Sparta he was nearly 27 years old. He quickly became a stalwart of the side and would go on to make 282 appearances for the club. During this time, Sparta twice 'won' the coveted fourth place behind the big three. Van Gaal was rarely injured and seldom missed a league game. He was absent for a prolonged period only once, during the 1981–82 season when he broke his left arm: 'I landed on my outstretched arm and I heard it crack. I said immediately: it is broken. At first, they didn't believe me because I still could move my fingers fairly well. But unfortunately, I was right.'

More problematic was his exhausting schedule. He had to teach at Don Bosco from 8 a.m. to 2 p.m. and then had to show up for training at Sparta an hour and a half later. In addition, he tried to improve his qualifications by taking on various courses in football and management, which took up a good part of the evening. On his regular, 200 km round-trip commute from his home in Avenhorn to Rotterdam, tiredness got to him occasionally and he had to pull over. Twice he crashed his car into the barriers when he dozed off while driving. Because of his teaching job in Amsterdam, van Gaal was unable to relocate to a home closer to his club. A few times he considered signing for a club closer to home – AZ Alkmaar, Haarlem or Volendam. Sparta, though, were determined to hold on to one of their most important players and the requested transfer fee of 400,000 guilders was enough to put these smaller clubs off.

Val Gaal played a technically developed and clean type of football. In all his Sparta years he only got five yellow cards and none of them were for foul play; it should come as no surprise that he received all these cards for his overly critical commentary on what he considered to be inadequate refereeing. This is also how he got his only red card. He loudly expressed his displeasure with a decision of the moustachioed referee, who then issued a warning to him. Van Gaal responded by saying, 'If you want to make it into tomorrow's newspapers, *moustache-man*, you should give me a yellow card.' The referee immediately obliged. 'If you want to make it to the front pages,' van Gaal continued, 'you should give me another one!' The referee duly obliged.

It is in van Gaal's nature to fully invest himself in the cause he is involved with: half-hearted commitments run counter to his nature. He learned the Sparta club song very quickly and, during an away game against Spartak Moscow, astonished the Russian spectators by singing the song prior to kick-off with Sparta's chairman and fellow player Danny Blind in the centre of the pitch. Although not all of his teammates were inspired by van Gaal's verbal outbursts, most were impressed with his level of dedication. When others would be gloating over a job well done after a win, van Gaal would already be preoccupied with the preparation for the next game.

When Petescu originally put van Gaal in midfield, the Sparta fans were not immediately enamoured with the player who was so fond of ball possession. But van Gaal ignored the complaints in the stands and in the press. 'I am strong with the ball and my passes are good,' he countered. 'I can really say that I am tactically solid. I can't help it if the public doesn't see that. Of course, I can shoot the ball forward as some others do, but the result is that you just lose the ball. So I just keep possession, and that may come across as arrogance.' Hoofing the ball upfield was against van Gaal's principles as a player, and continued to be anathema to him when he moved into coaching. He always insisted on a well-thought-out build-up of the attack.

It wasn't just among the fans and journalists that there were voices of disapproval. Among van Gaal's teammates, too, there were critics. Leen de Goeij, a former Ajax player, observed, 'Louis probably will deny this, but he really comes across as arrogant and assertive. Others may hold off on their commentary for a while, but not Louis. He had hardly arrived at Sparta before proclaiming that other players were inept. From the moment he was positioned in the first eleven, his influence was decisive. Of course, he did have the qualities to be a leader. But frankly speaking, I am not fond of those players that have to make comments parallel to those of the coach all the time. His insight into the game was good and he had great qualities as a playmaker. But towards the end of the first season he loudly began to correct his teammates – not only at training, but even at matches. He was respected by the younger players because they were open to that, but I honestly didn't like it. That boy lacks any self-criticism. Whenever the selection for the national team was announced, he was disappointed that he was not included.' Indeed, van Gaal seemed confident that he was ready to face a national challenge. 'Well, I admit that I don't have a large capacity for running. But that is really not a problem, as long as there are players who are willing to run for me, as at Sparta. If that would happen at *Oranje* [the nickname for the Dutch national side] I would say: Yes, I am ready for it. I possess the technique and the insight. It is up to [national coach] Kees Rijvers to decide if that is sufficient.'

Results under Petescu's reign were mixed, and halfway through the 1979–80 season he was replaced by Dutchman Joop Brand. Brand and van Gaal had met at a coaches' course at the Koninklijke Nederlandse Voetbalbond (KNVB – the Royal Dutch Football Federation) in Zeist and the young van Gaal often praised his colleague for his outstanding coaching qualities: 'He was the best coach I ever worked with. I would coach the same way he coaches. He has everything: he can teach, he knows how to interact with people, and still understands that as coach he is positioned above the players, lonely at the top. I rarely see coaches make purposeful substitutions. But he knows how to intervene before things go wrong. A coach has to be able to do that.' These early observations are telling of van Gaal's own priorities in football coaching.

Van Gaal's exuberance over Brand's training abilities notwithstanding, Sparta's results under his leadership were equally uninspiring and he was soon replaced by the Welsh coach, Barry Hughes. In many ways, Hughes was the polar opposite of van Gaal. As a coach, he is best remembered for his discovery of Ruud Gullit at HFC Haarlem, but he is better known in Holland as a performer of Mardi Gras hits and a guest on various TV comedy programmes. Hughes was always ready for a joke, for some comic relief. He gladly embraced his role as a clown, off and on the pitch, as is illustrated by the title of his autobiography, *Entertainer*. This did not sit well with the rather serious van Gaal. The Dutchman was devoted to the art of playing football with technical brilliance and tactical sophistication. Hughes, by contrast, was an advocate of the kick-and-rush style of football, with long passes to the front and a quick attack. He did not appreciate van Gaal's insistence on gradual and deliberate build-up play, seeing it as a waste of time and reducing goal-scoring opportunities.

When Hughes refused to listen to him, van Gaal went direct to the Sparta board, which angered his coach. Their relationship was troubled from the start, and in *Entertainer* Hughes expresses his frustration over the attitude of his midfielder. Yet at the same time he somewhat reluctantly acknowledged the positive impact van Gaal had on the team performance: 'He gave the impression that he personally had invented the game of football. He was pretty arrogant, a real smart alec. On the pitch I did not have so much trouble with him because he performed well. But as a person he was a hopeless case. With his type of character he did not have a good influence on the team atmosphere, although I have to admit that things steadily went better. That is also why he was my team captain during my last year. But he will never be my friend.'

Considering van Gaal's general effectiveness at Sparta, he probably ended up on the reserves bench more frequently than was justified. Several of his former teammates still think that van Gaal's meddling regularly cost him his place in the side. Hughes's view seems to corroborate that: 'I was not exactly the type of person who invites players to his office to discuss game strategies. I think van Gaal missed that because he was able to do that with Petescu. But I decide who plays and who doesn't, and I don't need anybody else's help with that. That is how I worked; I was a loner and did things without first debating with others. Louis tried to interfere with my way of working and that bothered me, to say the least.'

Despite Hughes's suggestion that van Gaal was not good for team morale, the outspoken midfielder was hard to beat as someone representing player interests. The young Wouter Holverda was one who was impressed: 'Louis was pig-headed, and most people do not like to work with such types. But he had certain qualities and everybody seemed to think that it was just fine if he would become the leader. And he really did that very well. He was the best player advocate we could have wished for ourselves. Of course he could criticise you during training in a most unpleasant way. Still, I always learned from that because even back then he did understand football very well. He does have a sense of humour. He would laugh intensely when we were kidding around. Then he would get red in the face, which caused us to crack up in turn.'

Defender Adrie Andriessen was amazed by van Gaal's perceptive-ness: 'If we could not get a grip on our opponent, he would say, "If you play 3 metres to the right, then I will play 3 metres to the left, and everything will be balanced." And he'd be right. First you'd think, what a weird guy he is. But once he was proved right on a few occasions, you got some respect for him and started to accept his directions. Louis would understand within a few minutes what was wrong. During the pre-match meeting we would have made plans, but he would change those at his own initiative during the game. He was the coach on the pitch.'

Understandably, van Gaal was not sad to see Barry Hughes go. He was replaced by Bert Jacobs, who, like Hughes, enjoyed joking around. But things clicked a lot better between the two Dutchmen, and Jacobs quickly recognised van Gaal's football intelligence and leadership quality: 'I immediately noticed that I was dealing with someone who was intensely involved with football and thought deeply about everything. I had never experienced a team captain who was so engrossed in his job. Later I also learned that he was a real personality. I got to know him as an intelligent and even erudite man. He read a lot and he knew what he was talking about. He was a leader off the pitch but especially on it. Through him I learned to understand what it means to have an "extension on the field". He was capable of coaching his teammates, and he thought ahead like a chess player. Because he and I had similar ideas about football, we worked together excellently.'

At Sparta, van Gaal also had the opportunity to extend his playing experience beyond the Netherlands. In 1983 Sparta got to the third round of the UEFA Cup, the only team out of the four Dutch participating clubs to make it as far. The 1985 tournament did not prove as successful, but the match against German giant HSV Hamburg, when Sparta scraped through as a result of some well-taken penalties, was memorable. Van Gaal found himself up against both Manfred Kaltz and Felix Magath, who would lead Wolfsburg to *Bundesliga* victory many years later, and with whom van Gaal would cross swords once more during their time in charge of Bayern Munich and Schalke 04. The year 1985 turned out to be particularly busy as Sparta also took a trip to China, right during the monsoon season. The hot and humid weather was something Louis and his teammates were ill-prepared for and it took a toll on their performance. But the increased stamina acquired in the Far East reaped its rewards during the following season.

By this point, Louis van Gaal had also become an active partici-pant in the Vereniging van Contractspelers (VVCS), the idiosyncratic players' union that is still around to trouble the KNVB bureaucracy and professional clubs in the Netherlands. Van Gaal was of the opinion that the rights of players were often not well represented and their duties poorly defined. In order to be effective in union work a person needs to be a bit of a lawyer-type: smart, outspoken and somewhat combative. In a community of quieter colleagues, van Gaal stood out as a person who had plenty of ideas about how to improve the lot of professional footballers and he was not hesitant in sharing these with his audience. In the association's magazine he explained, 'I apparently did this to everybody's satisfaction because I was asked again and again [to represent players]. As a result, you get certain traction in union work. I also wanted to understand more of what was going on. Then it is logical that you become involved in governing such an organisation.' He was eventually asked to become VVCS vice president.

Van Gaal was also instrumental in founding the Centrale Spelersraad, or Central Players Council, in 1985. This organisation became the official channel for representing player interests at KNVB headquarters in Zeist, and unsurprisingly van Gaal became its first president. In 1992, some time after he had already started coaching, he became the chairman of the equivalent association Coach Betaald Voetbal ('Coach Professional Football'), a position he held until he moved to Barcelona. These experiences further developed van Gaal's managerial and organisational talents. He made a significant contribution to improving the working conditions and remuneration of football professionals, and helped to make an environment that had been characterised by a lot of politicking into one more transparent and democratic.

During the 1984–85 season it became clear how much Sparta had grown dependent upon its playmaker. The team started struggling when van Gaal sat out some games due to an injury: 'Without van Gaal Sparta is Disoriented' read one headline; 'Sparta Vulnerable without van Gaal' was another. Van Gaal, though, was approaching his mid-thirties and exhaustion was becoming an issue. The commutes from home to work increasingly took their toll. Then in May 1986 the possibility of joining AZ Alkmaar opened up. Van Gaal had to apply all his powers of persuasion to convince the Sparta board to let him out of his current contract. He said, 'A farewell to Sparta hurts. I am a professional, but the club has become a part of my life. I have experienced everything there; you don't forget all of that lightly.'

The transition from his glory days at Sparta's centre to his new role at AZ was a difficult one for van Gaal. Accustomed to give directions to his teammates in Rotterdam, he had difficulty toning down his rhetoric and adjusting his mannerisms to his new environment. Almost from the start, some AZ players were irritated by the bossy and opinionated new arrival. Van Gaal's difference of opinion wasn't helped by the fact was that he wasn't quite the player he once was: at 35, he had slowed down further, which did not do much to improve AZ's performance.

The club had had high hopes for van Gaal when he signed. A few years earlier, AZ had enjoyed a lot of success on the pitch: thanks to the strong support of businessmen brothers Cees and Klaas Molenaar, AZ had risen to become Dutch champions in 1981 and reached the UEFA Cup final. Things had gone downhill after the Molenaar brothers withdrew their financial support from the club, and there had been some expectation that van Gaal would be the person capable of waking up the slumbering club.

Van Gaal's attempts to apply some revitalising shock treatment had the reverse effect and seemed only to create antipathy among the other players. Van Gaal concluded, 'The person van Gaal has not yet been accepted at AZ. Acceptance. That is the key word around which everything revolves at the club right now. That is hard to accomplish within a year, especially when you are a little advanced in years. At Sparta we were a mentally strong unit. We accepted each others' weak points and tried to mutually make up for them. But at AZ everyone looks after himself. I also got the impression that the bulk of the players don't want to listen. Maybe that has something to do with me; maybe I come across differently than I want to.'

Goalkeeper Hans de Koning seemed to think that van Gaal carried at least part of the blame for the team's lacklustre performance. 'As a player he was very dominant. He demanded that all the balls had to be delivered to him. Of course, he already was a veteran who had experienced much during his eight years at Sparta. Still, at times I had the feeling: Good grief, don't be so argumentative! Always criticising, that irritates players. It often led to friction and confrontations. You expect that when someone new comes in, he takes a bit of a wait-and-see approach to begin with. But with Louis that was not the case. He criticised from the get-go everything that was wrong in his eyes and occasionally did so in a really tactless manner.'

In December 1986, Louis van Gaal, 35 years old, went to the AZ board and told them, 'The body no longer does what the spirit wants.' The board asked him to wait a little because 'new developments' were in the pipeline at the club at the time. Soon after, the coach Han Berger was fired and replaced by Hans Eijkenbroek. Van Gaal, who did not yet have a coaching licence, was offered the position of assistant coach by chairman Arie Ligthart. Louis van Gaal's playing career came to an anticlimactic end in a game against PEC Zwolle, which was lost 3–1.

Van Gaal never quite reached the levels at AZ he achieved with Sparta, but the position in the dugout offered him a new opportunity, and one with greater responsibility than he'd initially anticipated. Almost immediately, Eijkenbroek found himself suffering from health problems. He was hospitalised and van Gaal was required to step up and assume leadership. Even when his health wasn't as bad, Eijkenbroek admitted that, 'If I had a bad day, I asked Louis to do all the work on the pitch. That meant that Louis was in charge. He did everything, from the preparation to the tactics to the pre-match meeting.' Though nobody said so openly, it seemed more or less a given that van Gaal would effectively be in charge from the beginning. Eijkenbroek was formally in charge because he had the required documents, but van Gaal was behind the wheel. This opportunity saw a metamorphosis in van Gaal. His uninspired performances on the Alkmaar field now made way for intense, hands-on management from the sidelines. The objective was clear: preventing relegation from the *Eredivisie*, and van Gaal was determined to do what he could to avoid this.

The van Gaal antidote for the malaise at AZ was to use the bullwhip on the team. He felt that because he was hard on himself he could afford to be hard on the team as well. And he was. The van

Gaal reign led to an entirely new regime at the club, with a strong emphasis on discipline. Latecomers were fined; after all, van Gaal was ever punctual himself. Players were required to park their cars further down on the parking lot, to make space for visitors nearer to the ground's entrance. Unpolished shoes were out, polite forms of address a must. 'The coach told every player in no uncertain terms what their qualities and shortcomings were, something that was not appreciated equally by all. But he did gain the respect of the players; the complaining ceased and they started to listen.'

Van Gaal explained why the straight-talking, tough approach was necessary: 'No excesses, simply the execution of tasks. Too much input leads to chaos, especially within the selection. I am, after all, the leader. I don't want to seem immodest, but that is how things have worked out naturally.' As a result, 'everybody knows clearly were the boundaries lie. I don't let things pass. That is also how I raise my children. That is very difficult, because it means that you sometimes have to do something against your feeling.'

Another bold innovation was that van Gaal moved seven players from the second team up into contention for first-team places: the first-team squad, as a consequence, grew to 23 players. By doing so, he provided plenty of opportunity to those vying for the same positions to learn from each other, and he turned up the heat in the team by creating competition. Sometimes the presence of stars in a team can give it a needed lift, both in confidence and in performance, but sometimes it can work the opposite way, suppressing budding talent at a club. Long-standing AZ players, previously confident of their place in the team, now found themselves on the bench. Whenever they were used as substitutes, they had to fight to prove their mettle and battle their way back into the first eleven.

This is one of the enduring trademarks of van Gaal's management style. In this, as in other things, he is amazingly consistent. At AZ he rattled the chains of a few who did not please him – midfielders who stayed in their comfort zone by making long passes to the front and defenders who sought security by hanging around the goalkeeper. He pushed them, sometimes using strong language to fire them up. According to Hans de Koning, training sessions became more intense under van Gaal than they had ever been before: 'But most of all, it was different. For example, he clearly focused on character development. He put seven people on the goal line and then asked someone to take a free kick from 7 metres. We had to figure out how we would keep the ball out of the goal by kicking or heading it away. We were not allowed to turn around but had to face the ball. If you got the ball in your stomach, that was just too bad: you were expected to have such commitment to the team effort. I remember that we thought he was a bit insane, but we did what he told us to do.

'I had never before experienced a coach who abruptly stopped play at training to correct our positioning. He explained how we ought to be positioning ourselves instead, how you can keep the lines open, and when you have to make a run. He taught us how to be sharper and to think a little more about our actions. The training never felt constrained. Afterwards, you always had something to think about. Pedagogically, he was very powerful. You could see that he was used to standing in front of a class and was accustomed to explain things in plain language.'

The media also noticed the change. 'Now there is a team,' ran one report. 'The players' compliments go to assistant-trainer van Gaal, who, within the time span of five weeks, transformed 11 disillusioned lads into a brilliant group.' The defensive approach was changed into a positive, attacking style, the type people come to watch football for, and the style van Gaal has continued to insist on throughout his coaching career. The assistant coach said, "This is the way I always wanted to play myself as well. Besides, this concept suits AZ perfectly well. It does not make any difference whether we play against Ajax or Excelsior [a team that commonly plays in the B league, *Eerste Divisie*]. And relegation is not an option.'

Indeed, due to van Gaal's efforts, AZ's place in the premier league was preserved. The club board was understandably pleased. Not only did AZ score goals and avoid relegation, but the supporters were happy and their numbers at games increased. But the ambitious coach did not stop at that; he wanted more. He kept knocking on the boardroom door, first with this demand, then with that. He wanted victory bonuses for the players; he was dissatisfied with the medical staff and wanted changes; and he wanted a gym. Nobody had ever heard of such a thing at a laid-back provincial club. As usual, van Gaal was ahead of his time: a decade later, AZ had one.

Unfortunately, the period of euphoria was relatively short-lived. Hans Eijkenbroek was officially still AZ head coach. The somewhat uncomfortable reality that his assistant was clearly more competent and had brought results the head coach had been unable to bring was not lost on most observers. Meanwhile, the team started losing some of its most reliable players, when a number of them were sidelined through injury. Van Gaal could not substitute as before, and penalising players for underperformance by dropping them became impossible. The result was that the discipline central to van Gaal's methods was compromised, and this affected the team performance and the results. The club chairman was faced with a dilemma and concluded that, 'Relieving van Gaal of his position seemed unavoidable. Players wanted to leave and there was no money to replace them. We had to make do with the existing selection. We had a lot of debts. Above all, I think that the Netherlands weren't quite ready for Louis van Gaal yet. What he wanted might only have been possible at Ajax. He thought that AZ was a top professional club, but the club structure was rather amateurish and the financial resources were limited. We were just glad that we could keep our head above water without the backing of the Molenaar brothers. The sponsors were small and for them supporting the club was more a hobby than an investment. Everything had to be done on the cheap.'

The board wanted to have a say in things. They felt that because they invested time and money in the operation of the club, they were entitled to have some influence on its technical direction: a situation not unusual at a football club. The financial room for manoeuvre for a club the size of AZ was somewhat limited. Provincial clubs in England, France, Spain, Germany and Italy can spend a multiple of what the finance director in Alkmaar can spend, particularly during the time of Louis van Gaal's first tenure at AZ. Even the bigger Dutch clubs, which have much less financial power than clubs in large European leagues, don't go on a player shopping spree just for the sake of playing a good tournament. They tend to focus on young and extraordinarily talented players: the club benefits from his skills in the short term and can resell them at a considerable profit later. This approach is understandable from a business point of view, but such policies can easily cause friction between the club management and the coach. The coach is interested in the immediate improvement of the team performance, whereas the club board wants to see a good return on its investment.

Van Gaal was not sympathetic to AZ's dilemma. 'At many clubs the rule applies, "He who pays the piper calls the tune." If a board member invests money in remodelling the cafeteria then he usually has a voice in deciding where to put the bar. That's often how it goes with a coach: board members would like to have a bit of influence on him as well, or at least appear to do so. To them governing a club is just a matter of investing some time and money. But I also demanded discipline from the AZ board. A board member has to work hard as well. If he says, "Oh no, it is just a hobby," then he should look for a different hobby.'

This view proved problematic for the club chairman: 'He wanted to change the club into a modern business. The board members invested money into the club, but in van Gaal's view they did not understand anything about football. If they gave some technical input, they were reprimanded by the coach. He spared no one, and told everyone straight to his face what he thought. That has its merits but also its downside. Sometimes in life you have to approach things a little more diplomatically. Louis was unable to do that and so made a lot of enemies, even among the players. He could explode in the dressing room and say to a player: "You can just get lost – I can replace you with ten others."' Understandably, the chairman and the coach did not become friends. Things eventually got so tense between the two that they would occupy seats on opposite sides of the aisle when they were travelling on the player bus, without a word being exchanged.

Van Gaal kept leading the training and coaching matches conspicuously and loudly. So loudly in fact that one board member, Wijnand Vermeulen, felt obliged to intervene during one match, when van Gaal upbraided a referee. He ran down from the stands and pulled van Gaal off the pitch. When the newspaper headlines ran 'AZ Board Fires Louis van Gaal' in November 1987, a month after the incident, it did not come as a surprise to many. Chairman Floor Mouthaan alleged in the *Alkmaar Courant* that the relationship between coach and players had turned sour: 'That is why we, after extensive consultation between board and technical staff, have asked van Gaal to resign.' Van Gaal, reacting in the same articles, disagreed with this interpretation of events: 'Asked to resign? They just fired me. Strange, really. The AZ board was very satisfied with me at first, and then I was suddenly shoved out of the way. Problems with players? I know that four boys in the selection have something against me, but I think that the majority are behind me. The board refused to listen to that group. They looked for a scapegoat [for AZ's low position in the table] and that turned out to be me.'

The issue is still a sensitive one for van Gaal, and reporters who have the audacity to bring up the episode find they have touched a raw nerve. Yet it is important to remember that the circumstances at the club were quite unfavourable and it was van Gaal's first experience as coach. Few people doubted his ability, but his uncompromising and unrelenting demands evidently undermined his relationship with many people at the club. After he left, few if any players contacted him to ask how he was. De Koning said, 'We knew that it had really hurt him. But we were too preoccupied with our own concerns. We wanted to keep our club in the premier league. In football there is no sentimentality: there are too many egoists around.' Later, there would be regrets at AZ, particularly when van Gaal's star started rising at Ajax. But at AZ he wanted total control, and the club was just not prepared to hand over the reins.

The episode is also demonstrative of van Gaal's enduring problems with the media. He was particularly offended by the portrayal of *Voetbal International*, which calls itself 'the only magazine that matters in Dutch football'. In a later interview with a reporter of the magazine, Kees Jansma, the humiliated van Gaal expressed his dismay over what he saw as undue interference of the periodical in the internal affairs of the AZ club management. '*Voetbal International* Decides Who Becomes Coach Where and Who is Fired' was the headline of the subsequent four-page article which resulted from that exchange. Van Gaal was especially galled that Jansma had had the nerve to call him 'authoritarian' and 'hysterical'. Van Gaal alleged that the journalist and his magazine were a primary cause of misconceptions among AZ board members: 'I respected you. I read your pieces. I had never expected such a condemnation of me as coach from you. When you, who are such a personality, cut down someone the way you did with me, it is no small wonder that board members start to parrot what you say.' 'That's how it is,' Jansma countered, 'I have seen you at work during two AZ games, with [head coach] Hans Eijkenbroek as a wounded fledgling on the bench next to you and you as a screaming and raging field marshal supervising the action. Not a bad word about your qualities as a coach, but from a human perspective I was put off.' Van Gaal responded, undeterred: 'I have set so much in motion at AZ: the scouting, the medical support, you name it. Yes, I am so arrogant as to think that I would find it incredible if professional football would now give me the cold shoulder.'

AZ ended the 1987–88 season in the fifteenth place and was relegated on goal difference to the *Eerste Divisie*. It took nearly a decade before the club would reclaim its position in the *Eredivisie*. As for Louis van Gaal, he need not have worried. Far from football giving him the cold shoulder, a new opportunity quickly arose at the biggest club in the country: Ajax.

AJAX AND THE 'DUTCH SCHOOL'

'Quality is the exclusion of coincidence.'
Framed saying on van Gaal's office wall at Ajax.

Van Gaal was originally asked to become Ajax youth co-ordinator for the 1988–89 season. But trouble at the club quickly changed this intended role. The flow of good performances of Ajax under 'Saviour' Johan Cruyff, including winning the 1987 UEFA Cup Winners' Cup, had slowed to a trickle during the following season. Key players were leaving: Marco van Basten moved to AC Milan and Frank Rijkaard left for Real Zaragoza. Cruyff blamed the board for having a poor transfer strategy and wanted to be fully in charge of all technical decisions, something the club refused. This resulted in Cruyff's move to Barcelona, where he engineered a series of unprecedented successes. Back at Ajax, Cruyff was temporarily replaced by a coaching triumvirate, which in turn was succeeded by the Swiss coach Kurt Linder. He did not last until October and was replaced by the duo of Spitz Kohn and Louis van Gaal.

This odd and chaotic series of managerial successions did not help build up Ajax's competitive edge, and it was up to this latest managerial incarnation to wring some success from what was left of the season. This they did with surprising efficiency, manoeuvring the team into second place in the *Eredivisie*. 'Louis is damned arrogant and we like arrogant people here,' was how Ajax chairman Ton Harmsen introduced his new appointment to the media. Van Gaal may not have agreed with such a character assessment, but his confident swagger made a positive impression in the halls of power at Holland's dominant club of that time. His first words as Ajax coach at the press conference announcing his appointment were, 'I am a straightforward, fair and righteous person. Which may sometimes seem harsh' – arguably proving Harmsen right.

Then Leo Beenhakker was appointed as Ajax's new coach. Beenhakker is a comparative rarity among Dutch professional football coaches, having never been a professional player himself. Although van Gaal is not averse to including some comic relief on the menu, he inclines to gravitas when it comes to things that matter to him. Beenhakker has a somewhat lighter touch. Cigar in hand, 'Don Leo', as he came to be known during his days in Spain, created many intriguing sound bites that have endeared him to the media. Both men, however, believe in hard work. In the 1980s Beenhakker coined the term *patatgeneratie* – the 'French fries generation' – to describe a group of self-indulgent players with poor work ethic, who had come of age in the newly affluent Netherlands. Prior to his arrival at Ajax he had helped Real Madrid to three consecutive national championships. But after experiencing several years of *rabia*, the 'fury' that drives the Spanish game, he returned to the cooler and more sedate Lowlands.

Beenhakker was of the opinion that van Gaal was not yet ready to be his assistant. Thus Louis went back to his original posting with the youth players. There, in the summer of 1989, he became acquainted with a budding generation of Dutch players of Surinamese descent – Clarence Seedorf, Patrick Kluivert, Edgar Davids and

Michael Reiziger. During the same year he was admitted to the coaching course of the KNVB, which, as a side benefit, included an apprenticeship with Johan Cruyff at Barcelona.

Under van Gaal, the educational approach towards the youth players at Ajax changed. He extended the training programme until the boys turned 20: 'We give young players the opportunity to prepare themselves for a career in professional football. The discipline and mental resilience of a player have to be perfected from his eighteenth to twentieth year. During that time he has to learn what he should and should not do later as a professional, and what his right place is on the pitch and in the group.'

In 1990 van Gaal replaced Spitz Kohn as Beenhakker's assistant. In *Ajax Magazine* he confessed that the move had not been as easy as some might have expected: 'It is very satisfying [to train the youth team] because you receive so much appreciation and respect from those boys. It really would have been nice to continue, but I think that in that case you don't get any further than being a youth coach. Ajax is the highest level you can reach. It is the best group you can train with in the Netherlands.' Prophetically, he added, 'I am so bold as to say that if the current group sticks together, they can also reach the highest level in Europe.' Beenhakker quickly learned that his new assistant was a perfectionist and micromanager who could not, and would not, leave anything to chance. But it also became clear that the two men, though both committed to getting the most out of the team, had different management philosophies. Beenhakker considered his players professionals who were aware of their responsibilities; hence, he did not mind when a player arrived a few minutes late for training. This, of course, was anathema to van Gaal, the disciplinarian. The two differed tactically as well, which regularly led to very lively and sparky debates at staff meetings. Van

Gaal, though, had learned from his time at AZ not to overstep his boundaries and to keep his proper place as the assistant coach. He fully aligned himself with the decisions of the head coach, at least in public.

Privately, van Gaal was itching to take the helm himself, somewhere. He tested the waters at the southern Dutch club Roda JC, at NAC Breda, and at his former club Sparta, where there was room for a new head coach. But things didn't work out: either his potential new employers were a little overwhelmed by the ambitious coaching objectives of the hard-driven Amsterdammer, or van Gaal himself hesitated to relocate, with the possibility of eventually becoming head coach at Ajax casting a large shadow over options elsewhere.

His hesitation turned out to be the right call: in September 1991 Beenhakker decided to reimmerse himself in Spanish football when Real Madrid made him a financially appealing offer. The board was not pleased, and Ajax chairman Michael van Praag even spoke of a 'betrayal'. Van Gaal was called upon to fill the ensuing vacuum, but his appointment did not go down well with the media. His spiky demeanour made him an unpopular choice, and *De Telegraaf* spearheaded a futile campaign to replace him with Johan Cruyff. The *Gemeenschappelijke Persdienst*, the Dutch associated press service, coolly observed, 'The gifted midfielder of bygone days hasn't changed a bit and comes across just as arrogantly as in the past at Ajax, Antwerp, AZ and Sparta.'

The boy from Watergraafsmeer was now centre stage at Ajax. The new role also meant a financial quantum leap – an annual income of close to 400,000 guilders. In an interview with *Playboy*, van Gaal confessed, 'I sat in my car and suddenly I realised, "I am technical director of Ajax." I began sweating profusely. That lasted for only one minute. Afterwards, I never again had that feeling.'

Things got off to a rather slow start and van Gaal's Ajax managed just 20 points out of its first 16 games. The supporters were not familiar with the tall former youth trainer and did not have a lot of confidence in him. Calls from the stands for 'Johan Cruyff' to return were interspersed by shouts of 'van Gaal, get out!' Van Gaal ignored them: 'Of course, I read the newspapers and hear those catcalls. But I will not change my attitude. After the departure of my predecessor I started doing things the way I felt I had to. Not because he did things badly, but because my ideas are just different from Beenhakker's. Besides, there is no reason for an adjustment. Our problem is not a lack of quality in the squad. The media are putting enormous pressure on us. You can't complain about that when you play with a team like Ajax, but it doesn't make my work any easier. What's worse, after every defeat, the pressures increase and player self-confidence decreases. There is plenty of motivation, but motivation alone is not enough.'

Van Gaal's controversial decision-making gave the fans and media more grounds for criticism. Jan Wouters, the 33-year-old veteran who had been brought to Ajax by Johan Cruyff in 1986, lost his place in central midfield and was expelled to the right flank, being replaced by Wim Jonk. Although the supporters recognised Jonk's quality, they did not take kindly to the perceived demotion of their favourite. Despite Wouters becoming Dutch Footballer of the Year in 1990, his role seemed to be marginalised. Relations between the two, each as headstrong as the other, were far from smooth, and at the end of 1991 Wouters moved to Bayern Munich. Van Gaal noted, 'We are going to miss Wouters. He was one of those people who opened his mouth. I really wished that everyone on the pitch would say something sometimes. That could prove to be very productive. There is no second Jan Wouters.'

Bryan Roy had even more difficulty aligning himself with the van Gaal vision. He was a media darling and appealed to the public through his individual brilliance. As van Gaal put it, 'The supporters have always adored Bryan because in the Netherlands the emphasis is on kicking the ball around nicely and not on all the other disciplines that I find equally important.' Indeed, Roy's accelerations around opponents would regularly bring spectators to their feet. Yet the coach put him on the bench for a time and even compelled him to play a game in the reserves. Van Gaal hoped that this humiliation would motivate the fleet-footed winger to submit himself to the new team discipline. 'That causes me pain,' van Gaal said, 'just as I feel pain when I see that Roy is not working on things he should be working on. Then I have to intervene. I have to take the boy off or call him to an account within the group – not in order to drag him through the mud but to help him.'

Whatever sympathy the coach may have had for the young player did not communicate well. Both the press and the public were in shock when van Gaal, in his trademark straight-talking manner, decided to call time on Roy as an Ajax player: 'During the past four years I have tried to improve his effectiveness. But I do not any longer see any improvement. I no longer believe in Roy. I have said this to the board as well. I informed Roy that he can start looking for a different club. I have tried everything with him, even the inclusion of individual trainings. He did not mind running for the team, but he could not think for the team. It was not possible to improve him. I blame myself for that.' He did not think that Roy was either lazy or selfish, but concluded that the player simply lacked football intelligence. Van Gaal was repeatedly called to account for his treatment of the young player: 'As coach it wasn't difficult, as a human being it was. As coach I know that I am right, as a person I am struggling with it. I know that I caused Bryan pain and I found that most unpleasant.' Unfortunately, these assurances did little to change the reigning perception among many that Louis van Gaal was a ruthless person.

Then striker Jonny van 't Schip announced that he no longer wanted to play on the right wing. Van 't Schip had been part of the proverbial Ajax furniture for a full decade and felt increasingly sidelined. Van Gaal, once again, was unrelenting. He believed he needed to play with two wingmen up front and was unwilling to adjust his strategy to suit van 't Schip's preference. The player disappeared from the team and eventually ended up in the stands. This was van Gaal policy: he and he alone decided whether and where a player was needed, not the player himself. In the van Gaal philosophy, the player has to be integrated with the team and the system.

What van Gaal was looking for was, as he put it, 'multi-functional players': players who could play with both feet, had both defensive and attacking capabilities, were physically strong, quick starters, had the necessary tactical acumen to function smoothly in different formations and, above all, use these skills as part of a collective team effort. He found them in people like Michael Reiziger, Ronald de Boer, Winston Bogarde and Edgar Davids. Davids in particular was the sort of player van Gaal wanted. The diminutive 1.68m midfielder was raised on a diet of van Gaal football philosophy and practice. He had the speed, technique and work ethic the coach wanted to see in his players, and he scored goals, especially when they were most needed. He was nicknamed 'the pit bull' by van Gaal in honour of his fierce style of play and midfield dominance. In many ways he was the ideal 'multi-functional player'.

No understanding of Ajax is complete without mentioning the godfather of Dutch football, Rinus Michels. The coaching legend –

'The General' – was proclaimed by FIFA as 'coach of the century' in 1999. Michels was one of the greatest coaches ever. He was also the inventor of 'total football', the influential tactical theory in which any player should be able to take over the role of any other player in the team. In total football, which Michels developed while head coach of Ajax, a player who moves out of his position is immediately replaced by a teammate. Thus, the team retains its intended organisational structure. No player is fixed in their nominal role; anyone can be successively a defender, a midfielder and an attacker. Total football's tactical success depends largely on the adaptability of each footballer within the team, in particular his ability to quickly change positions depending on the situation. The theory requires players to be comfortable in multiple positions and to be able to exert the additional effort required to make such transitions. Hence, it puts high technical and physical demands on them.

With its emphasis on attacking, total football became almost a religion for Dutch football fans. Yet it started out as something different. It was created by Michels not for aesthetic reasons but to win football matches. First at Ajax and later in the Dutch national team, his players were artists. But they were also extremely tough and aggressive. Their tactics – pressing, position-switching, relentless attack – were designed purely for victory. Total football was the result of a search for a way to break open entrenched defences. This required actions during the build-up and attack that would surprise the opponent. Frequent changes in positions, within and between the three lines – defence, midfield and attack – were encouraged. All players were allowed to participate in the build-up and attack as long as they were also responsible for their defensive duties. The main aim of this type of attacking pressure football was to regain possession as soon as possible after the ball was lost in the opponent's half during an attack. The trapping of the opponents in their own half is only possible when all the lines are pushed forwards and the team plays close together. This automatically means that the team gives away a lot of space in its own half and is vulnerable to counter-attacks. The coach plans to play mostly in the opponent's half of the pitch and the team therefore has to defend far away from its own goal. Consequently, the team cannot afford to lose possession during the build-up.

Total football and the attacking pressure that is part of it creates a spectacular kind of game. It is a feast for the spectators, and Dutch fans have come to almost expect it from their teams, especially at Ajax. However, it put great demands on individual players and the team as a whole. This approach requires years of selecting the right players and structured team building. The most compatible organisational form is the 4-3-3 or even the 3-4-3 system. The assumption is that the coach will carry the play forwards as much as possible. This is quite challenging and only a few coaches are audacious enough to fully commit to such tactics.

Johan Cruyff, the system's most famous exponent after Michels, said about him, 'I always greatly admired his leadership. Both as a player and as a coach there is nobody who taught me as much as he did. He was a sportsman who put the Netherlands on the map in such a way that almost everybody still benefits from it. There is no one I learned from more than Rinus Michels. I often tried to imitate him, and that's the greatest compliment one could give.' During his time as player, although Cruyff was fielded as centre forward, he wandered all over the pitch, popping up wherever he could do most damage to the opposing team.

The 1972 European Cup final proved to be total football's finest hour. After Ajax's 2–0 victory over Inter Milan, newspapers around Europe reported the 'death of *catenaccio* and triumph of total football'. The Dutch newspaper *Algemeen Dagblad* declared, 'The Inter system undermined. Defensive football is destroyed.' In 1972 Ajax won the European Cup, Dutch league, Dutch Cup, Intercontinental Cup and European Super Cup, one of only two teams in history to achieve the quintuple.

The Ajax van Gaal encountered, then, was a team steeped in the total football philosophy of Rinus Michels and further fired up by the the attack-minded Johan Cruyff. Everyone wanted to go forwards and join in the attack, including the goalkeeper. The *meevoetballende* goalkeeper, 'football-playing' keeper, drew the last man further away from the goal than more conventional playing styles warranted. Ajax's approach required a goalkeeper who did not comfortably remain in the penalty box, but who intercepted balls that fell behind the defence. He shared responsibility for the build-up of the attack and the rapid counters. This created an attractive but risky game. Van Gaal had to devise a strategy that would plug the holes left in the defence of such an attacking team. This resulted in a very controlled build-up of the attack, with intensive ball rotation. If the attack encountered too much resistance on the right, a shift to the other wing might be needed. The wingers had to be prepared to suddenly receive the ball on the touchline and carry it forwards, thus keeping the play wide. Every player had to be keenly aware both of his own position and that of his teammates. This required tight controls, and the entire team had to be able to shift over the field as a unit. In his minute definition of the tasks of each player and the formulation of tactical detail van Gaal proved to be a control freak. On his office wall he had framed his creed, 'Quality is the exclusion of coincidence.'

Sceptics suggest that the intense pressing and high offside trap that total football prescribes – in order to keep the field small when out of possession and as wide as possible when in possession to retain the ball – was really unsustainable. Particularly in modern times, the number of games and the pace at which they're played have become prohibitive in that regard. Jonathan Wilson alleges in his book, *Inverting the Pyramid: A History of Football Tactics*, that even the great Ajax of the 1970s couldn't really pull it off either. According to his research, 'Their team doctor had them on a steady diet of amphetamines, painkillers and muscle-relaxants.' Presumably, van Gaal's Ajax of the mid-1990s managed it only by virtue of having predominantly young players aged between 18 and 22. According to the sceptics, many of the modern players are primarily specialists, unprepared to play in every position the way the rapid swapping of positions of total football demands.

It takes a decade or so for teams to learn how to instinctively switch positions. Today, clubs go through players so quickly that they don't have the time to master the system, whereas the Ajax teams of the 1970s and 1990s had been staffed largely from within, growing up together and learning the system in the academy. These days, players know they're more valuable if they play one position well, rather than being passable at two or three. In total football, by contrast, the individual becomes a cog in the machine for the greater good. Self-sacrifice is irreconcilable with the modern footballer, and ironically the blame for that lies with Johan Cruyff, who became the first Dutch football star to cross over into pop culture.

For those who espouse the total football philosophy, the biggest problems are team building and strategy. It is important for the system to bring the skills of the team to the highest level through the establishment of clear relations between strikers, midfielders and defenders. Once players understand the core of modern football, they are able to use their unique qualities and skills for the team. Total football does not distinguish between defenders and attackers. In the past, a striker did not join the defence because he thought he had already done enough if he had scored a goal. In total football, it is a minus for the whole team if the strikers only attack.

Synergy, from the Greek *syn-ergo* meaning working together, is the term used to describe a situation where the final outcome of a system is greater than the sum of its parts. The opposite of synergy is antagonism, the phenomenon where two or more agents in combination have an overall effect that is less than the sum of their individual potentials. Synergy in terms of management refers to successfully tapping the full potential of individuals in the context of a particular group.

In modern football there is an abundance of talent, which, due to the virtually unlimited mobility in the international transfer market, is readily available to the highest bidder. But money alone does not guarantee excellence. The coach's challenge is how to make a smooth operating collective out of a loose gathering of individuals, no matter how gifted. The Netherlands, in particular, has often failed to take this hurdle successfully. The country has produced a surprising number of extraordinary players, yet Dutch teams have failed to be successful at decisive moments of most international competitions because of the tendency of Dutch players to play for themselves rather than the team. To get a group of bickering Dutchmen to perform as an authentic unit is no small feat, as many coaches in the Netherlands – both Dutch and non-Dutch – have learned the hard way.

Historically, the Netherlands has long found itself surrounded by its better-known neighbours of Germany, France and Britain. As well as being surrounded by great powers, the Netherlands is also embraced by water on many sides. The country is almost entirely flat, and in many places the land is well below sea level. As a result, the Dutch have frequently had to wage war with enemies of two types – political opponents and the natural elements. This has made them resilient, enterprising, tough and creative. The Netherlands was invaded on numerous occasions. The Spanish, the French and the Germans all marched armies straight across the little country, but all were successfully repelled eventually. In many places the Dutch have expanded their territory by reclaiming land from the sea through the creation of *polders*. The Dutch occasionally proclaim, somewhat presumptuously, that 'God created the world, but the Dutch created Holland.'

These permanent struggles with human neighbours and nature have made the Dutch tenacious, pig-headed and, in a way, rebellious. The Dutch call it *eigenwijs*, which literally means 'self-wise'. There is a natural inclination to want to defy the odds, and this trait is exquisitely personified in Louis van Gaal.

Whenever van Gaal has worked abroad, people understandably assumed that he would be in need of some advice because of his unfamiliarity with the local culture and football customs. Instead, he always insisted on following 'his way' – wherever he has worked he has unyieldingly stuck to his guns. Being a true Dutchman, he has no difficulty ignoring advice, no matter how well-intended some of it may have been. Van Gaal is a fascinating contradiction: an ultra-individualist utterly devoted to the collective effort.

Van Gaal's intense insistence on team unity at Ajax was initially not well received. The media were alternately repulsed, bemused and amused by what they thought would be a passing craze. Van Gaal attempted to explain his aims: 'Team building means: showing respect for your fellow man and showing respect for the qualities of your fellow man; mirroring yourself in those qualities and doing something with that. Golfing or bowling together is a part of getting to know each other in a different manner. The media unjustly emphasises such details. When I started, I developed an exercise of holding hands and heading the ball around. That was immediately ridiculed, as if this were the ultimate form of team building.'

Team building itself was of course not new, but the priority van Gaal gave to it was. He wanted input, but he wanted it within a framework of discipline. He eliminated freelancers, players who pursued their opponents all over the pitch. In his thinking it was particularly important that everyone kept his position so that there would be no defensive gaps. In van Gaal's philosophy the team comes before everything. His definition of 'the team' did not just mean the 11 or 14 players who had been involved in the game of the day, but also the reserves, the technical staff and other personnel, from the kit man to the cook. When Ajax won the Champions League in 1995, van Gaal went into the Ajax laundry room, put the cup on a washing machine and told the perplexed laundry women, 'So, this one is also for you!' Van Gaal was the pivot who created a 'we-feeling' among the people he worked with. There was one man absolutely in charge of 'the team', and that was van Gaal.

Van Gaal also put great emphasis on communication. Van Gaal constantly spoke to his players: before training, after training, during training. He would stop play dead in its tracks to point out some deficiency and lecture players on the right way – sometimes calmly, sometimes passionately. Van Gaal told his players that he wanted them to 'read the game', another expression that was made light of in the press. He tried to communicate that not only the coach but the players as well should have keen tactical insight so that they could make responsible decisions at decisive moments of the game. He claimed, 'You play football with your brain. Instinctual reactions are part of it, but it is important to always put the intuitive in service of the rational. Then you make headway. If you just play intuitively, you perform your tricks at the wrong moments.'

Van Gaal has often been accused of being a dictator by his detractors. Autocratic he may be, but it certainly is not true that he brooks no dissent. In response to such allegations he stated, 'I have always had trouble with people who criticise my approach as one of just drilling and player subjugation. Those who would thoroughly analyse my way of working could never come to such conclusions because it is contrary to my view of life. […] As you begin to communicate more and explain, they understand better. This shows in the way they are playing now. They are more aware of each other and interact better, on and off the pitch. At first, the match review was a monologue from my side, but now it is a dialogue. They offer solutions out of their own initiative and can comment on each other's positive and negative qualities. I think that is great because this is how you create the feeling of "we are a team".'

In addition to the focus on team building and communication, the scouting organisation at Ajax was also thoroughly reviewed. In van Gaal's opinion, 'There was no policy. Now [Ajax scout] Ton Pronk has his own network. Whenever we receive a tip about a player, we take a close look. All the data are put into the computer system. Based on those data he is assigned a ranking, for various positions. For one position he may end up being number one; for another position number three. Every candidate is evaluated in four areas: technique, insight, personality, and speed – "TIPS" we call that.' After Ajax's poor start under van Gaal's management, Ajax won its final 11 games, trailing the champions PSV by a mere 3 points. The doubters had been won over, and even the critics admitted that Ajax had a highly credible and competent new head coach.

Van Gaal had had an impact on his immediate environment: how the Ajax players played their game. But he also had a wider-reaching effect on how Dutch coaches thought about football and plied their trade. His style woke everybody up and forced them to re-evaluate their assumptions about how the game was played. Certainly, the flamboyance with which he introduced his ideas contributed to this revival; like him or otherwise, it was almost impossible to ignore the man. Under the influence of the van Gaal approach, Dutch coaches started to treat their teams as an organic whole. So while Rinus Michels is justly recognised as the founder of this integrated playing style, it is van Gaal who has been the coach to made it work more efficiently than any coach since.

THE
'IRON TULIP'

'The discipline of desire is the background of character.'
John Locke

In top-level games there are always instances when one moment of mental weakness from one player can decide the course of a match and, hence, the championship or tournament. The quality on the pitch is such that the opponent will immediately profit from a moment of inattention. It is down to the coach to get his players in the right frame of mind to avoid this. After all, the purpose of training is not just acquiring tactical skills but also the mental framework that underlies it. A coach who can convince his players of the necessity of this is invaluable. The best players know that football is played more without the ball than with the ball. The more they play with their head, the easier they will be on their legs, and the more energy they will conserve.

Such football intelligence is created from a number of match-related mental qualities. The emphasis varies from player to player, but to a greater or lesser degree they are essential for every top-level player: the conviction and willingness to be a winner; courage, self-confidence, and a controlled fear to lose; controlled aggression and stamina; the ability to accept and deal with defeat; to take and demand responsibility; to maintain team discipline and team spirit; and engender a sense of responsibility for the team. Naturally, a ball virtuoso will not become a fighter in duels with an opponent. The controlled fear to lose also has its limits. A true goal-scorer will not get thrown off balance by blasting a shot into row Z, but another player might be too scared to shoot or make a long pass. The solidarity players feel for each other has a positive influence on their mentality. This personal responsibility for achieving a good collective performance is the most important tool available to the coach to influence the mentality of his players.

The environment a coach creates at a club is crucial in achieving this. This is not an easy assignment, and there is no ready recipe for maintaining such a positive atmosphere: maintaining the set-up demands the constant attention of the coach. When holding a training camp that lasts for a few weeks, the coach has to deal with all kinds of problems. The quality of the hotel and the facilities must be exceptionally good. Another important aspect is to find a good balance between tension and relaxation. At such camps there are a number of 'empty' hours that need to be filled by a group that is exclusively made up of males, many, if not all of them, millionaires. Then there is the amount of time spent with family. It is usual, for example, that after a match the players of the Dutch national team always have a day they are allowed to spend with their loved ones. It gives the group an opportunity to break with the daily routine.

At Ajax, Louis van Gaal showcased his leadership style for the first time: that of a general commanding his troops in battle. What he says clearly sets the tone as to who is in charge, at training and in the dressing room. There are few things that irk the 'Iron Tulip' as much as a player who loses concentration. Even a single mistake is mercilessly berated. The furious speeches van Gaal would give at after-game meetings quickly earned him the reputation of being an enlightened despot – or perhaps not even that enlightened! Van Gaal himself does not give much credence to what he considered to be stereotypical characterisations: 'Of course, it is better copy to show van Gaal when he is cussing at players or ranting like an animal. People find this entertaining. But they do this, they just stick a label on you, and then I have to start explaining how it all works. Especially because these same media people don't show how I compliment a player every now and then. Apparently, that is not interesting.

'Some in the media write, "Van Gaal is a dictator!" No, I'm not. My rules are not narrow. Everyone can move within them, maintaining his own identity. I do not impose rules from above. I observe – and take measures. No individual is allowed to do as he pleases.' At the same time, van Gaal allows his stars a certain degree of freedom: 'With me, players of great creativity receive additional freedoms.' However, not only must their performance be at the right level, they must also observe van Gaal's rules of behaviour and do their bit for the team. When those conditions are fulfilled, 'It is not bad to occasionally miss training. But I explain that to the entire team. That is part of the holistic principle.'

Reporters and supporters were unaware of how van Gaal would warmly counsel his players in private conversation. He completely protected his charges, forming a shield around his team and keeping it safe from negative, distracting and harmful influences. At Ajax under van Gaal, everyone felt 'safe from the outside'. On the 'inside', van Gaal was not averse to letting a player have it if he did not do his very best. But that did not apply to those who went through a temporary dip in form. He was very good at telling the difference.

Football at the top level is brain over brawn; psychological sharpness gives a team its cutting edge. Concentration is essential for van Gaal. He assumes that a player who cannot focus for 60 minutes at training is in danger of losing his concentration during a game. Goals almost always come at a time when minds wander, and this has to be eliminated at all cost. In van Gaal's view, physical performance is relatively easy to improve, whereas mental sharpness requires much more attention: 'I want to keep the minds of the players fresh. They have to work a lot with their spirit. Players appreciate [short-term physical exercises] much more than the old mind-numbing endurance tests. I greatly value the solutions the players bring themselves.'

When the Ajax players completed an exercise in a perfunctory manner, van Gaal would become very angry: 'If sloppiness creeps into the game, we lose possession and must chase the opponent, which is, also mentally, very tiring. When I see that someone loses his concentration, I explode. They know that. And they never get angry over that. I think that they kind of like it that I have such a primal response. They realise they need it.' This same level of application was required during training: 'This is a profession, an occupation. We fool around a little here also, but not as often as elsewhere. Because I believe that training has to be an experience. If you go to training with the thought, "just nicely working with the ball", then you should not play at Ajax.' This type of demanding training was also necessary to drill players in basic game discipline and timing: '[How to] play the ball on time; be in space on time; the way you pass the ball to a teammate in relation to an opponent; thinking collectively during possession and when losing the ball. This kind of foundation has to be laid in a group when between 12 or 16 years of age. You cannot teach an old dog new tricks. With veterans you have to work on the consistency of their performance level.'

Team discipline was applied both on and off the pitch. It was unacceptable for a player to arrive even a minute late, and it was costly too: 350 guilders, quite a bit of money in those days. If the offence was repeated, the penalty was doubled. Shirts had to be tucked into shorts, and socks had to be pulled up: 'Those who don't have their shirt in their shorts want to stand out, or separate themselves. Why would you want to stand out when you are playing in a team? You have to perform well. Adapt yourself to the team. You stand out through your game, not through your appearance. If Clarence Seedorf wants to wear a white shirt, he has to be able to convince the group of the necessity of a white shirt. There really may be a reason for that, but that has to be communicated.' At press conferences, the players wore the Ajax suit, with matching tie and shoes. The jacket had to be buttoned up. Van Gaal would get irritated over details such as players not putting used towels in the laundry basket in the dressing room. If someone threw his towel elsewhere, he could take it home and wash it himself. Another van Gaal hallmark was that everyone, including the superstars, would lug around equipment, not only the supplies man or the reserves.

At team meals, everybody would start eating together. Reading newspapers at breakfast was prohibited. Van Gaal expected the players to talk to each other, preferably about football, but other topics would be acceptable as well. He wanted them to exchange professional ideas and learn from each other. Van Gaal guarded his turf strictly. Access to the *spelershome* – the player's area – was limited for reporters and even Ajax veterans were somewhat restricted in their movements. These former stars were allowed to drop in every once in a while, but weren't allowed to hang around. 'If there are strange birds around,' van Gaal explained, 'the players won't talk to each other. That is why the *spelershome* is closed from 12:30 p.m. to 2:30 p.m. Now my players play cards or backgammon. Those are social activities, which I haven't seen for about two years.' Van Gaal would also organise outings to build team spirit, including paint-ball, golf or bowling.

Perhaps van Gaal's experience as a teacher has contributed to his healthy understanding of the human being as an social animal, a *gestalt*. Van Gaal reflected, 'My first idol was Henk Groot, then came J. F. Kennedy, and next Rinus Michels. I got very disappointed by Kennedy. When I was still young I didn't see it, but he did a lot of things in his own personal interest, and not in the interest of the US and the world. Besides, he had all kinds of extramarital affairs. I am not a proponent of that either.'

When van Gaal interviewed a potential new player, the applicant would receive a thorough grilling; no subject remained untouched. He wanted to know the person's family background, what school he had attended and so on. Football topics would be discussed as well, but what van Gaal really wanted to know was what a person was made of. He wanted to understand the player's mind. Once a player was employed, the coach kept his ear to the ground concerning the player's family situation. Being the consummate family man himself, he understood that challenges on the home front could provide a major obstacle to a player's performance. It is in a coach's best interest that the home environment is harmonious. Van Gaal knew the names of players' wives and children and would regularly ask about the health of a pregnant wife and never miss a birthday.

In 2007, Louis van Gaal enlisted the services of a psychologist at his second spell at AZ. Leo van der Burg, whose agency more commonly instructed corporate managers, was to provide advice to the coaching staff on how to properly guide players. 'A person is not always in balance,' van Gaal said. 'I am working with psychology and neuro-feedback because I am always looking for better means to help players understand themselves better, and thus, control themselves better.' Van der Burg himself explained that, 'I try to help the coaches to look at the players in a certain way because many football coaches only see the game, but not the players. They can all play football, but what matters is that players are guided in a way that suits them. For instance, one player may need a lot of guidance, which will just confuse another. It is part of the coach's responsibility to able to deal with that.' Van der Burg primarily gave guidance and advice to van Gaal and his staff, rather than directly to the players. Van Gaal thought that was the way to do it. 'My players already have to deal with a number of people who evaluate them. That is why we use the services of a psychologist to provide the technical staff with insights that can help them instruct the players. He is a coach for the coaches.'

Van der Burg is of the opinion that most football coaches do not understand the value of psychological insight. 'Even on current coaching courses almost no attention is given to the personality of the player. Almost nobody knows how people function. We have more understanding of our vacuum cleaner or washing machine than about ourselves. In business that costs millions. Coaches try and look at the players, but they don't see anything. You can also look under the hood of a car, but if you don't have any knowledge you won't see anything.'

Van der Burg and his colleagues shared their thoughts twice a month with van Gaal and his assistants. Dwelling on the negative is futile, according to him: 'There isn't a single footballer who intentionally plays a poor game in front of 50,000 people. I often hear coaches complain after a game that they lost because so and so didn't reach their level. Wrong. As coach you have to ask yourself why you were unable to prepare them optimally for the match.' In that context, working on improving weak points seems rather futile. 'In Germany they once did research among left-footed players. They were asked to only shoot with their right. The result was that the right leg of those boys had improved by 3 per cent after those three months. But the left leg had declined by 30 per cent. So the expression "talent development" should be scrapped from the lexicon. You should allow players to do what they are good at. Let every player train independently to develop his strong points and make use of them. I also believe that training should consist of 80 per cent individual exercises.' This is an unconventional idea, but one that the more forward thinking van Gaal might be more inclined to listen to in earnest than many of his more conservative colleagues.

To understand how a coach can offer a complete and suitable education to his players, he needs to first understand and accept their true nature. People are made up of *mind* and *body*, and the mind, in turn, is composed of *intellect*, *emotion* and *will*. All of these four dimensions of the individual need to be nurtured and developed in a harmonious and well-balanced way. In sports training there is an excessive emphasis on the bodily aspect, with dire consequences. The individual must be understood as a unique human being with intellectual, emotional, volitional and physical powers.

Van Gaal is consistent – in his philosophy, in his demand for discipline, and in his emotional intensity – as Bayern Munich found out when he was manager there: 'He's the right man at the right club at the right time,' said chairman Karl-Heinz Rummenigge. 'This is the most professional working relationship we've ever had with a coach.'

'He's the father of the whole thing,' Franz Beckenbauer noted, and in more than just one way. Van Gaal the father-figure embodies the warmth and family-friendliness he likes to speak about. It was in keeping that Franck Ribéry leapt into his arms after scoring in Dortmund, and Arjen Robben joyfully knocked him to the running track at the Weser Stadium in Bremen after a winning strike. And while van Gaal was readying Martin Demichelis to come on as a substitute, with the player still grumbling about not being picked to start, van Gaal simply planted a kiss on the Argentine's cheek. 'A great guy,' Thomas Müller observed.

GOLDEN YEARS IN AMSTERDAM

'I don't need the eleven best, I need the best eleven.'

Louis van Gaal

Ajax's return to the European spotlight in the UEFA Cup, after a year on the sidelines, was going to last more than one or two rounds. Swedish side Örebro SK and German club Rot-Weiss Essen were swiftly pushed aside. In the next round, the Spanish side CA Osasuna was considered a tougher opponent, but two 1–0 victories came courtesy of Dennis Bergkamp. Louis van Gaal's plans for the team, in which the partnership of provider Wim Jonk and finisher Dennis Bergkamp was the main weapon, were becoming clear. The quarter-final brought the feel-good nights of European football back to Amsterdam, when KAA Gent were crushed 3–0. Semi-final opponent Genoa was beaten 3–2 in Italy, in one of the most spectacular European games Ajax had been involved in. The red Roman candles, the thousands of scarves, the singing and the pride all returned. Once again, Dennis Bergkamp was the man to finish it off in a nervy 1–1 draw in Amsterdam.

Ajax had reached the UEFA Cup final with a self-built team consisting of 'real' Ajax players, most of them from their own youth system. The two-game final brought Ajax to the Stadio Delle Alpi in Turin, where Torino FC saw Wim Jonk fire an incredible long-distance shot into the upper corner of the goal for a 2–2 draw. The second leg of the final took place at the electrically charged Olympic Stadium on 13 May 1992. The Italians pressed in another nerve-racking game, hitting the post twice and the crossbar once, three minutes before the final whistle. Ajax were depleted – Rob Alflen replacing a sick Bergkamp, Stefan Pettersson breaking his collar-bone against the corner flag – but somehow hung on. The final whistle was liberation – a scoreless draw meant that Ajax had won on away goals. Van Gaal had led Ajax to the UEFA Cup in his first season in charge.

Louis van Gaal had built something beautiful in a remarkably short period. Ajax's success immediately attracted attention from the bigger football leagues, in particular from the Italian *Serie A*. Inter Milan snatched the Jonk and Bergkamp 'super duo' away. John van 't Schip and Marciano Vink moved to Genoa, and midfielder Michel Kreek was signed by Padova. Van Gaal had to go back to the drawing board and start almost from scratch. That's what he did, believing that the next generation was even better than the previous.

The rebuilding process came at a price, and the 1992–93 season saw too many stumbles in the league and European elimination against Italian team Parma. But the KNVB Cup was won in a convincing manner: Feyenoord was destroyed at home in Rotterdam 5–0, and SC Heerenveen were swept off the pitch 6–2 in the final. The supporters, usually impatient during the building of a new team, were behind the van Gaal revolution. An amazing 80,000 people joined the official Ajax Fan Club, showing their faith in the new-look team that included Edgar Davids, Frank and Ronald de Boer, Edwin van der Sar, left-winger Marc Overmars and Finnish talent Jari Litmanen. A year later, van Gaal completed his squad overhaul with home-grown talent Patrick Kluivert and Clarence Seedorf, and smartly scouted Nigerian strikers Finidi George and Nwankwo Kanu. Ajax legend Frank Rijkaard returned to finish his career at his original club.

Van Gaal set about winning the *Eredivisie* and captured the Dutch title three times in a row between 1994 and 1996. The 1994–95 season has come to be known as one of the most successful in Ajax history. The club not only again became national champion, they completely dominated the league – winning 27 games, drawing 7 and losing none. Along the way they scored an outrageous 106 goals, which works out to 3.11 per game. The only game the team lost that season was the quarter-final of the Amstel Cup – as the KNVB Cup was now called – against Feyenoord. Striker Mike Obiku ended Ajax's campaign through a golden goal in extra time.

In 1994, Louis van Gaal had his first taste of the lucrative Champions League, the recently reconfigured European Cup competition. Ajax's achievements that season were extraordinary: they rolled through the competition without losing a single game and conceded just four goals in nine outings. First AC Milan, Casino Salzburg and AEK Athens were overcome in the group stage. Then Hajduk Split and Bayern Munich were hammered, respectively, in 3–0 and 5–2 wins in the Olympic Stadium. Just as remarkably, they beat Fabio Capello's AC Milan – the defending champions, who had thrashed Johan Cruyff's Barcelona 4–0 a year earlier – three times in the competition. In the final at Vienna's Ernst Happel Stadium, AC Milan were defeated by an 87th minute goal from 18-year-old Patrick Kluivert. Ajax's fourth European Cup was paraded in front of a crowd of over 250,000 at Amsterdam's Museumplein – the first time they had won it in 22 years and the three victories of the golden Ajax years, and the only time since.

The statistics, though, do not tell the whole story. There was also the way the team was schooled in the Ajax way, with the passing, movement, technique and all that entails, but at the same time, thanks to van Gaal, eliminating the self-indulgence which too often had infected the club. Then there was the fact that eight of the 13 men who appeared in the final against Milan were products of the Ajax academy. Van Gaal's Ajax played an intoxicating brand of football, predicated upon a tactical system that dispensed with orthodox notions such as 4-4-2 or 4-3-3, but rather featured a series of interconnected diamonds with two of the most intelligent football minds in the history of the game.

At the end of this extraordinary season, foreign clubs were again knocking on the doors of several Ajax players, but, following the lead of club favourite Jari Litmanen, almost the entire team decided to stay. The new generation believed they had to stick together because they weren't quite done yet. In the league, Ajax didn't concede a goal until the tenth match of the season and became national champion for the third consecutive year. They didn't remain unbeaten this time, but ended up with even more points than the year before. The Amsterdammers got their revenge for the Amstel Cup loss the previous season by winning the Dutch Super Cup against Feyenoord. The European Super Cup was won by defeating Real Zaragoza 4–0. In Tokyo, Danny Blind scored the decisive penalty in the shoot-out against Brazilian side Grêmio FB and Ajax won the Intercontinental Cup.

That season's Champions League campaign was almost as successful as the preceding year and Ajax topped their group with even more impressive statistics: Hungarian champions Ferencvárosi Budapest, Grasshoppers and Real Madrid were eliminated in the process. The Swiss were the only team to grab a point against Ajax.

Against Madrid, the referee overlooked two Jari Litmanen goals, both times missing that the ball had crossed the goal line. It didn't matter: the Ajax victory was enough for a standing ovation by the Madrid crowd and it was one of their best performances of the season. Even so, it didn't reach the exacting standards of Louis van Gaal: 'Because the game took place in an appealing tournament and a beautiful stadium people think it is fantastic. But I noticed a lot of mistakes. We should have won 5–0 instead of 2–0.' Borussia Dortmund did not have a chance in the quarter-finals, losing twice without scoring a goal.

Ajax's defence of their title seemed to be over, however, when Greek champions and semi-final opponents Panathinaikos won 1–0 in Amsterdam. But the Greeks were unprepared for the offensive display they encountered in the return match. Litmanen silenced the Athens crowd by scoring early in the third minute. Eighty-seven minutes later, the score was 3–0 and the second consecutive final had been reached. This time, though, it was not to be. Ajax gave their worst performance in a European game for over two years against a mediocre Juventus team in Rome. Even though a Jari Litmanen goal evened out an early Ravanelli strike, the penalty shoot-out saw Ajax stumble. Whereas Juventus were perfect from the spot, Sonny Silooy and Edgar Davids each missed, handing the trophy to the Italians.

This defeat aside, these stellar accomplishments did not only mean happy fans and glowing media coverage, but also increased revenue and a very pleased board. Prize money, better sponsorship deals and improved merchandising were part of the equation. On top of the customary hats, scarves and umbrellas, the Ajax store carried watches, bicycles and even pyjamas emblazoned with the Ajax logo. A very substantial part of the club's income was generated through the sale of players whose market value had increased exponentially in the wake of Ajax victories. Interestingly, players who left Ajax for higher wages elsewhere often did not perform at their previous levels. Van Gaal was not surprised: 'I think it is logical that players who leave Ajax do not reach their former level elsewhere. Nobody trains like the way we do, and nowhere are the qualities of the players put in harmony with one another as at Ajax. Abroad, a player has to once again fend for himself. He is evaluated according to his own qualities, and not, as with us, for his value for the team. At Ajax, individual weaknesses were covered by the team. That is the essence of team building. He can excel because of the team. Other countries are way behind us in that respect: what matters there is character. It is a matter of survival: one for all and all for one. At Ajax, day after day, we are working on making each other strong. […] What should I do with players who do not want to improve in training or won't even show up in the first place? Someone who does not understand the game and just stands still when he doesn't have the ball doesn't interest me. I don't need the eleven best, I need the best eleven.

'The players that left Ajax were raised in a system that demands playing for the team. People such as Dennis Bergkamp in Italy were confronted with an entirely different football philosophy. Suddenly, they have to fight for themselves with their own colleagues. Italian football bears little resemblance to Ajax football: the Italians want to win, whereas we want to win, entertain, and create chances.

'Players count for nothing,' van Gaal continued. 'The team is everything. I set more store by a player's character than by his on-field qualities, and particularly whether he is willing to give everything to the cause. There are some incredibly talented players who haven't got the character or the personality to suit my methods.

Litmanen, for example, was a different player at Barcelona than he was at Ajax. You have to adapt to a new culture when you move to a different club, and not every player is able to do that.'

The player deficit resulting from the uneven transfer flow – many more going out than coming in – was balanced by promoting more young players into the first team. Van Gaal explained that, 'Most of the boys I already coached in the A1 [youth team] and I knew what made them tick. When I became head coach, I just let them move up [to the first team]. [...] It has been proven that our continuous youth training programme has been beneficial: without it Ajax would not have survived.'

Ajax's youth system is impressive: during van Gaal's time, the club maintained 10 youth teams, with 160 youngsters in all, and all were striving to emulate the style of the great first team. A young number 9 would be trained in such a manner that he would be able to replace the first-team number 9, Patrick Kluivert at the time. Off the pitch, the attention to detail was just as focused: physical therapists, masseurs, doctors, dietitians, psychologists and private teachers were on hand to guide the young players physically and mentally. This operation annually required around 3 million guilders – a lot of money, but a lot less than an overpriced Brazilian transfer would cost. Besides, as van Gaal explained, 'A player who has been raised by us can much more easily find himself within the Ajax system than a 25-year-old top player, who can no longer change his identity.'

To make sure the well never ran dry, the football school was regularly replenished at so-called *talentdagen*, five-day 'talent days'. At Ajax's headquarters around 7,000 promising youngsters were on computerised databases, neatly sorted according to position. Of these, several hundred between the ages of 7 and 13 would receive a much-coveted invitation letter to prove their mettle for 45 minutes on the hallowed Ajax grounds. Out of these, 40 would be selected, and after yet another selective process 16 would remain as a reinforcement of the Ajax youth ranks. The computer tracking did not end there: every apprentice was sized up in 40 evaluation categories, ranging from ball control to social behaviour. Head coach Louis van Gaal's beliefs were passed on at an early stage: 'We are living in a *laissez-faire* society. But when you play in a team, you need discipline.'

After the Bosman ruling provided clubs everywhere with a severe financial headache, the Ajax model of self-reliance increasingly became in vogue, and club representatives from across Europe found themselves *en route* to Amsterdam to study their method. It seemed, however, that few other clubs were able to implement a similar system. Questioned by *Der Spiegel* about why it might be so hard for German clubs to replicate the Amsterdam style, van Gaal pointed out that 'people lack patience. The model has something to do with our mentality, the arrogance of the capital city, and the discipline of the small Netherlands. But it would be possible to copy the basics … [You] need to settle on a vision, a system: tactics and a structure that suits. Then you get the coach that fits the system, from the youth to the first team, with all working with the same idea.'

Van Gaal believed that training should not be a matter of keeping the players busy, or exhausting them. Training should be based on game analysis. Whatever was executed poorly during the match should be revamped at the training. As a van Gaal colleague at the KNVB later observed, 'Training should not be occupational therapy, but be focused on improving the team. You could compare it to a doctor who diagnoses an illness and prescribes medicine. In football you have to be able to make adequate analyses, and next choose the right medicine. Van Gaal has mastered this dimension in minute detail. If there is no existing exercise, you just make one up to cure the ill.' It was van Gaal, in the 1990s, who abolished the endurance test as a method of building up player stamina. Since then, almost all international top clubs only train with the ball. It has always been common for van Gaal to abruptly stop a training game to show an alternative game solution and proceed by practising the best tactics. He unfailingly has a particular goal at the beginning of a season and at the beginning of a week.

One of the most common criticisms heard of the van Gaal approach at Ajax is that it was a straitjacket approach that inhibited, even stifled, player initiative. Players were expected to execute the coach-prescribed task so minutely that there was no more room for creativity. According to this view, van Gaal's Ajax would take the idea of a sort of 'Clockwork Orange' to the next logical level of systemic perfection, with an emphasis on possession and quick ball rotation. Yet right from the start of van Gaal's tenure Ajax were heavily defeating his former teams, Vitesse 4–0 and Sparta 6–0, leading van Gaal to argue that the stereotypical view of his constricting playing style did not apply: 'At Ajax I took out players of the old mould and even in the defence replaced them with others who could take initiative. Every single Ajax player is creative. First of all, you have to do your job, be on time, and be polite. We respect each other, we trust each other, and we are honest to each other. Within such a framework, you can fully develop your identity and creativity. Discipline is the basis for creativity. Players like Kanu, Davids and Kluivert understood that.'

Nonetheless, in the experience of some players, this was an exhausting style of play. There was a certain lack of *joie de vivre*, particularly during van Gaal's last year at the club. The sheer joy of running with the ball, playing it around, seemed absent. Many football fans were frustrated by the continuous, controlled circulation football, with Johan Cruyff among the critics. Playing the ball back time and again to keeper Edwin van der Sar was not their idea of the beautiful game. The 1996–97 season, van Gaal's last at Ajax, was disastrous. The spirit and tempo were gone, and the team was a shadow of its former self.

Van Gaal had a number of explanations for the decline, not least the switch to a new stadium. On 28 April 1996 Ajax had played their last home game at De Meer, before moving to the Amsterdam ArenA, in the south-eastern suburb of Bijlmermeer. The move was not a happy one. Inexplicably, the pitch was of inferior quality to the one in the old stadium, and that was disadvantageous for Ajax, which, with its emphasis on rotation football, had to keep up the pace. Players also got injured more easily on the sub-par pitch. Indeed, there seemed to be an interminable list of injuries that season: Marc Overmars suffered from a severe blow to his knee and Patrick Kluivert was out of the running for most of the year.

Then there was, according to van Gaal, the 'European Championship syndrome'. Among European nations, the Dutch stand out as one of the most opinionated. This gives Dutch football its peculiar flavour: the Dutch seem to feel that they are the ultimate connoisseurs of the sport. This breeds an overconfidence in Dutch teams that the 'lesser' football countries will automatically falter when encountering Dutch superiority. During Euro '96 that was definitely not the case. The Dutch team was troubled from the beginning by nations such as the Czech Republic and Belarus in their qualifying group. A number of Dutch players seemed to be more concerned with their personal interests and star status than with team performance. It was an outfit, as one British newspaper observed, 'said to veer on the brink of rebellion if one of them woke up displeased with the hotel bedroom décor'.

The Dutch national team was leaning heavily on Ajax talent and experience. Within this group the Surinamese-Dutch players played a prominent role. At the time of Surinamese independence in 1975, the Surinamese were given the choice of Dutch or Surinamese citizenship. Some 200,000 out of a population of 450,000 left Suriname for the Netherlands – a level of migration staggering in scope. The Surinamese experience in the Netherlands was initially rocky, with high rates of poverty, crime, drug use and unemployment. Though the social and economic position of the Surinamese-Dutch has improved over the years, it would be a stretch to suggest that genuine integration has taken place.

For many in the Surinamese community, football was seen as a potential vehicle for upward social mobility. As with van Gaal, the innate football talents of many Surinamese boys were naturally honed on the streets of Amsterdam. The results were striking: in Ajax's Champions League final against AC Milan, the club fielded no less than seven black players, the majority of whom traced their heritage to Suriname.

Van Gaal's Ajax team had seemed to be made of steel, but cracks were rapidly appearing. Rumours circulated about Finidi George and Nwankwo Kanu being underpaid, as well as whispers about racial conflicts between the Surinamese and white players on the team. Many of the black Ajax players had long felt under-appreciated and under-remunerated. This eventually led to a minor exodus of Surinamese-Dutch talent in the mid-1990s: Clarence Seedorf sought his fortunes at Sampdoria while Edgar Davids, Michael Reiziger, Patrick Kluivert and Winston Bogarde all left for AC Milan.

In this volatile atmosphere of discontent, the interaction of black and white players during Euro '96 was anything but smooth. Patrick Kluivert, the flamboyant forward, complained of a lack of contact with national team coach Guus Hiddink, and the Dutch media happily fanned the flames of existing tensions in the team. In *Obsession Magazine*, several of the players, including Kluivert, Clarence Seedorf and Winston Bogarde, suggested that there were tensions between black and white on the orange team.

The 'cabal', or *de kabel* in Dutch, was the media name for five black Surinamese-Dutch players – Kluivert, Seedorf, Bogarde, Edgar Davids and Michael Reiziger. Throughout Euro '96 the Dutch campaign was marred by disunity and backbiting. There were a lot of personality conflicts at the cost of team performance. Some critics were of the opinion that, even if few football games were won during the tournament, the team had become 'world champions [at] bitching'.

The most noteworthy event was Hiddink's clash with Edgar Davids. Davids was very critical of Hiddink's management, saying the coach gave preferential treatment to white players in the team. Hiddink sent Davids home for proclaiming in a radio interview that 'Hiddink must take his head out of players' arses, so he can see better.' Davids had won the European Cup with Ajax the year before and was about to join AC Milan. Thus, playing at Euro '96 was important for him. Yet Hiddink sent him home after he made a big fuss about sitting out the second game. According to van Gaal, the incident had a negative ripple effect at Ajax, undermining the team morale.

This wasn't the only source of player tension. In the summer of 1995, Ajax's treasurer Arie van Os had had the bright idea to consult some older players about the future of the club. It should be no surprise that captain Danny Blind, well into his thirties, was invited to the discussions. But the de Boer twins, in their mid-twenties, were as well. Thus, the unfortunate and undesirable situation was created where the white players came to have a say about the remuneration of the black players. Then there was what became known as the 'Croky incident'. During the 1996–97 season Danny Blind and the de Boer brothers set up a sponsorship deal with the Belgian potato chips manufacturer Croky, without consulting the rest of the Ajax selection. The agreement meant that Croky would be allowed to put *flippos* – small disks with depictions of popular cartoon characters or celebrity personalities – in the snack bags of the company. In exchange, the team would receive 500,000 guilders which would be divided among its members. Bogarde, Kluivert and John Veldman, another Surinamese-Dutch player, took offence and refused to sign and thus threatened to sink the whole deal. Bogarde characterised the procedure as resulting from the unequal balance of power in the squad, because the opinion of the other players had been ignored. (In 2006, Winston Bogarde claimed on TV that the main cause of the tensions was the difference in salaries and power at Ajax. It has been claimed that Danny Blind, for example, was earning six times as much as club top scorer Patrick Kluivert.)

A combination of these factors was by itself not enough to bring Ajax down. Also important was the exodus of strong players like Michael Reiziger and Edgar Davids, with their replacements insufficient to fill the holes they left behind. Also, the unrelenting insistence on van Gaal's tactics seemed to be taking its toll. Van Gaal himself acknowledged in interviews that his system was very taxing for players. Particularly on the mental plane, the heavily structured game concept requires the utmost of players. It might have been no surprise that at some point Ajax began to suffer a type of 'van Gaal fatigue'.

Van Gaal left Ajax in 1997 after one of the most successful spells of the Amsterdam club ever. His last season as Ajax's head coach was a comparatively disappointing one, with a fourth place finish in the *Eredivisie* as a result. The Netherlands had got so used to Ajax's European glory that Ajax's run all the way to the semi-finals of the Champions League almost went unnoticed. The 1997 final was the first in three seasons in which Ajax was not playing. But there were no doubting van Gaal's accomplishments at Ajax, and these were properly acknowledged: there was a moving tribute to the head coach and he was knighted by the Dutch queen. The question now was whether he could replicate this remarkable success at his next club: Barcelona.

VAN GAAL
AND GOD

'If football were a religion, van Gaal
would be a true believer, an ayatollah.'
Gabriele Marcotti, Times Online

When José Mourinho left the pitch after Inter Milan's semi-final second-leg triumph over Barcelona, he went straight to the chapel in Camp Nou to offer his thanks to *La Moreneta*, the Catalan name for the famous statue of the Virgin Mary and Jesus Christ found at the Santa Maria de Montserrat monastery. It seems he was not the only man hopeful of some divine intervention *en route* to the final. In 2001, then Bayern president Uli Hoeness had a team scarf blessed in the chapel in the pilgrimage town Birkenstein in the heart of Bavaria. His prayers were answered as Bayern went on to beat Valencia in the Champions League final a few days later. Hoeness, now the club's president, made the trip again prior to Bayern's German Cup final victory over Werder Bremen and no doubt was hoping the good fortune gained from the visit would carry all the way to Madrid.

Louis van Gaal's religious observances are of a different nature. It seems that, on the pitch at least, and sometimes off as well, van Gaal conducts himself as the sporting equivalent of the Almighty, or at least his representative on Earth. The German tabloid press alleged that, soon after his arrival at Bayern, van Gaal liked to march around the dressing room declaring, 'I am like God! I never get ill and I am always right.' A few months afterwards, van Gaal put the record straight: 'I am not God. If I were God I would win everything all the time.'

Responding to intimations of their own divinity is something few other football coaches have had to do.

In the Netherlands, when he was asked if he had ever read the book, *Ik heb altijd gelijk* ('I Am Always Right') by the well-known Dutch author Willem Frederik Hermans, van Gaal responded in the negative. 'No. I know Hermans, but not that particular book. A catchy title. But I would never say that about myself. I would add the nuance: I usually am right.' On another occasion, it was suggested that the outspoken coach had taken a leaf out of chess giant Bobby Fischer's book. 'He who wants to be the best every day – and thus wants to compete with God – cannot always be nice and kind.' Van Gaal did not really bristle at the notion that he let himself be guided by Fischer's creed, while at the same time explaining that the idea was a pure media invention. 'But it is a nice saying. And that's the way it is, isn't it?'

If Louis van Gaal were asked to sum up his merits as a coach, he might reissue his classic statement, 'I am the best.' He is not alone in such expressions of supreme self-confidence. José Mourinho also passes up few opportunities to demonstrate his omniscience.

Raised in a strictly observant Catholic family, van Gaal kept going to mass even in Antwerp, years after he had left home: 'But I did not find any beautiful things there. It was a tic left from my education at home. We always had to go to church. We did go, but more because my parents wanted that. It is the same as –

even though that is comparing apples and pears – finishing your plate. I still finish my plate, even though modern etiquette doesn't require it any more.' Van Gaal's work ethic and principles come from his personal experience. 'How I am comes from my vision, my knowledge, and from my experiences with my family, surroundings, and my football career. That has nothing to do with religious faith. Actually, the principles of Protestantism are more in line with how I regard life than those of Catholicism.'

If any label could be applied to van Gaal, it might be that of humanist. No matter how many times he may be offended or disappointed, he continues to believe in the fundamental goodness of man. Maybe that is actually why he keeps getting offended: he refuses to become cynical. Certainly he has the opportunities to be so. During that nearly legendary season at Ajax, football was overshadowed by the passing of his first wife. In 1994, Fernanda was diagnosed with liver and pancreatic cancer. It was also a time when football showed its ugliest face, with opposition fans in Holland shamefully mocking him and his suffering wife. It must have hurt, but van Gaal bore the indignation stoically. Because he was the head coach of Ajax, van Gaal could easily get access to the best doctors and surgeons. But it was to no avail, and with hindsight he considered that all the medical interventions may have needlessly extended Fernanda's suffering.

After a painful and difficult last few months, Fernanda passed away at only 39 years of age. Their marriage had lasted some 20 years. Van Gaal explained that the faith of his parents gave him no comfort during his wife's illness and after her passing: 'That year, the passing of my wife was much more important than football was. And I show that; that is how I live my life. When I saw the suffering of my wife, I thought: That is not possible. God also has to respect the human being. It is the same with wars. If there would be a God, He should not permit this to happen.'

The author Harold Kushner wrote his book *When Bad Things Happen to Good People* when his 15-year-old son died after suffering his entire short life from an incurable illness. Kushner said, 'The facts of life and death are neutral. We, by our responses, give suffering either a positive or a negative meaning. Illnesses, accidents, human tragedies kill people. But they do not necessarily kill life or faith. [...] There is a crucial difference between denying a tragedy, insisting that everything is for the best, and seeing the tragedy in the context of a whole life, keeping one's eye and mind on what has enriched you and not only on what you have lost. [...] To the person who asks, "What good is God? Who needs religion if these things happen to good people and bad people alike?" I would say that God may not prevent the calamity, but He gives the strength and the perseverance to overcome it. [...] When a person is dying of cancer, I do not hold God responsible for the cancer or the pain he feels. They have other causes. When people who were never particularly strong become strong in the face of adversity, when people who tended to think only of themselves become unselfish and heroic in an emergency, I have to ask myself where they got these qualities which they would freely admit they did not have before. My answer is that this is one of the ways in which God helps us when we suffer beyond the limits of our own strength.' Kushner's book should be warmly recommended to Louis van Gaal and others who have not been able to maintain faith in times of tragedy.

BARCELONA

'Friends of the press, I am leaving. Congratulations.'
Louis van Gaal

Louis van Gaal's success with Ajax led to him taking over at one of the biggest clubs in world football: Barcelona. Under his leadership the club twice won *La Liga*, the Spanish championship. But unlike at Ajax, he did not win the Champions League.

On top of which, van Gaal was unable to win the hearts and minds of the Catalan fans, in part because he presided over what was seen as an unprecedented 'Hollandisation' at the club. In all, no less than eight Dutch players featured in the Barcelona squad. Furthermore, the systematic application of van Gaal's tactical discipline was at odds with the lighter Iberian mentality. Towards the end of his tenure at the Spanish club an unnerved and angry van Gaal concluded, 'I have achieved more at Ajax Amsterdam in six years than what would take a hundred at FC Barcelona.'

People resist change. This is one of the fundamental truths about human nature, independent of nationality or cultural background. It is in the nature of people to stay with what they are familiar with, to remain in their comfort zone. However, any dynamic business, including the business of professional football, must remain open to innovation. Sometimes it takes quite a bit of conviction and endurance to jolt an organisation out of its firmly established traditions. In order for a football coach to be able to bring needed renewal to an entrenched club or even national team culture, he must have a rich and varied background and international experience, and have the commitment to see changes through to the end. Only a coach who has been around, who is aware of international football realities and has witnessed their application, is able to do this.

The multinational makeup of modern top-league squads makes that a complicated matter. Language problems can create a murmur in the background, on the field as well as off. The coach needs to take the cultural background of the individual players into account when communicating with them. For example, it generally does not bother players from the Netherlands when a coach criticises them in front of the group. In fact, during games the players themselves will keep slacking colleagues focused by attacking them verbally and physically. Players who are brought up in a different culture might find this to be a humiliating experience. Spanish players, by contrast, tend to be touchier and have a harder time recovering when their pride is hurt. When a coach works in a country with a culture unlike his own, he needs to have a certain degree of openness to local characteristics, and, certainly, basic respect for the traditions of his host country.

The type of leadership a team requires not only depends on the football culture of that club but also on what state of development the squad is in at a particular point in time. A type of coach that is good for a team at one time might not be so good at another. When 'General' Michels left Ajax, he was replaced by a coach who gave the players more leeway. After all the years of tough coaching, the club needed a different touch. The star players were well schooled in the Ajax way by then; they knew all the ins and outs and started functioning better on the pitch when they were given a greater degree of autonomy under the new leadership.

The fact that Dutch coaches come from a country that, because of its small size and proximity to larger, more powerful neighbours, traditionally has had a lot of cross-border interaction, has given them an advantage over their peers from other nations. They have had a lot of practical experience in working with people from different countries. Their increasing popularity has caused a high degree of mobility which, in turn, has resulted in a high degree of exposure to various social customs and football traditions. An extension of this is the Dutch knack for learning foreign languages. Children in the Netherlands are required to study three foreign languages – English, German and French – for at least part of their high school years. At some point, they may select one or two of these for further study and drop others. This educational tradition was made necessary because of the large language areas that encroach upon a small area of Dutch speakers. And because the British, Germans and French will not (and usually cannot) speak Dutch, the Dutch will simply speak the other languages instead. It was no great surprise, then, that for the 2006 World Cup no less than four Dutch coaches were recruited to lead national teams: Dick Advocaat with Korea, Guus Hiddink with Australia, Marco van Basten with the Netherlands and Leo Beenhakker with Trinidad and Tobago. This was matched by no other nation in the world.

Dutch managers, then, find themselves in demand at home and abroad. They are often called in to manage less well-known but often similarly money-endowed countries like the Arabian Gulf states or African countries with poor populations and underdeveloped football traditions. Paradoxically, at least one of the reasons that these Dutch coaching wonders have learned the trade so well is that they often have had to work within certain financial constraints. Small Dutch clubs have always been waystations for talented players to pass through. Hence, clever scouting has to occur out of necessity. Van Gaal, never shy with words, has asserted that the Dutch league is tactically the strongest in the world. Though not all his colleagues go quite as far, most think that Dutch coaches have proven their value. The coaches seem to have the ability to respond to the qualities of almost any team.

As in many other countries, the best current Dutch managers were not always the best players in the past. Just after van Gaal joined Bayern Munich, British columnist Alun Goodmass observed, 'Van Gaal is the epitome of Dutch managerial opinionated arrogance and is loved by many in Holland and hated probably by slightly fewer … The reason many like him in Holland is that he is brutally forthright and the Dutch regard this as an essential trait to be proud of …

'He is usually seen on the touchline during games with a clipboard in hand, plotting his tactical moves to disrupt the opposition, readying his half-time revelations for his players. His substitutions are astute but are hard to swallow for some players who seem to be perpetually doomed to come on and save games from the bench. He operates a rotation system and knows no mercy with those who do not follow his path.'

Top football coaches are known to be compulsive record keepers. Van Gaal's journal contains detailed statistics on how many shots on goal and how many assists each player had logged during a season. Dutch coaches seems to be particularly fond of registering just about everything that happens on and off the pitch, before, during and after the match. Rinus Michels was obsessed with it and Dick Advocaat was similarly a chip off the old block. Speaking about his great mentor, he said, 'Day and night he thought about football. He made notes and stored all information. I started doing that, too. With me, that almost became like a disease.' Guus Hiddink, too, is known for his precise record-keeping of daily coaching concerns. A Korean-language publication detailing his management of the 2002 World Cup featured pictures of the pages of the log he kept during the run-up to the tournament. Pages are filled with Hiddink's neat and tightly written records of strategy, placements, and miscellaneous comments – at that time mostly in English, interspersed with some untranslatable Dutch jargon. He mostly wrote in pencil so that when a change was required he could erase his writing to neatly make the correction. Van Gaal's own writing habits, then, are not as odd as some in the media would have you believe.

The successes of the Barcelona 'dream team' that won the European Cup in 1992 set a very high standard for the club to live up to, but defeat in the final two years later marked the end of a cycle. Despite the achievements on the pitch, the controversial departure of manager Johan Cruyff in 1996 brought to light divisions at the club. He was followed by Bobby Robson, who coached the club for a season until he was replaced by Louis van Gaal. He arrived to some pomp and circumstance, being proclaimed as the successor to Cruyff and his style of play.

Playing at Camp Nou – with its near 100,000 seats making it the largest stadium in Europe – is a daunting proposition. Van Gaal's time in charge of Barcelona was not easy and he had to fight to make his players understand his unique football vision. It was at Barcelona that the world realised that van Gaal's genius came at a price. His belief in tactical rigour brought him into conflict with many of his players, and his inability to relate his ideas to the local media and the fans meant the team always seemed on the verge of imploding. His critics depicted him as a kind of footballing zealot, a man wedded to his tactical dogma.

Not that his tenure was unsuccessful, by any means. The 1997–98 season was his first year at the club, and he managed to win three trophies: *La Liga*, the *Copa del Rey* and the UEFA Super Cup. Van Gaal won the league title during the second season as well, which meant that after two seasons as manager van Gaal had been able to bring the team back to the pinnacle of Spanish football. His third year in charge, however, proved to be the most difficult. The team finished second in the League and were beaten in the semi-finals of both the Champions League and the *Copa del Rey*, leaving the club trophyless.

Louis van Gaal's Barcelona team gave the Catalan people the result they wanted more than any other – victory in *El Clásico* over Real Madrid in the capital. His chosen players, his hit-and-run tactics, destroyed Real Madrid's unbeaten start in a pulsating 3–2 triumph. They will have loved that in Catalonia, where football is the expression of political separatism. But Barcelona is not like most football clubs. Van Gaal was working for for a club president who had removed 12 coaches in 19 seasons; a president whose previous appointment, Bobby Robson, was replaced because he only captured the Spanish Cup and the European Cup Winners' Cup and finished second to Real Madrid in the league. At Barcelona, that is unthinkable. When the club president sees the white handkerchiefs of disapproving fans and hears calls of *entrenador fuera* – 'the coach must go' – he gets rid of the coach before the fans get rid of him. 'It is not a sane mentality at Nou Camp,' remarked Rinus Michels, who coached Barcelona years before van Gaal's arrival.

Van Gaal's tenure was not helped by a tense relationship with Rivaldo. Rivaldo had moved to Barcelona from Deportivo de La

Coruña in 1997 for 4,000 million pesetas – more than 20 million euros. The fee was not undeserved: in his first season at Barcelona, he was the league's second highest goal scorer, with 19 goals in 34 matches. Rivaldo might not have been a part of the triumphant Brazilian team at the 1997 *Copa América* tournament, but he was a key player in the successful defence of the title in 1999. Jointly with Ronaldo, he earned himself the distinction as top scorer in the tournament with five goals and was named the Most Valuable Player of the tournament. In 1999 he was again the second highest scoring player in *La Liga*. In the same year he won both the FIFA World Player of the Year and European Footballer of the Year awards.

One of the tasks of the football coach is to set acceptable limits to individual performance and mould the team into a unit that makes best use of the strengths and skills of each individual player. To a greater or lesser degree, each player feels he is 'a kingdom unto himself'. The star players feel this most strongly. It is a major task for the coach to unite these 'kingdoms' and so to create a strong team. Every player wants to shine and thus tends to establish conditions that are most conducive to their own performance. That is common human behaviour but, in a team setting, the individual is of secondary importance; the interests and success of the team are primary. Players may shine, but only in the best interests of the team.

Individual submission to team interest will go pretty smoothly as long as the team is on a winning streak. But when things threaten to go wrong, players have the tendency to look for high ground to save their own image. The many little 'kingdoms' have to be melded into one team, with the willingness to bundle all the available resources into one to battle the common 'enemy'. Only one person can achieve this: the coach. He has two different and seemingly conflicting tasks. On the one hand, he has to respect the integrity of each little 'kingdom', and, on the other hand, he has to win over all the players so that they will sacrifice themselves for the common goal: the result of the match.

One unhappy player can cause knock-on effects. The catalyst is often the star player, who is also the darling of the fans and the media. Something of this occurred between Rivaldo and van Gaal, and in their third season at Barcelona the two fell out. The stand-off was the result of Rivaldo's refusal to play as the left-sided forward in the vintage Ajax 4-3-3 schema van Gaal was committed to using. The South American star wanted the central role, which eventually led van Gaal to put him on the bench on several occasions. He insisted that Rivaldo, part of a stellar front three that also included Luis Figo and Patrick Kluivert, forget his dribbling skills and focus his attention instead on his coach's belief that efficient passing won matches. Telling the World Player of the Year to stick to his position on the left wing or make space for others instead of roaming around freely may well have been integral to van Gaal's tactical plan but was not the best way to survive in the Catalonian quagmire. Replacing those superstars with a busload of former Ajax players did not endear van Gaal much to the locals either.

Van Gaal sometimes complained that when Barcelona won all honour and glory went to the players, but when the team lost he was condemned in front-page articles. About Rivaldo he said, 'There is somebody to whom I have given too many chances. I thought he would make the difference. If that person does not do that then the equilibrium is the dressing room is gone. That was my biggest mistake this season. This culture needs stars. Now I have two players that rank among the 10 best in the world. At Ajax in 1995, when I did not lose a single game, I had nobody on that list.

I cannot change this culture. It is a culture of "We are the best."But of course, that does have to be proven.'

Another Brazilian van Gaal managed to alienate at Barcelona was the midfielder Giovanni. The arrival of van Gaal saw the international relegated to the substitutes' bench at Camp Nou, later prompting him to sign for Olympiakos. In 2010, the player minced no words expressing his disapproval of his former coach: 'Van Gaal is arrogant, proud and has a problem. My life with him was horrible. The Brazilians did not want him; he put me down and also fought with Rivaldo and Sonny Anderson. He always gave us the excuse that we were not training well. I know that he must have some trauma. He has no idea of football, does not know anything. In the time I was with him he always did the same training. He's crazy.' The Brazilian's resentment has not dissipated over the years. When Bayern were beaten by Mourinho's Inter in the 2010 Champions League final, Giovanni said would have liked the defeat to have been far more severe: 'If it were up to me, I would have liked it if Inter won 15–0 with five goals from Lúcio.' Lúcio was another Brazilian who was 'slighted' by van Gaal, who sold him to to Inter after the new coach made clear he did not need his services.

Van Gaal does not think he has problems with players with outstanding talent: 'I have worked with super players who do have the ability to take responsibility. Players like Cocu, Xavi, Iniesta, Puyol … And that's why Barcelona does so well now. The core is made up of players who are able to be critical of themselves. These boys all started under me. I love working with players like them; I can't stand the big-name players who only excel when the TV broadcasters are around or when the sun shines …' The ultimate van Gaal player is Andrés Iniesta. Van Gaal says of him, 'He sees the game so well, he can play in different positions ... Xavi has that too, but Xavi is more static. Iniesta has that sparkle in his game. Xavi is more like I was. Technically perfect. Tactically strong, but too slow ... Like myself. Iniesta is the player I wanted to be, but wasn't ...' For his part, Xavi says, 'Van Gaal is a rather special coach. I hold him in high esteem, partly because it was he who gave me the chance to play in *La Liga*. He trusted me, and it is not forgotten. He can be a bit difficult, but he is true, one cannot take that away from him. With him, if you work well, you play.'

Van Gaal's time at Barcelona boasted two individuals who would go on to become Champions League winning managers themselves. Pep Guardiola, Barcelona's captain under van Gaal, observed his immaculate attention to minutiae: 'He really notices every detail.' José Mourinho, a young interpreter in Catalonia in the late 1990s, wrote scouting reports for van Gaal. Opinions in Barcelona are divided as to what role van Gaal had in laying the foundations for the club's later successes. Under Guardiola's management, the team was built around an array of home-bred players, including Xavi, Iniesta, Puyol, Valdez and Messi. Some suggest that Guardiola learned the art of management from his one-time boss. In this version, Barcelona was just not yet ready for the innovations that the headstrong Dutchman tried to bring about – their realisation only occurred later. Others, meanwhile, see an older influence in Barcelona's modern style: that of one of van Gaal's predecessors, Johan Cruyff.

The sporting failures of 1999–2000 convinced club president Josep Lluís Núñez that it was time for van Gaal to go. In May 2000 Louis van Gaal's resignation was announced, relinquishing the remaining time of his contract and with it a very sizeable sum of money. Van Gaal had a contract at Barcelona until 2002. During the remaining time he could have earned an additional 10 million euros. To the dismay of his wife, Truus, he rejected a considerable sum of buyout money, however: 'I leave with my head held high, and I will not receive a single peseta. Others did do so and caused themselves a lot of grief.'

Van Gaal left the club with a good record but struggled throughout to connect with the Catalan fans. His tenure at the Camp Nou was also blighted by a poor relationship with the press, which undermined him and helped lead to his departure. His failure to master the Spanish language often led to him losing his cool at press conferences, and when there was nothing much to report the Catalan media often turned to baiting van Gaal to criticise his tactics and philosophy. As in the Netherlands, van Gaal clashed with the media, and when he left, he uttered immortal words: '*Amigos de la prensa, yo me voy. Felicidados*' – 'Friends of the press, I am leaving. Congratulations.' In the end, there were more enemies then friends, more tiffs than trophies. With almost no one left to alienate, van Gaal left for a new challenge, and one that would see him returning home: to coach the Dutch national team.

BONDSCOACH

'I find it hard to bear a loss and find it
terrible when something doesn't succeed.'
Louis van Gaal

The Dutch have an unrivalled record of pressing the self-destruct button when it comes to major football tournaments. Johan Cruyff did not show up for the 1978 World Cup, Ruud Gullit blew out the 1994 World Cup, and the squad fell apart at Euro '96. David Winner's book, *Brilliant Orange*, is full of all sorts of fascinating theories about why Dutch footballers always mess it up in the end. In a chapter called 'Death Wish' a political scientist blames it all on Dutch suspicion of national pride: 'We think winning is a little bit ugly,' he says. 'It's only for other people who need it to compensate for some other lack.' Former player Wim van Hanegem is on record as saying that the Dutch seem to have an allergy to authority, leadership and collective discipline. 'If things around the national team are quiet, everyone thinks everybody is sick. If we don't have a problem, we have to create a problem.' The psychoanalyst Anna Enquist suggests that, 'There is some kind of death wish in our football connected to our Dutch, Calvinist shame of appearing good. Our Calvinist culture makes us deeply ashamed of being the best.'

When Sir Bobby Robson moved to the Netherlands to manage PSV Eindhoven, he described the move as 'a culture shock'. The

Dutch penchant for tactical debate surprised him. He lamented, 'An English professional accepts the manager's decision, but after every match here the substitutes come and visit me' – to interrogate the coach as to why they weren't playing. In 1990, when he was England manager, he observed, 'The Dutch play football very well, but what they do even better is shoot themselves in the foot. As opponents we always bank on this second quality.'

In the mid-1990s, Louis van Gaal announced that after the year 2000 he wanted to become *bondscoach*, the Dutch term for the national team manager: 'I have a particular vision of how a *bondscoach* is supposed to function. Well, I don't see that happening. Even if it were just to prove my way is right, I would like to give it a try.' Van Gaal is somewhat fond of making predictions. He's given statements that did not materialise, such as the prediction that he would stop coaching at 55, but the national coach dream, however, did come true.

Van Gaal was named as the new Dutch national coach on 7 July 2000, soon after the European Championship 2000 tournament. He succeeded Frank Rijkaard, who quit after his team was knocked out by Italy in the semi-finals. 'You see before you a very happy person,' he said after the KNVB announced at the Amsterdam Hilton it was giving him a six-year contract. During the term of his contract, the federation was to assess his performance every two years. 'At first I wanted to take a sabbatical year [after leaving Barcelona],' van Gaal said, 'but I've always thought that if the opportunity came for me to become national coach I would grab it with both hands.'

As with Bobby Robson at PSV, but in a different way, becoming national coach was something of a culture shock for van Gaal. To his surprise, he discovered that the squad took international breaks between club duties as leisure time and an opportunity to catch up with old friends instead of training seriously on patterns and playing style. Van Gaal's grand ambitions on the training pitch flew in the face of indifferent team members, who wanted to qualify as effortlessly as possible. This difference of opinion and the disagreements that ensued resulted in the only absence of a Dutch team for an international tournament since the mid-1980s.

When the draw was made for the 2002 World Cup qualification groups, the Netherlands were placed in a section featuring Portugal, Ireland, Estonia, Cyprus and Andorra. The first home game, against Ireland, ended in a 2–2 draw. A month later, Cyprus was decisively defeated in Nicosia, 4–0. Then the Dutch were beaten 2–0 by Portugal. It was a disappointing performance: the trademark Dutch style had almost disappeared, and most of the Dutch attack got stuck in the Portuguese midfield. Despite beating Andorra 5–0 in Barcelona and further victories against Cyprus and Estonia, the Dutch could not make amends in the return fixture against Portugal, only managing a 2–2 draw.

Prior to the Estonia match, an unwanted distraction was provided by Edgar Davids and Frank de Boer, when samples of their urine showed traces of the anabolic steroid nandrolone. The results weren't conclusive, in that similar substances can naturally be present in the human body, albeit in minute quantities. So when the controversial findings were made public, national team coach van Gaal backed up his players. 'The result from the tests by counter experts is not yet known, but no matter what, I unconditionally believe in the players.' Nevertheless, he was somewhat taken aback that he had been unable to reach Davids to discuss it: 'I was surprised because Davids has two mobile phones, of which one was without voicemail. I have called him a few time times, left messages on the phone with voicemail, and called him on his landline. So far, he hasn't returned my calls.' Frank de Boer, on the other hand, contacted his coach immediately when the initial doping test proved positive. Van Gaal remained terse about the troubles of his two lead players: 'We will first wait for the results of the independent inquiry involving the dietary supplements and what kind of food the players have been served at Dutch national team trainings.' Eventually, though, Davids was suspended by FIFA. Frank de Boer was initially suspended for 12 months before a UEFA appeals body cut his ban after finding that contaminated food supplements were 'more than likely' responsible for the positive test.

The crunch match for Holland's chances was the return match against Ireland. Van Gaal set out for Dublin in good spirits: 'I am satisfied with the selection. We have a well-balanced group. The Irish in principle will always play the same game. You can't change the culture of a country just like that. They will rely on their own qualities and will play aggressively. That mentality is in their blood. That was also how they played against us in Amsterdam. It is our task to respond to that and I have a lot of hope that we will be able to do that. The team knows no doubt, but we should not forget that Ireland has not lost during the last five years. In that light it is strange that we get more respect from the people in Ireland than the Irish team. We are a big name, but that does not mean anything. We will have to prove ourselves. We may impress the public, but we certainly do not impress the Irish players. They are boys who all play in the English Premier League.'

When the Dutch arrived at Lansdowne Road in 2001, it appeared that it would just be an inconsequential stop-off on the way to the World Cup finals. Van Gaal considered the possibility of defeat in the build-up, but only in relation to coach Mick McCarthy who, he suggested, would be under pressure if Ireland lost. As it turned out, van Gaal's footballing beliefs were secondary on a day when wildness prevailed and logic was dumped. He seemed desperate, probably because he was, and after 10-man Ireland went ahead through Jason McAteer with just over 20 minutes to go, he sent on forward after forward in search of a goal. Ireland, however, held on. The elimination of Holland from the World Cup was a huge deal back in the Netherlands. As van Gaal said, 'For Dutch football this is a disaster. Here we lost the World Cup. We had the chance to finish it off. You have to win, especially when you are playing 11 against 10. We had one man more in midfield. We created two good chances but thereafter played along with the game of the Irish.' The post-mortem in the press was full of opinion as to who was responsible. The *Algemeen Dagblad* wondered, 'The central question is: can van Gaal be blamed? The tactical changes during the qualification duels were not logical, but none of them had a decisive influence on the game. In the away game against Portugal it really was Frank de Boer who caused a penalty, making it 2–2. And during the qualification game against Ireland, the seed for the loss was sown when Kluivert and Zenden missed great chances for a safe advantage. That does not mean, however, that the functioning of the coach should be questioned; a coach who was presented a year ago accompanied by a drum roll.' *De Volkskrant* suggested that, 'Van Gaal has thus far been unable to convey the spark of his ambition to the players. It would be too much to assign him sole responsibility for the fiasco of the national team. Too many of his stars have failed at decisive moments.'

De Telegraaf was harsher in its criticism: 'What a disgrace that *Oranje* [the nickname for the Dutch team], despite the presence of a collection of world-class players, who are playing for the best and most prestigious European top clubs, could only garner two points in four encounters with Portugal and Ireland. It was 16 years ago that our national football pride last missed qualification for a major tournament. Then *bondscoach* Leo Beenhakker was heavily criticised. [Now there] were tactical blunders with the same result [as in 1985]: The Netherlands, one of the best football nations in the world, will be sidelined as a spectator at the World Cup next year.'

The *Brabants Dagblad* used even stronger language: 'In the aftermath of the game, van Gaal defended himself by pointing to the poor condition of the pitch and the noise in the stadium that made communication – his forte according to his own evaluation – impossible. That was bullshit. Communicating about how you play 11 against 10 you do before the game, for example, during one of those many little cosy hours at a training camp or during one of those special, secretive trainings. Van Gaal should be ashamed.'

After the débâcle, Louis van Gaal addressed the Dutch supporters in an open letter on his official homepage: 'You are very disappointed. But take my word for it that the hangover was the greatest in the Dutch dressing room in Dublin. The players were broken. But we must go on. That is why we begin [the final qualification match] against Estonia with the European Championship in view. Give the players a fair chance.' Van Gaal fielded exactly the same eleven as at the notorious game against Ireland, evidently to give players a chance to redeem themselves. Estonia were defeated 5–0. The grace van Gaal had asked for from the supporters was nowhere in sight, though. When the ball was inadvertently played over the sideline a few times, the Dutch spectators responded with catcalls and whistles. The win was meaningless anyway because Portugal won its match against Cyprus 3–1, ruling out any theoretical possibility that the Netherlands might still be present at the World Cup.

Criticism of van Gaal wasn't confined to the media. Leo Beenhakker issued the judgement that 'Van Gaal did not achieve his objectives and should draw some conclusions from that.' Marco van Basten launched a scathing attack on van Gaal, claiming his tactics were responsible for the national side's failure to qualify: 'Van Gaal has never played for a national team himself, so maybe that was the problem. He wanted to be in control too much while they were only together for two or three days at a time. That is simply not long enough.' Years later, van Gaal returned the favour by providing a thorough critique of van Basten's failures at Euro 2006.

A disenchanted Louis van Gaal resigned from his position as national coach effective in February 2002 following the Netherlands' failure to qualify for the World Cup. In his own inimitable manner van Gaal responded to media inquiries at a press conference: 'The players had a different vision than I; then it is time for the *bondscoach* to stop. Whether I failed or not? I certainly have failed. Because I have the final responsibility. The KNVB objective was to make it to the World Cup and then reach the best eight. We failed to accomplish that, the players' group and the technical staff.' An emotional van Gaal provided further detail and background, sometimes with a loud voice and clenched fists, a penetrating look and sometimes teary eyes. 'It is a very sad day for me. A year and a half ago, I was very happy. Then I considered it an honour to become *bondscoach* and I had the ambition to become world champion. But we didn't even make it to the tournament. That is sad. Very sad and very disappointing – for the Dutch public, the KNVB, and the sponsors.

'Twice [the Dutch national team] had the chance to become world champion. But in the 2002 World Cup we did not even achieve the minimum goal, a place among the best eight. For me this is a very sad day. All of us, the players and the staff, have failed.'

Van Gaal felt the chemistry between the players and himself was not right: 'I always look to the present and the future, not the past. I never had the chance to take part in a major tournament with the Netherlands and that's a real shame, but I resigned because some of the players refused to accept my methods. I am who I am and I have my own ways. I'm not going to change and I have no desire to.'

After Holland's unsuccessful bid to qualify for the World Cup, van Gaal took to the air in the form of a nationally televised, hour-long speech in which he sought to give an account of his greatest coaching failure, which became sort of a classic in media-land. Van Gaal said he received a lot of support from fans, colleagues and technical staff, all wanting to change his mind about him throwing in the towel. But according to van Gaal, 'The most important thing is to continue as one, the players' group and the technical staff together. That is why I have spoken with a number of players. Not in order to ask them whether or not I should leave, but in order to find out what their vision for player management is. They have a different idea about professional supervision than I do. I want to exclude coincidence; I do not believe in a looser approach. In the short term you might get some results with that, but in the short term you always come up short. Under those conditions, I will not be able to get those extra 10 per cent out of a player; and I see that ability as one of my qualities. So then I decided it was better to quit.'

Van Gaal was not only responsible for the national side at the KNVB but also for the development of what was called the 'Masterplan'. In the mid-1980s, Rinus Michels had offered his thoughts on youth football in the Netherlands. One key belief was that kids' football should not replicate the adult game. Another was that it should be enjoyable, with everyone involved and lots of chances to score. Across the Netherlands, his ideas are still used. At the age of 5, games are 4-a-side. At 9 they progress to 7-a-side on half-sized pitches. Finally, at 13, they play 11-a-side on regulation pitches.

While *bondscoach*, van Gaal took the time to revise the Michels model. He spoke of the pyramid structure and getting the amateur and professional games working together. Academies were rated on a four-star basis, a youth coaching diploma was introduced and clubs were licensed depending on the number of development teams they had.

Perhaps the key strand of the Masterplan was the focus on enjoyment.

The Masterplan was for all – boys and girls, the talented and the awkward, immigrant children and the physically impaired. The intention was that everyone would achieve his own maximum potential, with enjoyment of the game being the central objective. This was a task that came to van Gaal naturally, having been a teacher and having invested much time and energy in the restructuring of the youth programmes at Ajax and Barcelona.

For decades the failure of Dutch youth teams had been a mystery. While the full national side, most of the time, brought fans to their feet at European and World Cup tournaments, the youth teams stumbled time and again. But in recent years a quite spectacular turnaround came about. The U-17 came in second at the European Championships in 2005 and again in 2009. In 2005 they came third at the World Cup. The U-21 team won the European title in 2006, the first time ever for a Dutch youth team, and the feat was repeated in 2007.

Foppe de Haan, the under-21 coach from 2004 to 2009, has referred to Louis van Gaal as the architect of these successes. In 2001 van Gaal presented his Masterplan with the objective of raising the level of all of Dutch football. At the time, the sceptics considered it a paper tiger, while believers praised van Gaal. De Haan evidently is a member of the second category: 'Of course you had top talent in the past. Just look at the group of van Basten at the youth World Cup in Mexico. But that was just a snapshot. The total average was too low. Today, that is higher. And we are winning prizes.'

Van Gaal would have liked to stay on as technical director to work on the implementation of his Masterplan. The KNVB did not permit that, however. Henk Kesler thought that, 'On February 13, against England, the spirit of Louis van Gaal should no longer hover over the Dutch national team.' Thus van Gaal left on 1 February. At that point his future was up in the air. 'I don't see myself *bondscoach* again. There is only one country where I could be federation coach and that is the Netherlands.' Then again van Gaal also said he was going to retire at 55. In 2014, he had the chance to take the Dutch side to the World Cup finals after all.

AT BARCELONA
AND AJAX AGAIN

'Here at Ajax lies my heart,
A club, fascinating, and set apart.'
Opening lines of van Gaal's poem, dedicated to
the 'love of his youth', Ajax, at the time of his
instalment as the club's technical director.

In the spring of 2002, the Dutch newspaper *Het Parool* passed on the following titbit of information to its readers: 'All the archives of van Gaal have been transferred to his new Catalonian home town Sitges.' The fact that the coach had 'archives' that needed to be 'transferred' was cause for merriment among some of the Dutch media. Bert Wagendorp in *De Volkskrant* noted that everyone probably 'has a few stuffed envelopes' with historical mementos, but only van Gaal has 'archives' plural: 'The Spanish doubtlessly have already assigned a team of translators to turn the trove into Spanish.' But van Gaal patiently explained his motives by asking the rhetorical question, 'How else can I better show that I am happy here?' in Catalonia. Sadly, van Gaal's happiness with Barcelona during his second spell at the club was to be of even shorter duration than the first time around.

Barcelona's Champions League campaign of 2002–03 began well. They cruised through the first group stage and started well in what was then the second group stage. Bayer Leverkusen were unable to bring the Catalan train to a halt and Barcelona became the only one of the 32 teams in the competition to win six group stage games in a row.

In *La Liga*, however, things looked substantially less rosy. After a heavy 3–0 defeat at the hands of Seville in December, the fans expressed their anger at the management, primarily club president Joan Gaspart. Gaspart was treated to a sustained tirade of calls for his *dimisión!* (dismissal) and *fuera!* (out). Unthinkably, a mere two points separated Barcelona from the relegation places. The Spanish daily *Marca* was of the opinion that 'Barça was Witness to its Own Funeral' while *Sport*'s headline claimed that 'This is a Total Crisis – It Does Not Get Any Worse.' Perhaps a little prematurely *La Vanguardia* wrote, 'The public at Camp Nou has issued its verdict – it no longer wants a van Gaal and a Gaspart.'

Gaspart's response was defiant, stating that 'I don't think about resigning, and neither will I dismiss the coach.' Van Gaal also did not think that backing out would be the answer to Barcelona's woes: 'Resignation is no solution. The most important thing is the unity of coach and team. I will speak with the players and lead the team out of the crisis.' The players in turn seemed to back him up. Carlos Puyol said, 'It is up to the players to get out of the situation that we have manoeuvred ourselves into. The change of coach won't do us any good. The solution is a victory in the next game and the start of a series of successes.' Van Gaal himself was at a loss to explain the difference in performance level between the Champions League and *La Liga*. 'It is hard to explain the difference between the games against Newcastle and against Seville. It is simply unbelievable;

we are disheartened. We have to work harder than ever before to overcome this bad situation.'

After the Christmas break, a goalless draw against Malaga was followed by another heavy home defeat: this time Barcelona losing 4–2 to Valencia. Gaspart again expressed his confidence in van Gaal, but the pressure to move the Dutchman out seemed to be unrelenting and increasing. Eventually, van Gaal's position at Barcelona became untenable, despite a successful Champions League campaign: at the time of the announced exit of the controversial Dutchman, Barcelona had won all of its 10 European tournament fixtures. The final straw was the 2–0 loss against Celta Vigo at the end of January. The result left Barcelona in twelfth place, 20 points behind leaders Real Sociedad and still only 3 points from safety.

Joan Gaspart decided that enough was enough and released van Gaal, replacing him with Radomir Antić. Looking back on the Dutch coach's brief second spell at Barcelona, defender Oleguer Presas thought that 'Van Gaal short-changed himself. When the performances declined, there was only attention for his image. He is a sociable person, but he did not think it was necessary to show this aspect of himself to the outside world. More and more people got the idea that he was a hard trainer.' At a press conference a tearful van Gaal bade the fans farewell and apologised for the club's poor standing.

After his dismissal at Barcelona, van Gaal briefly worked as a football analyst during live matches on Holland's public television network NOS. Never one to shirk the chance to return to an ex-club, he returned to the scene of his greatest triumphs as a coach – he returned to Ajax, but this time as technical director. Van Gaal started the press conference of his ill-fated tenure with a poem, declaring his love for the club.

The position had arisen when Leo Beenhakker unexpectedly announced his resignation from the post. After several weeks of persistent rumours, it was announced that Louis van Gaal would return to 'his Ajax'. Following Beenhakker's departure, the brief of the technical director in Ajax's club structure changed a little. Whereas Beenhakker was jointly responsible with head coach Ronald Koeman for major purchases, van Gaal was to focus more on the development of the youth system – one of his strong points – in co-operation with the youth system director, Danny Blind. Major transfers would be dealt with separately by Ronald Koeman and general director Arie van Eijden.

Arie van Eijden was delighted with van Gaal's return: 'The appointment of Louis van Gaal is a new impetus for the club policy we launched three years ago. It is not a matter of a *new* policy. Louis van Gaal will continue to refine the Ajax youth system with Danny Blind. Louis will be the link between the Amsterdam ArenA and De Toekomst.' De Toekomst – 'The Future' – is the name of the sports complex where Ajax's youth and amateur teams play.

Ajax chairman John Jaakke was also a happy man: 'We went very carefully in appointing a new technical director. We have taken much time to fill up the vacancy of technical director in the best possible way. That the choice for Louis van Gaal was made with great unanimity vouches for the continuity of our club's strategy.' Ronald Koeman, head coach of the first team, who had worked closely on a daily basis with Leo Beenhakker, was also enthusiastic about the arrival of the new 'TD': 'The arrival of van Gaal is a very good thing for the club and myself. I have the firm impression that this is the final stop for Louis van Gaal. He's said goodbye to his career as a coach.' Van Gaal himself confirmed Koeman's thoughts: 'Just read some of my old interviews. I've always said I wanted to stop coaching at 55. Well, I did so a little earlier. […] I have come home. This is my club. I will start working on the sidelines for now. I want to take my time and look around first.'

Unfortunately, the honeymoon was quickly over. Several conversations between the Ajax leadership and technical director van Gaal showed that the two sides were at odds over the proper management of the club in general and the role of the technical director in particular. The co-operation with head coach Ronald Koeman was never harmonious, and the two had a quite different view on how the first team should be coached. Ajax did not fare as well in the Champions League as it might have, and the relationship between van Gaal and Koeman was not helped when the chairman sided with the coach after a disappointing performance against Bayern Munich. In most cases, when there is a conflict between a superior and a subordinate in any business, the subordinate is fired and the superior, as the guardian of long-term development, stays. Consequently, some thought that in the stand-off between van Gaal and Koeman, the Ajax board should have sided with van Gaal instead of Koeman all the more because van Gaal's insight into football matters was superior to that of Koeman.

Van Gaal could not accept that Ajax's European ambitions were compromised. The leadership thought that the club should be satisfied with competing for the UEFA Cup, but van Gaal disagreed: 'I think that a club like Ajax should be able to play in the semi-finals of the Champions League once every five years.' The real sore point, though, was that the hard-driven football man felt caged by the restrictions placed upon him in his capacity as technical director. He thought his authority was too limited in comparison with that of the first-team coach, particularly when transfer policy was concerned. Van Gaal wanted to have a larger say in the buying and selling of players. A particular bone of contention was van Gaal's intervention in the feud between Zlatan Ibrahimović and Rafael van der Vaart (Ibrahimović had injured Van der Vaart during an international between Sweden and the Netherlands: Van der Vaart claimed he'd done so deliberately). Van Gaal solved the dispute by selling Ibrahimović, something that Koeman did not appreciate.

When van Gaal finally decided to go, he explained his position eloquently while showing his sadness over the imminent departure: 'I have made my request to be relieved of my duties in the interest of Ajax. This was not motivated by the disappointing results of recent days. What matters is, among other things, a difference of view concerning technical policies and the jurisdiction of the technical director at Ajax. Everyone who knows me well understands that I like clarity. Making compromises does not fit well with my character and I anticipate more differences of opinion. In light of this I have decided to clear the way. I sincerely hope that by doing that I will serve the best interests of Ajax. I would have liked to grow old at Ajax, but unfortunately that is not to be.'

Kevin Garside wrote in the *Telegraph*, 'This is what can happen when success is explained in mystical terms, when the coach is accorded Svengali status imbued with magical qualities beyond the ken of mortals. When the magic fades it does so inexplicably and is seen as a terminal development. It was a mistake to return to Barcelona and then Ajax in technical roles distanced from the dugout.'

Only when van Gaal resumed the tracksuit at AZ Alkmaar did his footballing genius reawaken. In other words, only when van Gaal returned to his football roots and dealt with its essence – how to play the game well – did his talent shine.

VAN GAAL
AND THE MEDIA

'In old days men had the rack. Now they have the
press. We are dominated by journalism.'

Oscar Wilde

Complaints about the media are not limited to today's
parents, teachers or sports coaches, but have been with us for
a long time. Coaches the world over begrudge the treatment
they receive at the hands of the press. These complaints are not
without reason. The sports media, maybe more than any other,
is expert at churning out nonsense in quantity. That sports
coverage and celebrity scandal-mongering are commonly linked
in a profitable but second-rate press is an international reality.
Spectator sports are not always known as an arena of measured
analysis and calm reflection.

As a consequence, much that has been said and written about
the flamboyant man from the country of windmills and tulips is of
dubious quality and reliability. Despite the sheer volume of articles
and broadcasts, the picture of van Gaal portrayed has not necessarily
become much clearer. On the contrary, news reports have added
to the confusion through their ambiguity and contradictions, and
have given van Gaal some ground for offence.

The media are, fundamentally, a profit-motivated institution. They are in business, just like professional football clubs are. However, the interests of the press and the clubs are often diametrically opposed. Whereas the coach is interested in maintaining an environment of stability and tranquillity, the media are interested in the opposite. Few sports magazine readers would be interested to learn that, say, Ajax had a peaceful afternoon of training: conflict and scandal sell many more copies. Hence, in top football clubs even the walls have ears.

The media are constantly on the lookout for the latest morsel of sensational news – it's their business. A good observer can quickly recognise the existence of tension or a conflict within a team; some players will not play at the service of others, will not make the runs they usually make, and neglect their basic tasks just a little more easily than under normal circumstances. Off the field these tensions also produce small irritations. Journalists often are excellent hunters for news that seems spectacular and in most cases can find someone to do their dirty work. Usually, there is someone ready to complain. The danger of losing the much-desired tranquillity will then start looming at the gates of the team.

In football, as elsewhere, the results speak for themselves. If a coach loses games, he quickly becomes the villain; if he wins games, he is usually the hero. Even though van Gaal might, due to his slightly abrasive manners, have started with a 'debit on his emotional bank account' (in the words of Stephen Covey), the critics were soon, if not permanently, silenced. In van Gaal's first year, Ajax won the UEFA Cup out of thin air, knocking two Italian teams out of the running in the process. During the semi-final against Genoa, no Genovese player had yet had a touch when Ajax put the first ball in the Italian net, within a minute of the start.

The final score was a completely unanticipated 3–2, and Dutch newspapers fell over each other to heap praise on the performance. When Ajax went on to win the final, the ordinarily staid and ever-critical Dutch press was jubilant.

Soon enough the relationship between van Gaal and the media turned sour, however. Eventually, things got so bad that the Dutch reporters' association Nederlandse Sport Pers (NSP), decided to remind the flamboyant coach of his public duties. In a letter from the association, van Gaal was lectured on etiquette: 'The press conferences of Ajax are being disgraced by vulgar shouting matches. This aggressive approach perhaps guarantees success with young, docile players, but is inappropriate at a press conference at which adult people are present.' The missive was immediately countered by the coach at a subsequent meeting with the media. Holding the incriminating document in the air, van Gaal, akin to a schoolmaster disciplining an unruly class, asked the assembled journalists who had signed it. No one had the courage to raise his hand. Van Gaal thought the letter was not only ridiculous but also insulting to him and his players: 'I object sometimes because I find the question dumb, not the questioner.'

At some point, it seemed that van Gaal realised that his intense and aggressive way of communicating did not win him friends and influence people in a positive way. He admitted that media experts had advised him to soften his rhetoric a little, but added, 'Maybe they are right. But if I put this side by side with my character, I say "no". I react the way I react, with my heart on my sleeve. I am prepared to improve myself, but I refuse to be untrue to myself. Nobody can take away my forcefulness: I am a fighter.' Perhaps he had given up hope of changing his image because he had more or less been typecast since his time at Sparta: 'One [school of] thought [was that] I was a fantastic player, a tall slowpoke who was able to carry the team; the other thought I was a tall slowpoke who also was arrogant enough to tell everyone how they should play football. That image was only reinforced when I started working at Ajax.'

Underneath the media exchanges was a cultural chasm. Journalists saw the straightforward and conservative van Gaal as authoritarian and intolerant. In reality, van Gaal is more of a political anomaly – a conservative disciplinarian with a football philosophy in which the collective is central. Perhaps, then, it was no surprise that the media did not understand him. They could not understand that van Gaal was not enamoured by the so-called permissive society, a society which, in the coach's view, condoned vandalism and stimulated apathy. He thought that a lack of order, authority and respect were causes of this. There had to be clear rules that were clearly enforced. This would create clarity, fairness and calm. By the nature of their profession, most journalists have a dislike of order; they critique it. They do not support the governing powers; they question and challenge them. The Dutch media in particular is suspicious of people who they think are putting on airs.

Another reason for the innate Dutch tendency towards social democracy is the Protestant-Christian root of the country. 'Before the glory of God all men have fallen short.' These collective shortcomings make, one, all people equal and, two, overconfident individuals suspect. People with 'attitudes' are not taken seriously, at best, or ridiculed, at worst. Though most Dutch men and women are quite secular-minded these days, this original Protestant egalitarianism has left its mark on people's thinking. No one should assume that he or she is any better than anyone else. The Calvinistic brand of Christianity has brought along a host of other 'Dutch virtues', such as honesty, reliability and a strong work ethic. Van Gaal, as one of the old school, embodies all of them. He is honest and direct with all his co-workers, and straightforward towards both his superiors and his subordinates. He is devoted to his job and committed to the responsible fulfilment of the tasks required of him. Above all, he is a very hard worker.

The sports media in the Netherlands, because of its size, is something of an old boys' club. Everyone knows everybody else, and hence consensus, or rather stereotyping, is rather quickly established. In van Gaal's case, this did not turn out in his favour. In the early stages of his career he was often ridiculed in the media for the unorthodox jargon that he used. His constant use of the term 'team building', for example, was a novelty reporters were not yet accustomed to. Van Gaal said, 'In the first weeks the results were not good, so van Gaal could be ridiculed. I think you have to come with arguments, evaluate someone's way of working, instead of falling over a word like team building, which is not commonly used in football. That short-sightedness irritated me a lot; and always this shallow reasoning about the scoring. The press thinks: few goals are made; therefore, the play is bad. You can look at it the other way around: considering that the play is excellent, there should be more scoring. Do you sense the difference?'

Van Gaal has had difficulty recognising that the relationship between the media and football clubs is a symbiotic one. In the Netherlands the media sell copies thanks to Ajax, but the reverse was equally true; Ajax, its corporate sponsors, its players, and, yes, its coach, are advertised and promoted by the media. The media helped to make Ajax, Danny Blind and Louis van Gaal famous and rich. But this reality seemed lost on van Gaal. To him the press was the enemy that needed to be checked, and if at all possible stopped at the gate: 'By nature I am mild-mannered, but I quickly get hot when I notice that the media turns up with "facts" that do not exist, or when I notice that there is antagonism. Ajax's success is based on investment and dedication. I sometimes sense a lack of appreciation for that. Moreover, I feel that there are some people who take delight in us falling on our face.'

When van Gaal suspected that some reporters weren't being serious and upfront there were consequences. He blacklisted them. Journalists who had, in van Gaal's view, produced inaccurate reports or been overly critical were still allowed to ask questions at press conferences, but they were denied interviews: 'When journalists ask dumb questions, then I mercilessly attack them because they did not do their job well and they harm my players.' When *Voetbal International* reporter Ted van Leeuwen asked a 'dumb question', van Gaal gave the celebrated response, 'Are you really that dumb, or am I so clever?'

Van Gaal, then, has a very ambivalent relationship with the media. For one, he really yearns for attention. On the other hand, he is rarely pleased with the attention he gets. In this, he is not alone. There is at least one other Dutch football coach who has had a rather strained relationship with the Dutch media, and that is Dick Advocaat. When I worked on my biography of Advocaat, I interviewed Frans Leermakers, the historian of ADO Den Haag, the club where Advocaat started as a youth. Leermakers made a lucid observation that is also very much applicable to Louis van Gaal: 'At times, Dick had a lot of trouble with the media. Because of his honesty and because he is a little inflexible, he does not come across well when it comes to PR. It's just not in his character to be media savvy. Frankly speaking, in such a conflict you always lose. When you reach such a high level, you really become some kind of public property, and you can't avoid the things that are happening on the fringe of the games. Also, if it weren't for the media, Advocaat would never have become as famous and wealthy as he is now. Of course, he did not deserve to be treated badly. He really is too much of a football expert for that, and really a very nice person besides. And the players always backed him up.' Leermakers suggested there was an element of inconsistency in the coach's demand to be left in peace by the press, because in the end not only the media profit from some commotion, the clubs and those who work for them do as well. It would serve disgruntled football coaches well to remember the old adage, 'There is no such thing as bad publicity.'

Of course, the media regularly go overboard and fan the flames of petty conflicts, disseminate unconfirmed reports or make patently false allegations. As a result, van Gaal has always had very firm guidelines for his players on how they are to interact with the members of the fourth estate. Item one on the list is that it is unforgivable to hang 'dirty laundry' outdoors. Whatever is discussed in the dressing room is purely confidential and should stay in-house. If anyone had problems or complaints, they should go and see van Gaal.

To instruct his players on what they should and should not say, van Gaal even organised media training for his charges. The result was that interviews with Ajax players henceforth produced soporific articles; the only one who caused firestorms, and was permitted to do so, was the head coach himself.

The playing style of Ajax during the van Gaal years was in many ways a reflection of the coach's character. The pre-eminent concern in circulation football was maintaining possession and control. Others might be of the opinion that such a game concept dealt a death knell to spontaneity, creativity, unpredictability and joy, elements which make football so attractive to both players and spectators. But that mattered little to van Gaal. Football education at Ajax also manifested this predilection for control, and was based on scientific, or at least verifiable, data. Player development was carefully stored in a computer and analysed. Deviance from the pattern would be immediately registered.

Likewise, van Gaal would never grant an interview without the firm assurance that he would be allowed to read and edit the article prior to publication. He would never consider leaving the details of a contract at a new club to financial advisors.

Van Gaal's biggest concern with the media was showing signs of weakness. He seemed to assume that the world beyond the immediate environs of the safe Ajax grounds was infested with people of ill will. This worldview helped to turn van Gaal's encounters with the media into confrontational exchanges, with a defensive coach on one side and an edgy press corps on the other. This created a degree of antipathy on both sides.

On one occasion, van Gaal was invited to appear on Sky Sports as a studio commentator. Possibly knowing that an appearance fee and a free trip to London might not be enough to convince the great but suspicious coach, it was suggested to him that this could be an opportunity to gain a 'better profile' in the English Premier League.

'No, thank you,' van Gaal said pointedly. 'I'm quite happy with my bad profile.'

Van Gaal has received, according to his own tally, tens of thousands of requests to appear on talk shows, game shows and so forth, but has always declined: 'I am a football coach. I only want to talk about my profession; I don't participate in the rest … I have been asked, but I don't have time for it. Do I have to fake some smiles on TV? I don't think I should change myself. I am not dissatisfied with myself.

'I am happy when I am happy, and I am sad when I am sad. I laugh when I laugh and I cry when I cry. I am not going to laugh because I am appearing on television. Fifteen years ago everyone wrote that I had received media training, because things were quiet around me for some time. A little while later something happened again and then all the reporters had to acknowledge: Louis van Gaal did not get any media training.'

At Ajax, then, players received media training. Rightly so, according to van Gaal. But he felt he didn't need it because he was of the opinion that he 'dealt with the media in a very good manner'. Van Gaal's limited faith in the Dutch media is because he sees the enterprise as dominated by personal connections with certain individuals; the dominating and thwarting influence would often be that of Johan Cruyff. Van Gaal believes that the space given to Johan Cruyff and Marco van Basten as national coaches was never given to Dick Advocaat, or to van Gaal himself. Van Gaal believes the reason to be that the former two were superstars as players and Advocaat and van Gaal weren't.

People close to van Gaal say that in a personal conversation it is possible to say almost anything to him. But what is said in public is a different matter altogether. His pride and his perfectionism makes him extremely sensitive to criticism. Van Gaal does not want to make mistakes, and if he does make one he does not want to read about it in the press. The media variously characterised the 'Iron Tulip' as a person lacking tact and social skills, a despot, a megalomaniac or a raving lunatic. Meanwhile, van Gaal himself thinks he was just misunderstood as a person and insufficiently appreciated as a coach. At a memorable press conference, on 30 September 1991, he was asked what sort of coach he was. While self-consciously looking over all those present in the room, he slowly, deliberately said, 'I am a very consistent, honest and direct person. And sometimes that strikes people as being hard.' Based on this reply, some came to the conclusion that he was pedantic. In turn, the coach said in an interview with *Voetbal International*, 'Over the past two weeks I have learned that I should not be too quick with speaking about myself. I think the press has to get to know me. People who have been around me for a while and who know me treat me differently. In my approach to the media over the last two weeks I have made mistakes. This is the least developed area of the person van Gaal. I do not know what kind of media are coming at me now. I will have to study this and develop in this area.'

Truus Opmeer, van Gaal's second wife, says that 'Before I knew him, I thought he was a grumpy, arrogant guy like the rest of Holland. But he isn't. Most of the stuff he shows on television is not that good, I agree. He can be so agitated and all. I would do that differently. And he does have a funny side. But his work is his life and he takes that seriously. Very much so. And Louis thinks people attack him all the time. He needs to laugh more, he looks better when he laughs. Louis says I'm right, but he doesn't want to change. He feels the others need to change. I just stopped watching his interviews. Last year, I was ready to call these presenters and reporters and tell them my opinion, but I can't of course.'

Van Gaal has always made it clear that his relationship with the media was a professional one. Consequently, there is not much of a bond between the members of the press corps and the coach, as there might have been between journalists and managers such as Willem van Hanegem or Guus Hiddink. When van Gaal was once asked what he thought of the Hiddink charm offensive at press conferences, he responded, 'I explain much more than

Hiddink does. He never says a great deal. Hiddink is a master of not answering questions. I always answer questions.'

At a press conference in Barcelona, van Gaal once upbraided a journalist for being excessively negative. In halting Spanish, laced with those hard consonants the Dutch do not easily shed, he expressed his dismay that, 'You are always negative, never positive.' The scathing condemnation, broadcast across the media, is considered a classic to this day. In terms of his communication skills, van Gaal came to be considered an Iberian version of Giovanni Trapattoni – flamboyant, engaging, and somewhat linguistically impaired.

Van Gaal's struggles with the media were still evident when he joined Bayern Munich. One needn't understand any German to realise van Gaal was really not happy with Sky reporter Dieter Nickels questioning Bayern's passion after a match against league opponents Nuremberg. Van Gaal found it incomprehensible that the interviewer would doubt the quality of his team's play, and explained that the goals simply didn't come. In reaction to the journalist's follow-up questions, his vexation rapidly increased until it reached a full-scale pitch. In Holland, friends and foes have learned to live with the outbursts of the idiosyncratic football master, but the encounter quickly became somewhat of a media classic for the flabbergasted German audience. The *Bild Zeitung* ridiculed the episode under the headline 'Louis van Gallig!' ('Gallig' meaning sharp or caustic).

When he was interviewed by well-known Dutch journalist Steffie Kouters in 2006, van Gaal began by asking, 'You know the conditions for this interview, don't you?'

Kouters replied, 'I suppose that you want to read it before it is published.'

'Not only read,' van Gaal responded, 'I also want to be able to change things in it. It has happened that I completely rewrote a piece.'

'I would find it very unpleasant if you were to do that.'

'Me too,' replied van Gaal, 'because that is a lot of work for me.'

'You are a suspicious man, aren't you?' Kouters asked.

'Not at all,' van Gaal disagreed. 'Do you think you can have this kind of conversation with just anybody? Someone who shows so much of himself? I am naïve. Truus tells me that about a hundred times a year. I believe in people. I have a positive view on life. I assume that you will make a beautiful story of this. And if it isn't, that means that I hit my nose once again. That's how I go through life.' That he comes across as harsh and unfriendly is not his fault. 'That has nothing to do with me, the person Louis van Gaal. That is the result of the selective image that the media show of me.'

Kouters received a national award for her interview. A seasoned professional in the field, she later confessed to being quite nervous. She told van Gaal, 'When I came in you looked at me with some mistrust, because I am from the media. You aren't really the kind of person who says with a smile: come on in and have some coffee.'

Van Gaal replied that 'This is a necessary evil for me. I do this interview because my press officer asked me to. […] I am different from the way I am seen publicly. I find that a pity.'

'Don't you ever think,' Kouters asked, 'I am a little guilty of contributing to that?'

'Of course I am a little guilty of that,' van Gaal agreed. 'It would have been easier if I would have just been an actor. If I would be able to do it again, I think I would do it differently; although I don't know if I would have been able to. I would have made my life a little easier if I would have been less sharp, and would have beaten around the bush a little more, would have magically put a smile on my face more often.'

AZ REPRISE

'A false balance is abomination to the Lord,
but a just weight is His delight.'

Proverbs 11:1

Drive north from Amsterdam and pretty soon buildings are replaced with lush green meadows, the famed black-and-white dairy cattle are omnipresent, and the pungent smell of cow manure fills the air. The country is unchangingly flat everywhere, with no mountain or hillock to break the monotony of the straight line of the horizon. It is a great place for riding bicycles, something that almost every Dutchman or Dutchwoman does daily. In fact, there many more bicycles in Holland than there are cars, and separate bicycle paths are a standard fixture, running parallel to roads for motorised traffic, even alongside rural highways.

After a drive of about 45 minutes, if the traffic's good, you reach Alkmaar, a city with a population of about 100,000 people which the Dutch think constitutes a 'city'. But indeed, in 1254 famed Count Floris V granted Alkmaar a town charter, which even today the Dutch consider an important achievement. By contrast, the seat of government Den Haag (or The Hague) never did, and hence is derided as Holland's largest 'village'. Alkmaar is located in a typical Dutch *polder* landscape, close to a major nature reserve with dunes, beach, woods and water; water is everywhere. Its greatest claim to fame used to be its cheese market, which is a major tourist draw. But in 2009 Louis van Gaal changed what the city was known for by making AZ national champions for the first time in nearly three decades.

In 2005 van Gaal accepted the position of head coach at AZ. His predecessor Co Adriaanse had done wonders at the club, but was known to squeeze all the potential out of his teams like lemons and leave before they invariably implode. The sign that graced van Gaal's office at Ajax – 'Quality is the exclusion of coincidence' – didn't make it to his new domain at AZ. Not that this changed his view of coaching; it continued to be his fundamental creed. Van Gaal, the man who wants to keep everything under control.

The relocation to AZ had looked like an inspired move as van Gaal relished getting back to some intimate coaching work, forming a new team in his own image. Soon after van Gaal's arrival, AZ discovered that it had a new fan, none other than Chelsea coach José Mourinho. In his weekly column for the Portuguese sports daily *O Record*, Mourinho explained why from now on he would watch all of AZ's matches: 'Van Gaal is a great coach and a great person. From now on I am a supporter of AZ Alkmaar. Louis van Gaal is working on his comeback and his success is as good as guaranteed.' Mourinho added, prophetically, 'It won't be long before he will return to a big club in one of the major leagues.'

During van Gaal's stint at AZ Alkmaar, the club was dubbed 'the Dutch Chelsea' for the apparent similarity between freewheeling banker and AZ owner Dirk Scheringa and the extravagant Chelsea owner, billionaire Roman Abramovich. Some £600 million has come out of Abramovich's deep pockets to fund his pet project in West London, and, like his Russian counterpart, Scheringa seemed to regard AZ as his personal toy. Yet, in reality, the spending of the DSB bank owner was quite modest by comparison. Like Abramovich, who turned to some heavy-duty Dutch coaching help in Guus Hiddink, Scheringa turned to Louis van Gaal to get the provincial club to the top of the league. AZ eventually went on to win the league not by buying big-name players, but by playing good football, as van Gaal explained. 'Ajax has more individual skills, and that's logical … They have more money to spend. We talked with Huntelaar before Ajax got him. Same with Makaay. Hunter went for Ajax, Makaay for Feyenoord. Alves also decided to follow the money. And that's the difference. And that's why it would be a tremendous result if we'd win the title.'

Under van Gaal, the emphasis at training changed: 'With me, players have to understand why they are doing something. With every exercise I explain why I am doing something. That is how we prepare for the match. I explain the build-up of the opponent so that they can feel it, and also so they won't be caught off guard during the game. Still, they say that I don't train hard enough; not as hard as Co Adriaanse. But I train smarter. I build things up deliberately, so that they work with greater concentration. On the pitch, players have tasks that come together with their position, and I explain that to them, so that they are committed to their position.'

At the start of van Gaal's tenure many felt there was little progress to be made at AZ, but the new coach managed to bring the team to a consistently higher level. After two years at the helm he had come within seconds of the Dutch title. In the 2006–07 season, he reached the last day with his AZ leading Ajax and PSV on goal difference. All that was needed was for AZ to beat bottom of the table Excelsior, to win a first *Eredivisie* title in 25 years. Van Gaal watched in impotent horror as his goalkeeper was sent off and his side lost the game and title. Some critics – ever present in van Gaal's wake – suggested that this tragedy may have been of his own making. During the season he insisted his team could not yet be considered as favourites for the title, and that they were working for the long run. However, this had a negative effect on his players, who seemingly could not believe the championship was within their grasp even when it was staring them in the face.

Van Gaal said afterwards, 'It's always a real disappointment to lose out on a championship in the final match [of 2007]. The club needs a title to confirm the progress it has made. It's the next step that we have to take if we want recognition in the Netherlands. We only have a budget of 16 million euros, compared with 65 million for Ajax and 60 million for PSV, but we have been in the top three the last two seasons and we got to the final of the cup, which we only lost on penalties. The president is a wealthy man but he doesn't want to bump up the budget for the sake of just spending more. Money isn't the be all and end all. Ajax, PSV and Feyenoord all pay two to three times the wages that we do, but the gap is closing. When you develop players and bring them on, you get real satisfaction out of it, so no, I don't feel frustrated. We have other things acting in our favour, such as the quality of the football that we play. We like to attack and that is a selling point for us. When I won the league for the first time with Ajax, we did it on a low budget, and we can do the same here. If I didn't believe that then I would never have come here.'

Before the new season van Gaal told his top scorer, Dutch international Danny Koevermans, that he would have to take a back seat as his new signings would be preferred. Koevermans could not take the strike force to the next level, the Champions League, the manager explained. At that time AZ hoped to sign Brazilian top scorer Afonso Alves from Heerenveen, along with a couple of younger talents. Alves did not come, while the designated talents failed to make an impact. A disgruntled Koevermans left Alkmaar for PSV, where he ended up playing in the Champions League. Meanwhile, AZ languished in the lower regions of the league, having much trouble finding the net. Talk of the top four evaporated.

Perhaps as an ominous sign of things to come, van Gaal had an accident in the autumn of 2007 and was confined to a wheelchair for a while. At a reunion of the ALO, the Academy of Physical Education, he broke both his ankle and fibula when he attempted to give those gathered a live demonstration in pole vault jumping. According to his own interpretation, he completed the exercise perfectly but slipped on the smooth soles of his shoes because he was wearing footwear that was ill-suited for such daring physical performances. As a result, the 56-year-old coach landed awkwardly on the gymnasium floor and ended up with a double leg break – 'I was crazy enough to think that I was still 18.' He received surgery on the day of the accident at the Alkmaar Medical Centre. Van Gaal must have damaged his leg quite badly because no less than six pins were inserted to support the broken bone. His leg was put into a cast, and for the next few weeks he had to be wheeled around in a wheelchair. But he was released the next day so he could attend the AZ–NEC game at the DSB Stadium. He admitted that his presence at the game came unusually quickly after the surgery. Patients who undergo full anaesthesia ordinarily stay in hospital for three days: 'Just to make sure, I swallowed a substantial dose of painkillers on the way to the stadium. I wanted to be there, no matter what. But I did not want that they would see me suffer.'

Van Gaal issued a dose of black humour when he suggested that he had intentionally broken his leg to give his assistant, Edward Metgod, the opportunity to prove his mettle. But although Metgod was on the touchline leading the AZ team, van Gaal was on hand watching how his team humbled the visitors 4–0 from an otherwise empty executive box. He was in contact with the dugout via walkie-talkie, but before the technical staff had managed to establish a satisfactory wireless connection AZ had already scored the first goal, a header from Simon Cziommer. For their next game, away at Eindhoven, AZ put in a request with PSV to allow the wounded coach to supervise the action on the pitch from an elevated lodge position at the Philips Stadium. The answer was negative: because he was a potential fire hazard liability, van Gaal would have to stay on ground level. The Philips people tried to be accommodating and suggested removing two chairs from the dugout to make space for the wheelchair.

During this period, team manager Piet Hartland became van Gaal's chauffeur, driving the coach from his home in Noordwijk to training in Alkmaar and back, with van Gaal in the back seat, injured leg across. The physical training he left to his assistants, but Friday pre-game training, with specific instructions aimed at overcoming the next league opponent, was done by van Gaal himself – on the pitch, wheelchair and all: 'In football your legs are very important. But coaching you just do with your head. It would only be bad and problematic if I had a head injury and couldn't properly communicate with the players. But that I can still do very well. Only, instead of interrupting the game and going to a player, the player now has to come to me. But I have never missed a single game in my entire coaching career. When I'm sick, I still come.' At Barcelona he once broke his metatarsal bone: 'You can easily find pictures of that because I just continued to work. I could understand the Spanish interest in that, but it was news even in England. I thought that was really exaggerated. As a coach I have won the Champions League, but I have never received as much attention as when I am now sitting in a wheelchair. The Queen, baking a cake on "national volunteering day", is covered on page 8 of the newspaper, and I, with something as unimportant as this, am on every front page.'

Despite such unexpected setbacks, van Gaal stayed upbeat: 'When I got here, they were still playing in an 8,000 capacity stadium which hardly ever sold out. Now we have a new ground with room for more than 20,000 fans, and last season we sold out almost every match. That's already an important step. The aim is for AZ to become a big club domestically and recognised throughout Europe on the same level as the big three over here: Ajax, PSV and Feyenoord. The president wants to work in stages so that every aspect is covered, not just the results on the pitch. Having said that, the fact that we are ahead of the big three in the UEFA rankings thanks to what we achieved last season is an essential element in the progress we are making.'

The season turned out to be a horror for AZ and van Gaal. Plagued by injuries, poor morale, and new signings not gelling with the other squad members, AZ had to battle against relegation for a while, before ending the season with an anonymous mid-table finish, an underwhelming eleventh place in the *Eredivisie*. Van Gaal, characteristically defiant, initially refused to take the blame for the team's decline. As amusing as his rants often were, they irritated other managers, players and fans to the point where people actually enjoyed AZ's and van Gaal's losing streak. Some criticised chairman Dirk Scheringa for not sacking him. Van Gaal, meanwhile, announced his intention to leave, a decision that led to a host of players expressing their desire for him to stay. To many people's surprise, ahead of the final league game against Sparta Rotterdam, van Gaal bowed to their wishes and reversed his decision.

'After talks with the board and the directors of the club,' van Gaal said, 'it seems everybody wants me to stay at AZ. A lot of players came to the club because I am the coach. Leaving now would not be fair on all of them.' Van Gaal began turning his attention to the next campaign: 'We have learned a lot this season. We really have to be sure that players are getting better and, if not, look for better players. We also have to be strict about transfers. If there is uncertainty about getting a player, we should focus on getting someone else.' He identified a lack of leadership as a major handicap at the club, adding he would be seeking an experienced campaigner in the transfer window: 'That kind of player we really missed this season, although the last of couple of weeks it looked better … It is a shame that we probably won't play European football next season, but we know what we want. We took one step back this season, but I am confident that we will make two steps forward next season.'

To the amusement of his critics, van Gaal and AZ continued where they left off by losing the opening two fixtures of the 2008–09 season: NAC Breda beat AZ 2–1 in Alkmaar and ADO Den Haag overpowered them 3–0. But in their next league match van Gaal sparked a turnaround. His motivational speech inspired AZ to pull off a shock 1–0 win over reigning champions PSV Eindhoven. From that point on, AZ played like a team transformed. Free-flowing attacking football, spectacular goals and intelligent movement, van Gaal's trademarks, were once again in abundance. Results like the 6–0 hammering of Sparta Rotterdam and the 5–2 defeat of Willem II Tilburg illustrated this change in fortunes.

A combination of unwavering commitment and incessive tinkering with the team finally got AZ where van Gaal wanted it to be. Goalkeeper Sergio Romero developed into a class act in the capable hands of van Gaal and his staff. Gill Swerts and Niklas Moisander were attacking full-backs in the Ajax tradition, covering the entire wing and playing impressively both attacking and defending. The heart of the defence was formed by veteran Kew Jaliens and the talented young Mexican Héctor Moreno. In midfield, van Gaal could select Dutch internationals like Demy de Zeeuw and Stijn Schaars, as well as Belgian internationals Maarten Martens and Sébastien Pocognoli. Australian international Brett Holman was also available. The true revelation in midfield, however, was Nick van der Velden, who came in from minnows FC Dordrecht. Up front, the style of play and physical build of Belgian powerhouse forward Moussa Dembélé was similar to that of Zlatan Ibrahimović. Signed from Willem II, he turned into a prolific goal scorer, scoring numerous spectacular goals.

The new van Gaal system withstood its greatest test at a reborn PSV in February – well, for one half anyway. Hounding PSV when they had the ball, AZ dominated possession in the first half, resulting in two goals: Gill Swerts was able to head in a Stijn Schaars corner before Demy de Zeeuw was tripped up in the box. De Zeeuw missed his penalty but Maarten Martens converted the rebound. The team sat back back in the second half, allowing a spirited PSV to squeeze two goals past them. The 2–2 draw was a fair result, but the match was important as it ended the claims that AZ led the *Eredivisie* by default because PSV, Ajax and Feyenoord were having an off-year. By this point in the season, AZ had gone undefeated for five months and the draw was their first failure to win in almost three.

The players request for van Gaal to stay turned out to be proved right: AZ went on to win the championship for the first time since 1981. The club won the title by 11 points, and was the first time in 28 years that a team other than PSV, Ajax or Feyenoord had been champions.

Only one person wasn't surprised by the turn of events: when van Gaal officially opened the city's famous cheese market in 2008, he met a fortune teller who told him, 'AZ will become champions on 19 April.' As the club did not have an *Eredivisie* fixture that day, van Gaal took little notice of his prediction. Come 18 April, and AZ had a chance to take the crown but surprisingly lost to Vitesse Arnhem. But on the following day – yes, 19 April – their closest pursuers, Ajax, lost 6–2 to PSV Eindhoven and the title belonged to AZ.

In his column in *De Telegraaf*, Guus Hiddink heaped praise on van Gaal's AZ: 'I agree with Louis van Gaal's assertion that AZ can handle the level of the Champions League. When I consider how fantastically the team has performed in the Netherlands this season, then I think they will also be able to prove themselves at that higher level. I feel that AZ has earned respect for the manner in which the club has continued to develop itself, with the impending title of national champions as a just reward. It is good for Dutch football that for a change a different club becomes champion.' More praise came from van Gaal's old rival, Johan Cruyff: 'First of all, of course, congratulations to AZ. As the result of a strong series the Alkmaar players have become, surprisingly but deservedly, the champions of the Netherlands. Special compliments to coach Louis van Gaal, who personally redeemed the last season in an excellent way. When I realistically look at the title of AZ, then I must evaluate the team less critically than Ajax, PSV and Feyenoord. Considering the means they have in Alkmaar, the performance has been very good. The foundation for this was especially laid in the defence. With 17 goals against in 31 matches, you can perform on the European level.'

The Alkmaar cheese-carriers' guild does not have its own patron saint, or its own altar in church like many other professional guilds such as the cobblers, coopers, coppersmiths and tanners. However, a biblical text from 1622 is still the motto for the guild of Alkmaar: 'A false balance is abomination to the Lord, but a just weight is His delight.' It could well be the motto, too, for Louis van Gaal – a straight dealer who believes that honesty and hard work have their just reward. At AZ, they certainly did.

THE LOUIS VAN GAAL MENU

'Louis is a warm-blooded human being.
It's sad that not a lot of people know this.'

Truus van Gaal-Opmeer

After flopping as coach of Holland, van Gaal decided that defences had become too sharp to succumb to endless passing. He began focusing on the instant when a team loses the ball. It's the moment when the opposition's defence might be out of position. When AZ became champions, this was the moment when they struck. To some, AZ's counter-attacking methods appeared to be the opposite of the traditional school of Dutch football tactics. On closer inspection, though, there are more similarities than differences. Built on the foundation of total football, AZ's game was to sit back and wait for its opponents to overstretch themselves and then break out. Their skilled, lightning-quick strikers were sufficiently superior to capitalise on only a handful of chances. Van Gaal's system gave the individual more room for improvisation, and was less stringent about formations – he had his team play in at least four different shapes during the winning season. AZ still applied asphyxiating pressure on its opponents, but did so largely in its own half, rather than over the whole field. When the team gained possession, players tried to move up the field in three passes or fewer, usually ending in a through-ball for the strikers to run on to. They attack, in other words, in short and quick bursts and then dedicate themselves to letting the opposition do the work.

'It's a footballing philosophy more than a system,' van Gaal explained. 'A system depends on the players you have. I have played 4-3-3 with Ajax, 2-3-2-3 with Barcelona and I can play 4-4-2 with AZ. I'm flexible. The philosophy stays the same, though. The coach is the team's focal point, so preparing the tactical formation is essential. Every player must know where he has to be and support his teammates. [...] I don't think that you can adapt it to every possible situation. You need the right mindset, and it depends on how the players see the coach and vice versa. The coach is the focal point of the team but you need to have an open mind, and so do all the players. Everyone needs to work together to achieve a common goal. Preparing your tactical formation is essential. This is a sport played by 22 men, and there are 11 opponents out there playing as a team. Each individual needs to know who he has to beat and be there to support his teammates.'

One of the things van Gaal did at AZ was to dramatically expand his management team – its size nearly doubled during his tenure. Not only was the medical contingent increased, but significant attention was also paid to the technological side of things: 'I am always working on knowledge management, and I want people in my staff who complement me. I consider measurement very, very important, but I cannot do everything myself. That's why I use a physical trainer. What I see in those boys, he confirms. The same thing applies to my PowerPoint presentations and game analyses. Those are made by a computer guru and my assistants.'

In van Gaal's training, the primary objective is education, the learning process by which players improve. This was of particular importance at AZ because the club was in no position to buy expensive players, people at their peak. Instead, the club acquired players at the level below – good players with good learning potential. From 2008, the video-analysis computer specialist Max Reckers worked with cameraman Kees Verver to support the learning process. Verver filmed by special camera – one that produced images notably larger than those that are commonly presented to TV viewers and hence provide a much clearer overview of the positioning of each player. While Verver filmed, Reckers codified hundreds of game situations into dozens of categories on laptop. In the post-game processing, the images were dissected into some 2,000 'events'. Individual players then received a video digest of relevant images – incidents in which they were personally involved. Van Gaal would then provide further feedback, based on his interpretation of the footage.

Video analysis also played a significant role in the game preparation. Recent games by the upcoming opponent were taken apart, analysed and categorised in the same manner that AZ games were treated. Thus a wealth of information was generated that van Gaal could use as a basis for training for the forthcoming match. This became the basis for game simulation where 11 AZ reserves were instructed to play in the style of the opponent, countered by AZ's basic 11. The training was likewise filmed and would become the foundation for a follow-up 11-versus-11 training match. The result was that an upcoming match was already 'played' twice before it actually took place.

Van Gaal's video team used sophisticated systems for game-tracking: *SportsCode* to register ball contact per player, and *Sportvu* to determine the real-time position of every player – their average playing position throughout the match (curiously, the latter was developed by the Israeli army to track the movement of tanks on the battlefield). Van Gaal gave his pre-game instructions to his team, and team performance was then evaluated based on whether players followed instructions. Compliance was sometimes valued even more than the actual scoreline. Thus, paradoxically, van Gaal considered the performance of his team in that early 2008–09 defeat against ADO Den Haag 'very good'.

'I am interested in the total human being,' van Gaal explained. 'I don't think passing the ball from player A to B is what it's about. That's the easy part. To form a good team, you need to gel a group of individuals together. Last year, we lacked a leader on the pitch. You need to approach a team sport as a collection of cogs that you then gel together into a football machine. No machine … That's not a good word … You need heart and soul too. But you need to know what drives people, who can they play in service, how do I approach and motivate this kid. I made profile descriptions of all my players and we now have a shared language I can use with my coaching staff. I once told a player: "You don't improve here, I can't use you any more. It's over." That night, I couldn't sleep and I knew I was wrong. I went to him the next day, and said: "Listen, I couldn't sleep. I was wrong. You will keep your place in the team." The world is getting complicated. We live in the zap culture. One push on a button and you know everything, and kids start doing that when they're 12 years old. I need to work with those circumstances and I can't do it alone, I need specialists in many fields to guide these players.'

Though van Gaal is a firm believer in technology, he considers creating harmony within the team of primary importance. To that end he employs some rather down-to-earth methods. At AZ, just as during his early days at Ajax, he organised game evenings for his team. 'And they still find that great! They are all games with an interactive character, so that you get to know each other also under different circumstances, together with the wives and the board members. We play cards, we do a quiz. And singing together we do as well; everyone participates. If you present them in the right way, people will always enjoy those games. Because you go back to interaction: looking each other in the eyes, with a smile on the face. I am the show master!

'I need day-to-day contact with the boys. It keeps me young. I want people around me, I need to communicate. I can be alone for a day, but the next day I start to become jittery and the third day I go crazy … I get two or three calls per month. Reasonable clubs too. Sometimes they call me four times in a row … I am sorry Bayern Munich always came at the wrong time for me. That's a club I'd like to work with, and I could have, I suppose …' But in the heat of the 2008–09 season, working with AZ gave van Gaal satisfaction enough: 'The level we sometimes reach at training reminds me of Ajax and Barça. The interchange between players and coaches is good and we have confidence this season. That's important. Last season, we were mostly the better team but we couldn't score. The pressure starts and you start to make mistakes, which adds to the pressure. Now, we don't have trouble scoring and everyone relaxes into the game. We only conceded 11 goals, which has everything to do with our ability to score up front.'

Van Gaal is more flexible than his critics are willing to acknowledge, although this is something he has learned over time: 'When I was a new coach, I tried to impose certain aspects of the game on boys who played intuitively, and that did not work for them. I have learned that this type of player benefits less from structure and systems, and needs to be given more freedom. Moussa Dembélé was an intuitive player whom I left alone to a considerable degree, for my style. Moussa had a lot of freedom. That had two advantages. He operated better and he also recognised that I treated him differently. But he wanted to be part of it, so he asked me things. Because of this approach, he became a player with a much broader orientation.

'I am "two in one": a harmony and a process coach. I build a relationship with the players. In that relationship it is clear what my vision is and how we can realise it within the team. I always do that in a relational atmosphere. I do not believe in war and punishment. This is a very lengthy process that really never ends. There is a certain distance between the players and me, and that is good. But players from 16 up to 35 make up the group. Some are still on their way to adulthood, so I fulfil a fatherly role. But I can also be a tormentor. I conduct myself according to the circumstances. But the precondition is that there has to be a relationship. That is why I rarely scold players; I am more emotional and direct. When you work in a punishing way, you correct someone based on his behaviour. But someone's behaviour is part of his identity, so I don't think that is useful. I rather look for solutions in communication. It may be necessary to penalise, but in the end the player has to want to make the right choice. Otherwise you get an unworkable situation.'

Despite his strong and sometimes haughty public persona, van Gaal has had aspiring coaches jostling for placements under his wing. Patrick Kluivert, who successfully completed his professional football coaching course (*Coach Betaald Voetbal*), did an internship under van Gaal at AZ. Adam Sadler, the former Norwich City assistant manager and then the number two at Gateshead, visited AZ as part of his Pro Licence: 'I had sky-high expectations,' he admitted, 'but Louis van Gaal exceeded them. He was welcoming and open. He's a man of integrity and strong moral values who demands maximum concentration. He doesn't let players relax.'

At the Amsterdam Sportgala, Louis van Gaal was honoured as the Dutch Coach of the Year for 2009. Fifty-one coaching colleagues cast ballots in his favour, in recognition of his accomplishment of making AZ Dutch champions: 'This is fantastic, also because the media have contributed to this,' said van Gaal, in a terse reference to his often strained relationship with the press. Van Gaal thanked the AZ players, board, and former AZ chairman Dirk Scheringa: 'The lines were short at AZ. Things haven't been going so well with Dirk Scheringa this year,' referring to the débâcle surrounding the bankruptcy of Scheringa's bank, DSB – Dirk Scheringa Bank.

There were rumours that van Gaal had ambitions to be England manager, but van Gaal played these down. 'The Dutch media made a mountain out of a molehill. I've actually got a contract with AZ until 2010. I have a clause in it which enables me to leave earlier but only to coach a national team. I drew up a list of five possibilities as the club didn't want to have a whole host of countries knocking at their door. England was on the list, and since the job was available the media made a lot of fuss about it. I'm happy here, there's real chemistry between the president, the players and the staff and I like the overall atmosphere at the club. My ambition at the moment is to take part in a major international tournament with a country and to win it. I've won almost everything there is to win at club level. What I feel is missing is the experience of a Euro or a World Cup at the head of a national team. AZ definitely wants to keep me on and I've always finished my contracts out of a sense of loyalty.' Van

Gaal suggested that AZ boss Scheringa might want to turn him into a Dutch Alex Ferguson: 'The president is looking to build for the long term with me and he wants to keep me on until I'm 65, but I don't want to be coaching a national team at that age and definitely not when I'm even older.'

If the England job was ruled out, another possibility seemed more enticing – to take over at Bayern Munich. Van Gaal had a good conversation with the AZ leadership, represented by chairman Dirk Scheringa, technical director Marcel Brands, general director Toon Gerbrands and treasurer René Neelissen, as to whether the successful coach should be permitted an early departure or required to complete his term at AZ. According to Brands, 'We don't want to lose Louis, but we understand we cannot hold on to him at all cost.' Van Gaal made clear that Bayern was the club of his dreams. Twice before he had come close to making the move to the club: once when he was working with Barcelona, and the other time when he decided in favour of the Dutch national team. In the programme bulletin of the final league match of the 2008–09 season against SC Heerenveen, van Gaal 'begged' for leniency from chairman Scheringa in allowing him to leave before the term of his contract expired. According to van Gaal there was a verbal agreement that he would be allowed early departure should AZ win the national title: 'Top European clubs like Bayern Munich, Chelsea or Real Madrid cannot be compared with AZ. That is why I hope it will be possible to talk with Dirk about him giving me this contract year.' If that would not happen then 'it would be difficult to maintain credibility, both for me and for the AZ board'. The coach bade farewell to his players and the technical staff by saying, 'I wish everybody a good vacation. Maybe we'll see each other again in June for the first training. Maybe we won't.'

On 8 August 2008 – 08-08-08 – which just so happened to also be his 57th birthday, Louis van Gaal said 'yes' to Truus Opmeer. The couple were married in the town of Albufeira on the Algarve in Portugal. The ceremony took place on a clifftop, with splendid views of the sea, under steely blue skies. Truus van Gaal-Opmeer commented, 'I wanted to get married in De Kuip [Feyenoord's stadium], but Louis said, "Please suggest something normal next time ..." The wedding was wonderful. It was important to me, not so important for him. He always regarded me as his wife, but the media kept referring to me as "Louis' girlfriend" and I didn't like that. We got married late [after a fourteen-year-long relationship] and mainly because I wanted to get hitched and get married in Vegas, just the two of us. Louis wanted a big celebration. He said, "If you have something to celebrate, celebrate!" And he hadn't asked me yet. He did last year [2008]. Just before Christmas. He couldn't go down on his knee because he'd just broken his leg. I think a secret marriage would have been wrong. Louis' daughters from his first marriage belonged there as well. Their mother died and then their dad would marry secretly ... No. I'm a Feyenoord fan and I wanted to get married on the pitch in De Kuip. He didn't get that. But I said, "Hey ... I'm the bride, OK? It's my city." But we got married in Portugal instead, where we have a home. We flew our friends in, 80 guests. I was nervous, more than thrilled. All the details, the flowers, the table setting, all that stuff.

'Louis can't help himself. He believes in himself and his methods. I told him recently, "We have a nice house here, and a nice house in Portugal. Why do you still want to do it? Stop. Go and do motivationals or analyse on TV. Make good money and don't carry any responsibilities." Two years back, English TV offered him a job. I liked it. Good money, interesting lifestyle. But he refused.

I'd thank the Lord if he quit. I know what we'd do. Louis would probably take up studying, something like psychology. He golfs, we play tennis, although tennis isn't that good for us. We play doubles and he keeps on yelling, "Run", "Hit the ball!" "Just play tennis," I tell him. Louis is a homebody. He doesn't want to go to the movies. And he doesn't get it either. If we watch a DVD he'll go, "What a silly story." And I tell him, it's just a movie! He can be so serious. Louis likes basic Dutch food. I light a candle, a glass of wine. He doesn't do a thing in the house; he doesn't even know how to make coffee. He likes me to spoil him and I like to do just that.'

Since 2000, Louis and Truus van Gaal have been ambassadors for the *Stichting Spieren voor Spieren*, the 'Muscles for Muscles Foundation'. The website of the organisation explains that the couple is 'very involved, often present at a variety of events, and very important for the entire organisation'. Under the theme, 'Healthy muscles dedicated to help ill muscles', the objective of the organisation is to generate funds for the treatment of children with a variety of muscular diseases. In 2009, at the organisation's fifth gala, a benefit evening to collect money for research and treatment, van Gaal said, 'I know how important it is that money is constantly generated to finance scientific research. Besides, it gives a lot of satisfaction to brighten the future prospects of children with muscular diseases with this kind of investment.' Partly due to the imposing presence of van Gaal, €400,000 were collected during the evening – a record sum according to the organisers. Chairman Gerard Hoetmer said that the charitable group could not have wished for a better ambassador: 'Louis is not only a world-class coach, but he is also able to see the relativity of things. In addition, he is also an enormously warm person. Inside the organisation we witness at first hand how involved Louis is and how close he is to the children. He is not only a top sportsman, but also a top human being.'

Van Gaal does not advertise his charitable activity: 'When I do something like that, I do it for a good cause. Only because of that. Not for the sake of my image.' This is typical van Gaal. He has featured in commercials for the Dutch branch of the German consumer electronics brands Media Markt and it was assumed that he had given his income from these endeavours away. Media probings into the matter, though, led nowhere: 'It's nobody's business what I do with that money. I will never respond to that. But that commercial I did for Media Markt does say something about the appreciation there is in the Netherlands for the things I said in my confrontations with journalists. All those sayings are now used in the advertisment. I think that is great. A compliment.'

With all things going well for him, the question remains: is Louis happy? The coach's exacting standards make life difficult – for those around him, and, apparently, for himself. Halfway through the 2008–09 season, van Gaal offered this appraisal: 'Well, we lead the table, I just married Truus, my children and grandchildren are healthy, so … My wife wants to spend more time in Portugal where we have a second home, but I told her not yet! I don't see myself sleeping in and playing a round of golf every day.' In AZ's restaurant there is something that's called The Louis van Gaal Menu: mashed potatoes, endives, slow-cooked skirt steak and bacon bits with a garlic gravy: 'They had made mistakes. I had asked for endives stew, but it had turned into kohlrabi stew. But I don't like kohlrabi. If it is a Louis van Gaal menu, then it has to be a Louis van Gaal menu.' Hearty Dutch fare, with a bit of extra thrown in, the three-course menu costs €28.50.

'By nature I am a gourmet. I grew up in an affluent family and things weren't bad for us. But because I reached a certain level, I have developed that gourmet inclination. I no longer drink bad wine.' Thus speaks van Gaal, ever the perfectionist. The builder and the man of details. The AZ training field is covered with a white sort of blanket. 'Did you see that cover on the field? When we train it goes off. After training it immediately goes back on. Twice a day, eight people pull on that thing, often including the stadium manager himself. That is unheard of, fantastic. Everyone pulling on the same rope – that's what matters.' Louis' dessert in his menu is homemade custard with fresh mandarin, whipped cream and crispy chocolate: 'Actually, chocolate custard is even better, but the mandarin parts will slip into the chocolate and that doesn't taste too good. Mandarin in custard is tasty, delicious even.'

Truus says, 'He thinks I spend too much money. How many coats do you need, he tells me? I tell him to move to Spain or Italy because the money is so good there, but he doesn't get that. He doesn't care about money. When he turned 50, I gave him an expensive watch. He didn't get it – "I already have a good watch." That's typical Louis. We never fight or bicker about domestic stuff. Our life is great. I'm good with his daughters and I play grandma for Louis' grandchildren. I love it. I also have a picture of Fernanda [Louis' first wife] in the room. Why not? She is grandma too. I never pushed myself as the new mother. Kids can only have one mother. I bought the two grandsons a little AZ jersey. You should have seen Louis' face. Proud and emotional. Louis is such a warm-blooded human being. It's sad that not a lot of people know this.'

AT BAYERN MUNICH AT LAST

'Der Tod oder die Gladiolen.'
Louis van Gaal, quoting a Dutch saying meaning
'Death or the gladioli' – essentially all or nothing.

The 2001 *Bundesliga* title and the Champions League triumph in Milan four days later made amends for the 1999 disaster in Barcelona, when Bayern were robbed of victory by Manchester United through two stunning injury time goals. During the first decade of the twenty-first century, Bayern were reconfirmed as the team that always succeeds; both they and most of their domestic rivals became convinced that Bavarian hegemony was almost an unshakeable law of nature. '*Mia san mia*' – we are who we are – is the club's self-confident mantra. It celebrates 'Bayern-ness' as a byword for success. This sense of superiority, an unapologetic sense of entitlement and a high-pressure environment, have undoubtedly helped the club attain its special position within German football. Perhaps, though, the real power lies in others' awareness of '*so sind sie*', or 'that's how they are', the deeply ingrained fear of deferential opponents, many of whom start the campaign dreaming only of finishing second.

A few years laters, however, and Bayern were struggling for consistency, having been managed by four different coaches in three years. Dutch midfielder Mark van Bommel was named Bayern's first-ever foreign captain, and the ever-changing side had evolved to include twice as many foreign internationals as domestic ones. By 2008–09, Bayern's confidence was dented to such an extent that some despaired over a prolonged identity crisis at the club. 'We are who we are' had given way to a nervous 'Who are we?' under Jürgen Klinsmann's management, and after only 300 days at the helm he was deemed surplus to requirements. Bayern was desperate to get back to basics after the failed experiment, with president Uli Hoeness eager to sign 'a football teacher' who would bring out the best in a team with considerable potential. And so the call went out to Louis van Gaal.

Van Gaal's self-belief seemed to be well-matched with that of Bayern's of yore. In an interview in 2007, van Gaal had told FIFA, 'I am who I am, and I have my own ways. I am not going to change and I have no desire to.' He repeated his mantra when he arrived in Munich on 1 July 2009: *Mir san mir!* We are who we are! And I am who I am: confident, dominant and honest, a workaholic, innovative, but also warm and family-friendly. That's why I think I'll fit in.' He presented himself with a 13-strong management team to photographers. Then the season formally started with a little light training – 'to get to know each other', as van Gaal explained. He wanted to 'write history' with Bayern: 'Our goal is to win titles, in the championship and the cup, and maybe, just maybe, we will win the Champions League at the end of the van Gaal period.' He warned, however, 'That cannot be accomplished in a month; maybe it can be done in two years.'

The Germans were not required to pay compensation for van Gaal's release from AZ. Instead, Bayern offered to play a game 'for free' in Alkmaar as an expression of gratitude for handing over the popular coach. After van Gaal signed a contract running until June 2011, club chairman Karl-Heinz Rummenigge declared, 'We are happy that in Louis van Gaal we have managed to acquire an experienced and successful coach.' Throughout his career, the Dutchman has made no secret of the fact that he is a Bayern Munich admirer. The club had knocked on van Gaal's door before, but he had repeatedly rejected the advances because they came 'at the wrong time'.

Van Gaal thought that his system-based coaching style and Bayern's organised corporate structure would make a good match. Unlike most other European top clubs, which are run by businessmen, the people in charge of Bayern are real football men – people van Gaal could work with: 'I think that I will fit well there. When I went to Barcelona, I could also have gone to AC Milan. Despite the very substantial salary in Milan, I chose Barcelona. [Likewise,] at Bayern you can become champion and achieve something in the Champions League.'

Van Gaal did his best to adapt to his new environment. He endeared himself to his adoptive nation by insisting that all who plied their football trade in Germany – coaches and players alike – learn the domestic language. Though he learned German in high school and even took an intensive refresher course just prior to his arrival in Munich, his German was far from perfect. He continued to intermittently amuse and bewilder his audience, enriching the language with novel vocabulary and mind-boggling syntax. Even so, his labours were recognised by the German magazine *Die Deutsche Sprachwelt*, and he was chosen as one of three *Sprachwahrer des Jahres* 2009 for his exemplary dedication to the preserving the German language (*Sprachwahrer* translates as someone who is 'faithful' to the language).

In his book, *Lass Mal Sitzen*, German psychologist Reinhard Wolff analyses the unique phenomenon of the Dutch speaking (or trying to speak) German. The good-natured abuse of the German language by the western neighbours has produced comical expressions in the past, but Louis van Gaal seems to have taken the confusion to an entirely new level of sophistication. According to Wolff, van Gaal's maxim '*Der Tod oder die Gladiolen*', has become so popular in Germany that it may actually receive a permanent place in the German vernacular.

Undaunted by linguistic challenges or cultural barriers, and armed only with a Dutch–German dictionary, van Gaal settled in to his new role. He had warned that the redevelopment of Bayern as he envisioned it might well take up to two years. He then proceeded to outline his 'holistic principles', and taught some of the van Gaal philosophy to the uninitiated: 'I don't see players who simply kick the ball from point A to point B, I see humans who react to their surroundings. Training has more to do with the brain than the feet.'

Van Gaal cautioned that the first few change-filled months could be problematic, a prediction that came to pass. Bayern failed to win their first three league fixtures, as van Gaal's philosophy of short passing and strict positional discipline took time to take hold. When he assumed control at the beginning of the season, it took him at least 10 matches of tinkering before he settled on his preferred line-up – 10 matches during which the team seemed rudderless and the coach's credentials were questioned. Indeed, for the first four months of the season van Gaal and Bayern Munich looked incompatible. The new coach was accused of adopting an authoritarian approach that had apparently left his players afraid to express themselves, and the Bavarian side struggled to find form. Van Gaal's experimental start – his juggling formations and tactics, all the way to an outlandish 3-3-3-1 line-up in a Hamburg away game – was feared by many to only exacerbate the existing crisis. Eventually, however, results were to prove him right; though not without pain, misunderstanding, and a very generous helping of criticism from just about everyone along the way. Once the coach found his formula an impressive winning streak began, and neither van Gaal nor the team looked back.

During those tough early months at Bayern, the German media criticised van Gaal for curbing his players' creative instincts by imposing too many tactical restraints. Renowned former Bayern defender Willy Sagnol admonished, 'Bayern players are not small children!' References were made to his background as a teacher, the implication being that his style was unsuited to top-level football players. It was an accusation van Gaal had heard before and quickly dismissed: 'The media know you have been a teacher so they like to give you this label,' he said. 'I'm not the schoolmasterly type.' The flexibility van Gaal showed highlighted this point. Realising his team found it difficult to take on board all of his many instructions, he softened his stance slightly and urged his players to take on more responsibility themselves: 'I had to change the way I communicated,' he said. 'At first the players thought they had to carry out my instructions to the letter. But they have to adapt to different situations. It was an unfortunate start, but I changed my team talks and now it's better … My way of working was something the players had to get used to. I demand they use their brains because I believe football is played largely with the mind. I'm very direct and emotional, and I make corrections immediately. You try to teach students in a certain way, using aspects of your character. It's exactly the same with football players. Tactical team play is the most important thing. Bayern is a big club. Clubs like Barcelona and Chelsea can go out and sign almost anyone. But we're trying our best to build a very good team.'

It was approximately 15 years earlier, during the reign of coach Giovanni Trapattoni, that Bayern first earned the nickname *FC Hollywood*. At the time, the epithet was given in response to the recurring appearances of several Bayern players in the German tabloids, and it was a name made more appropriate by the antics of Trapattoni himself. Over the years, these cameos became increasingly rare, and the nickname had eventually wore off ... until the arrival of van Gaal. He had been brought in to improve Bayern's image, both domestically and in Europe. Bayern made no secret of their desire to become kings of Europe for the fifth time since 1974. The club board also wanted to confirm a distinct identity, a clear sportive culture and definite philosophy such as that maintained at Arsenal or Barcelona, or at Ajax, during the years when Louis van Gaal reigned supreme at the Amsterdam club.

The prospect of another year without any silverware was too much for defender Philipp Lahm, who criticised everything from Bayern transfer politics to on-field tactics in an interview with the *Süddeutsche Zeitung*. He criticised the club management for a lack of vision and the absence of a football philosophy. Ironically, when Louis van Gaal corrected that deficit – instilling the fundamentals of a consistent and coherent philosophy of football – he was criticised by many at Bayern as being intransigent and out of touch with local realities. But Lahm sided with his coach by saying, 'You shouldn't just buy players because they are good.'

It's rare to see Bayern players publicly questioning the team and it was almost unthinkable that the source of such straight talk would be mild-mannered Lahm. Yet, he was one of the few people who had both the courage to speak out and at the same time kept faith in his manager. When was asked whether he regretted not moving to Barcelona when he had the opportunity, he replied, 'I definitely do not regret it, because I still am of the opinion that something can really develop at Bayern. Why should I go when I believe that I can have it here, at home, at the club I grew up in? But you do have to critically analyse the situation. It definitely has to do with the reality that over the last few years we had several coaches who had different ideas. Clubs like Manchester United or Barcelona establish a system, and then they buy the people for that system. You target specific players; that is how the team develops.' The Bayern management was not amused and fined Lahm for presumably speaking out of turn. But then they essentially followed his advice and stuck with van Gaal.

Since the start of his first season at the club, van Gaal had struggled to communicate his football ideology to the Bayern squad. No matter how competent the group was, few seemed to really grasp what he was talking about. There were a few mutineers, with Luca Toni being perhaps the most notable case. Van Gaal said, 'Football at Bayern is of the highest level and every player who comes here promises to give it their all when they sign a contract. Football is not about individuals, it is a team sport. It is not a hobby, it is a profession and that is the difference. We have rules and we have to work within these rules. Luca Toni did not stick to the rules. He had to fight for his place along with Ivica Olić and Mario Gómez. Every player, whether they are a world champion or whatever, has got to accept that he doesn't play.' The majority seemed to be OK, but nonetheless confused, bewildered and overwhelmed. While Philipp Lahm suggested that the club needed 'a philosophy', Franck Ribéry said that 'his [van Gaal's] philosophy was hard to understand'. He also complained that 'in training no one is laughing. Everything is too serious.'

By late October, rumours suggested that van Gaal would be sacked if Bayern were unable to beat Eintracht Frankfurt in their next match. With four minutes left and the two teams level with a goal apiece, van Gaal chose to do the unthinkable: bringing on defender Martin Demichelis for striker Luca Toni. The home crowd of 69,000 fans roared their disapproval, but the coach ignored them, sending centre-half Daniel van Buyten up front to partner Mario Gómez. It was a gutsy move, but it worked: two minutes from full time the Belgian defender nodded in Thomas Müller's cross, and Bayern came away with the three points. It proved to be the first of several season-defining moments for van Gaal and Bayern.

Tensions within the team were never far from the surface. They'd occasionally spill into full public view, such as when Luca Toni had to make way for Arjen Robben at half-time during the game against Schalke in November. The volatile Italian did not take kindly to that and left the stadium. Van Gaal expressed surprise and displeasure when he learned of Toni's exit after the closing whistle: 'When such a thing happens, that is not good. We'll have to talk about that.' The match ended in a draw, leaving Bayern in eighth place in the *Bundesliga* table. The fans remained unhappy, while the media chorused that this was Bayern's worst start in the *Bundesliga* for 15 years. President Uli Hoeness spoke of 'nervousness' in the team ranks, but honorary president Franz Beckenbauer, putting on a brave face, felt that van Gaal should at the very least be given time to prove himself until the winter break. Few were upbeat but Philipp Lahm felt better times were ahead: 'Many still have a mixture of respect and fear [of van Gaal]. But he certainly is no monster, and he does not demand absurdities from us. It takes more time, but I am convinced that he is a good coach.' Unlike when Bayern was adrift under Klinsmann, Lahm had 'hope, because I can recognise structure. We are on the right path with this coach.'

Lahm's, though, was a rare voice. As restlessness at club head-quarters outweighed discipline, the Bayern management were increasingly critical of the Dutchman and his methods. Uli Hoeness said, 'A large concern like Bayern can no longer be controlled by just one person. Louis van Gaal is of the opinion that he has to organise everything by himself. But an individual cannot handle all of that. I cannot keep saying that everything is terrific when we are in eighth place.' Beckenbauer called upon the individualistic Dutchman to learn 'to delegate responsibility'. He felt van Gaal was insufficiently willing to enter public debate because the coach 'preferred to be clearly recognised as the authority'. The management likewise questioned van Gaal's tactics, suggesting that it might better to shift from the 4-3-3 system preferred by van Gaal to a 4-4-2 system.

Uli Hoeness, above all, wanted to see progress: 'I do not insist on a time-frame. What matters to me is that he and the team are capable of making headway. When we have the feeling that the relationship between the team and the coach is dysfunctional or that it blocks the development of individuals, then we have to think. The coach must be able to keep everyone happy, even those that do not play.' The club's director of sport Christian Nerlinger increased the pressure further by insisting that results had to improve dramatically by Christmas: 'You have to simply win the four remaining games before the winter break. The curve has now got to turn sharply upward. Teams like Mainz cannot be allowed to remain above Bayern in the long term. Van Gaal knows the job, but he now needs to get things right.'

Van Gaal was displeased by these public comments, and said so: 'The pressure that is built up by the media on club, players and coaches is almost unbearable. Everyone at the club and in the media are much too impatient in terms of the team. Of course everyone makes errors in his profession, and not every transfer has worked out so well. On the other hand, I sometimes wonder about the speed with which people are assessed. I had predicted it at the beginning of the season that we would need a few months' patience until everything worked out. The trophies are handed out in May. [...] When I started in 1991 with Ajax, in the first half of the season people only wanted Johan Cruyff. That wasn't fun for me. The players needed time to adapt to me, to know who I was as a person and as a coach. With Barcelona in 1997, it was the same. It took four or five months before it was much better. It was similar with AZ, and exactly the same with Bayern. I am confident that we have changed the situation at Bayern now. But I have always kept my faith in the players and also in my philosophy.'

Occasionally, there were flashes of what the Promised Land might look like, such as when Dortmund was destroyed 5–1, Wolfsburg defeated 3–0 or Frankfurt humbled 4–0 in the race for the DFB Cup. This was a playing style where players fitted into a team like cogs in a well-greased clock, and the ball was circulated in perfect control until the inevitable opening presented itself. The project required perhaps more faith then some of the wayward were capable of mustering. Franck Ribéry had his moment of enlightenment in Dortmund. He dropped his previously critical attitude towards his coach by leaping into his arms in victory celebration after scoring a beautiful goal. 'It was difficult for me to stay on my feet. Franck has shown that he loves this coach,' confessed van Gaal later with a smile.

By mid-December, Bayern had climbed to third place in the table. The team cruised to a comfortable 5–1 *Bundesliga* win against Bochum, and van Gaal was very satisfied with his side's performance: 'My players concentrated very hard in the build-up to the match and kept their concentration once it kicked off. It was a big task after the 4–1 [Champions League] win in Turin, but I'd say winning 5–1 here in Bochum isn't too bad. We prepare well for every match, with videos, team talks and individual chats. I think we saw some of that coming through today. We're back to within two points of [frontrunners] Leverkusen now. I'm very satisfied. […] I always believed we could do it. Enjoying a lot of possession is the Bayern way of playing football. The more possession we have, the more chances we would normally create. I'm the kind of coach who has a philosophy. The philosophy needs to be absorbed, and that takes time. It's a process.' It wasn't just on the pitch where things were feeling more settled: van Gaal was getting accustomed to German culture, and particularly the food: 'I love the local culture over here. Even as a meat eater, I've never eaten as much meat as I have in Germany. It's very wonderful indeed.'

CATASTROPH GAAL, THE TULIP GENERAL, GLUCKS GAAL

'Van Gaal has a philosophy, which he's employing.
There are not many trainers in the world who
possess the same quality he does.'
Christian Nerlinger, Bayern sporting director

Non-stop sunshine, 30-degree heat, palm trees, a breathtaking skyline featuring the newly-opened world's tallest building, and dramatic contrasts typified by the muezzin regularly calling the faithful to prayer from the neighbouring mosque – Dubai would have been a fine choice for a holiday, but Bayern Munich weren't there to relax, but for a serious workout. In their six days away as part of a mid-season break the squad completed 10 intense training sessions and a gruelling fitness test.

'I think we made a very good choice with Dubai. The climate was excellent, the training facilities were pretty good, and the hotel was nice. Every player gave 100 per cent, all the players were hungry, the mood in the dressing room is excellent,' van Gaal summarised.

The team pulled together impressively. 'The players worked hard and I'm very satisfied.' So satisfied, evidently, that he decided to show his softer side, and announced that he would not impose a curfew during the remainder of their training camp in Dubai: 'I'm not saying they must be home by one o'clock. It is important for the head to be free. It is also important for the team.' Defender Daniel van Buyten reacted positively to the news and praised van Gaal: 'Van Gaal is working very purposefully. Behind each exercise there is an idea. We have worked well and we have had fun doing it.'

The club captain when van Gaal started at Bayern was Mark van Bommel. He is an engaging conversationalist, and when explaining things he regularly ventures into comparisons and proverbial expressions. Sometimes he translates just a little too directly from his native Dutch into German, which provides his German audience with some amusement. The mood in the team was very good, van Bommel said after the training camp. 'There is no sour apple,' he commented, perhaps in reference to the disappearance of Luca Toni to Italy. The first-choice eleven became settled, with changes only possible as a result of injuries or suspensions. Gómez spoke of a strong competition, but that he had identified a great 'we-feeling'. 'This collective thinking,' added Bastien Schweinsteiger, 'can be the decisive factor for success.'

After the productive week in Dubai, van Gaal was confident of a decent opening to the second half of the campaign: 'We've had a very good training camp. I think we're in a position to continue where we left off before Christmas. I have a good all-round feeling.'

What was remarkable about Bayern's season was that what became the first-choice starting eleven turned out to be markedly different from what was expected when van Gaal was appointed. Van Gaal was still settling into his new job when he made it clear Lúcio, the captain of Brazil's national team and a team regular for five years, did not fit into his plans. Within weeks Lúcio was sold to Inter Milan, leaving a huge hole in central defence. Van Gaal insisted that the Belgian Daniel van Buyten was the man to fill it. Van Buyten had appeared in just 18 matches in the previous season – including four off the bench – compared to Lúcio's 43 starts in all competitions. But by mid-February no one was questioning van Gaal's decision and van Buyten had started all 21 of Bayern's *Bundesliga* games to date. Not only that but he started five of six games in the Champions League – he was suspended for the one he missed – and had a total of seven goals, as many as Lúcio notched in his five seasons at Bayern. The Belgian confessed, 'I've definitely improved under this coach. He's getting things out of me which I didn't necessarily think I had.' Van Gaal obviously believed he had a suitable replacement in van Buyten or he would not have been so quick to part with Lúcio. 'He has really blossomed,' forward Mario Gómez commented. 'He clears everything at the back, and he is scoring vital goals at the other end. I think he has taken a big step forward, even at his age.' Bayern rewarded van Buyten, aged 32, with a two-year contract extension. Van Buyten, a towering presence at 6ft 5in, deserved it. He went on to reward van Gaal and Bayern all season.

It was no secret that the relationship between van Gaal and Italian striker Luca Toni was rather more strained. Although van Gaal's initial preference for a lone centre-forward may have contributed to the loaning out of the former Bayern star to Roma during the winter break, the Italian striker clearly had a hard time fitting into van Gaal's system. The coach also demoted incumbent goalkeeper Michael Rensing in September, opting instead for veteran Hans-Jörg Butt. Full-back Edson Braafheid, originally hand-picked by van Gaal, did not live up to expectations and was loaned to Celtic.

Then there was winger Franck Ribéry, the *Bundesliga* Player of the Year in 2008 and widely considered Bayern's brightest star at the start of the season. It turned out to be a campaign to forget for Ribéry, who was tormented by injuries and issues off the pitch, including uncertainty over his contract, which was to expire in June 2011. The result was that Ribéry, so instrumental to Bayern in the previous two seasons, was no longer a regular starter in *Bundesliga* matches. Yet amid all this, van Gaal's Bayern, after a shaky start that saw it take a precipitous dive in the rankings, thrived in the second half of the season. Part of it was due to van Gaal's reliance on veterans such as full-back Phillip Lahm, midfielder Bastian Schweinsteiger and, above all, winger Arjen Robben, who arrived from Real Madrid in the summer for around €25 million.

Robben's transfer was considered by many as something of a gamble. Nobody questioned his skills or his flat-out speed, but there were doubts over his ability to avoid injury. In fact, his injury record was so bad he had come to be known as 'the man with the glass ankles': the 26-year-old player had only managed 30 league starts in a season just once in his career. But amazingly, Robben remained healthy and was instrumental in bringing Bayern to new heights. Ahead of the *DFB-Pokal* final (the German equivalent of the FA Cup), he offered his thanks to Bayern's medical staff, which he believed played a tremendous role in helping him to the stellar level he achieved at his new club: 'Fitness is the most important factor for me. I've been very consistent since the midpoint of the season. I used to have a lot of trouble with muscle strains. There was obviously an underlying reason, but we've come to grips with it recently, largely thanks to Dr Müller-Wohlfahrt and the club's outstanding medical team. They all matter to me a lot.'

Van Gaal said, 'The fact Robben came to Munich at all had to do with Franck Ribéry. I had originally planned to have Ribéry as a number 10 in a midfield diamond. But he didn't want to play there, but on the left wing. So I changed the system to a 4-4-1-1 and I needed a right winger. Robben was on the market. As always, the players phone each other. Before I called Robben, Mark van Bommel told me that he wanted to come. He had already had countless phone calls with him, and sent many texts. So I didn't have to do much. The problem was that Robben played on the left wing for the Dutch national team. I only had one place for him on the right wing. So I asked him if he'd play on the right for Bayern. He immediately said yes. The fact is, if Ribéry had been happy to play in the number 10 position, then I would probably not have brought Robben to Bayern.'

As well as using a core of experienced players, van Gaal also confirmed his uncanny ability at promoting from within. Holger Badstuber, a lanky 21-year-old defender, and Thomas Müller, a 20-year-old attacking midfielder, were both products of Bayern's youth academy and largely unknown to the general public. Both, though, became mainstays of van Gaal's side. Müller in particular emerged as one of the most exciting young talents in the European game. Tall and commanding, he often sits between the midfielders and the centre-forward and is especially adept at making late runs into the penalty area. When he scored a hat-trick against Bochum, he brought his season's tally to 19, a tremendous return for one so young.

Bayern's fluidity in attack made it easy to forget that, just a few months earlier, van Gaal's job had been in jeopardy. But Bayern reclaimed its poise, and that was largely the result of van Gaal's daring insistence on a specific system and an unlikely mixture of stars and previously unknown young talents. Previous great Bayern squads had typically consisted of players who rose to prominence with other clubs and were bought by Bayern when they were in their prime. Van Gaal instead focused on home-grown youngsters. It isn't easy to come into Bayern's squad with a name like Müller, but Thomas's season would have done even his namesake Gerd proud. At the back van Gaal put his trust in Holger Badstuber and 19-year-old Diego Contento, also a product of Bayern's amateur ranks. Contento only received his first professional contract at the start of 2010.

Bold personnel moves are nothing new for the idiosyncratic Dutchman. But even by van Gaal's standards, they required an extraordinary amount of conviction, considering what they meant for the rest of the squad. Mario Gómez, bought from Stuttgart for around €25 million, became just part of an ensemble cast of strikers that included Miroslav Klose and Ivica Olić, rather than the week-in, week-out centre-forward his transfer fee might have suggested. Van Gaal demoted star striker Klose to the role of Mario Gómez's substitute. Müller's rise has consigned Bayern's other big off-season signing besides Robben, Russian midfielder Anatoliy Tymoshchuk, to the sidelines. To appreciate the scale of van Gaal's daring, consider this: he kept on his bench the German national team's most prolific goal-scorer and a player who cost a reported €10 million transfer fee to play a team that included three teenagers.

Van Gaal shrugged off his willingness to prefer Müller and Badstuber to bigger names by pointing out he gave Clarence Seedorf his Ajax début at 16. Van Gaal is a radical proponent of the 'performance principle' – in the positive and negative sense – and he has developed an uncanny capacity for unearthing performance potential. He recognised and nourished a greater number and variety of young talent into stars than any other coach. Unlike Arsenal's Arsène Wenger, who develops known young stars after acquiring them for sometimes hefty transfer fees, van Gaal picks the fruits directly from the tree. The young superstars from the legendary Ajax class of 1995 were for almost a decade some of the hottest commodities in the football world. Bayern Munich doubtlessly would not have minded replicating this tradition. At the start of van Gaal's first season, no one at Bayern would have believed that the team would still be in the running for three trophies by spring without significant contributions from Toni, Gómez, Braafheid, Tymoshchuk, Ribéry and Rensing. But that was exactly what happened.

During his time at AZ Alkmaar van Gaal said this about his way of working: 'It's more about a philosophy than a system, and the system itself is always dependent on the players.' Discipline, structure and organisation are the three pillars on which he bases his approach to every new game. Bayern's dominance stems from possession of the ball throughout the match. By mid-April, Bastian Schweinsteiger, Philipp Lahm and Holger Badstuber were the three leading players in the 'touches per game' statistics in the *Bundesliga*. What was more, the pass completion rate of the team was excellent: 83 per cent of passes reached their mark in the league matches, and even in the opponents' half Bayern was achieving a 76 per cent pass completion rate. Bastian Schweinsteiger was the best passer in the league in the opponents' half, completing an exceptional 80 per cent of his passes. A further key to Bayern's success was discipline in defence. The Bavarians received the fewest yellow cards and conceded the least goals from set pieces. Sporting director Christian Nerlinger stated, 'There was enormous pressure from outside but Louis van Gaal was as solid as a rock. He stuck to his principles during a difficult situation and that paid off. Now you can see things working.'

So while Bayern had suffered a shock when they were beaten 2–1 in Mainz in August, they redeemed themselves with an impressive performance against Mainz in late January, cruising to a comfortable 3–0 win. Van Gaal claimed, 'That was our best home display so far. I don't think you can ever beat Mainz easily: their goalkeeper stops everything you throw at his goal. But he finally went and made a mistake in the second half. We created a lot of chances and kept the pressure on their keeper. I thought we were very good in possession against a totally defensive team. I'm very satisfied because I've seen some good goals scored by a very good Bayern team.'

Once Bayern's attack began to click, results began to follow. Following a defeat to Hamburg in their seventh league match of the season, the club went on to pick up an incredible 30 out of a possible 36 points in their next 12 matches. This included a run of 7 consecutive wins, during which they scored a total of 23 goals, an average of more than 3 a game. The combination of Philip Lahm and Arjen Robben was the engine that kept Bayern's attack running. The play between the two dazzled teammates and opponents alike, with no one being able to solve the riddle of how to stop them.

Bayern rose to the top of the league for the first time since May 2008 and the fans were treated to a show both before, during and after the match against HSV Hamburg as the club celebrated its 110th anniversary at the Allianz Arena. Hamburg had been something of a bogey team for Bayern: they had never lost in the Allianz Arena before. It promised to be a match with a heavy Dutch influence, and Mark van Bommel was looking forward to the encounter: 'It's an all-orange match, with lots of Dutch guys on the field and the touchlines. It'll be a laugh,' he said, considering the possibility of as many as five Dutch players turning out for the watching national coach, Bert van Marwijk. 'Orange is a great colour, especially in football,' Arjen Robben added, before considering a reunion with Hamburg striker Ruud van Nistelrooy. 'I know him well. He's my friend. When he's fit and in the groove, he's still one of the best in the world.' Van Gaal chipped in, 'Football is only ever a contest between one team and another, but on Sunday it'll definitely be a game among Dutchmen.'

In the end, it was the French connection that proved decisive. The game was still goalless when Franck Ribéry picked up the ball at pace with 13 minutes to go. He isolated Guy Demel, turned inside and unleashed a shot that was later clocked at 112 km/h. It rocketed past Wolfgang Hesl and into the near side of the goal. That goal was enough to secure three points and first place in the table – for the first time in 22 months, 652 days, or 57 rounds of matches. Bayern's rise to the top coincided with the festivities for the anniversary – fireworks and festive music on the grounds. Van Gaal let his team join in with the celebrations, and suggested he would be celebrating longer than any of them. 'I am always the one who switches the lights out at the end.'

Bayern were moving forward on all fronts. In the Champions League they faced Manchester United for a place in the semi-finals and went into the second leg on the back of a crucial league victory against rivals Schalke. Despite being reduced to 10 men as a result of Hamit Altintop's first-half dismissal, the team produced an outstanding second-half defensive display to silence the 60,000 strong Gelsenkirchen crowd. It was their most important domestic match of the season and van Gaal's men managed to hold on to their 2–1 advantage for all three points. The former Dutch international Willem van Hanegem was full of praise for van Gaal's management: 'Halfway during the away game against Schalke he ended up with 10 men on the pitch. But even then he holds on to his vision: to impose your will while playing football. And they got chances too, but it remained 2–1, a remarkable win against one of the frontrunners. I see that Bayern is beginning to look a little like Ajax of 1995. Louis is still missing a Danny Blind or Frank de Boer, guys who are able to defend but who also know how to intelligently attack. A better goalkeeper wouldn't hurt either. But in general you now really enjoy watching Bayern at work.'

The same toughness was displayed in the victorious German Cup final against Werder Bremen and in the first leg of the Champions League semi-final against Lyon. Van Gaal said later, 'I have never witnessed such an overwhelming percentage of players believing in my philosophy. This team can become even better. We have not yet reached our full potential,' adding that Bayern had played a disciplined game against Bremen for 70 minutes. 'The discipline is in the brain. The most important thing is to maintain it over 90 minutes. All the conditions are there [at Bayern] and it is only a matter of time before we operate like that.'

Van Gaal's side closed in on a 22nd championship after a lacklustre 1–1 draw at Bayer Leverkusen. A tough string of recent games had clearly caught up with them and the team looked exhausted. 'Not just the body, the head wasn't quite right any more,' admitted Philipp Lahm. Thomas Müller was clearly held back by Hans Sarpei in the box shortly before the final whistle, but no penalty was given. 'We wouldn't have deserved the win anyway,' van Gaal admitted. Yet they had survived a tough run of matches unscathed. 'Their football was never perfect, and rarely first class,' wrote *Kölner Stadt-Anzeiger* in praise of the designated champions. 'From Robben and Ribéry to Butt and Badstuber, the distribution of quality is very uneven in the squad. But their inner core is made of titanium. Even if everything else fails, they never lose their belief that an existence without success is pointless.'

Bayern held on to their position at the top of the *Bundesliga* thanks to a helping hand from Hannover, as they inflicted a surprising 4–2 defeat on Schalke. When it was Bayern's turn to play Hannover themselves it was a different story, the team recording a 7–0 home win against the relegation candidates. Robben scored his first hat-trick for the *Bundesliga* side since joining from Real Madrid, while Croatian striker Ivica Olić and Germany's rising midfield star Thomas Müller both scored twice. Van Gaal was clearly pleased. 'I'm delighted with the way we let the ball do the work. That's the most important thing. If we do that, we have players who can make the difference. Arjen Robben can make the difference, as can Franck Ribéry, and so can Thomas Müller. They all proved that. Obviously, it's good for Arjen to score three, but I have to look at the game as a whole. It was a wonderful display, and it was clearly pleasing to the crowd.'

Meanwhile, van Gaal did not exempt the 'twelfth man' from some disciplinary correction. Despite the glow of victory surrounding the team the coach still found time to criticise the Bayern fanbase. He complained about fair-weather supporters at the treble-chasing club, saying they only backed the team when it was doing well. He suggested that the Allianz Arena crowd came only to be entertained: 'It's very bad,' he told reporters on the eve of the decisive *Bundesliga* match at home against Bochum. 'It's like Barcelona and Ajax, a "theatre" public. Of course, the last three weeks have been a surprise, but when we win everything it's easy to have voices. I think the public must also get behind the team when things go badly, and that is something I haven't experienced,' he added, exempting the

South Curve supporters from his criticism: 'They are always getting behind the team.' Bastian Schweinsteiger also suggested that there was room for improvement. 'When things were not going well [early in the season], we were immediately being whistled at in the Allianz Arena, but that sort of thing does not happen in England. I would like to have the whole stadium behind us even in difficult times.'

Christian Nerlinger said, 'Louis van Gaal is a superb leader of this group of players, day after day. You can clearly see how the team has developed, his signature is obvious. Even away from home, we've controlled the possession, we've made our opponents do the running, and we've dominated the game. The team has become a unit and has come on as a good footballing team in a way we couldn't necessarily have expected. The first 20 minutes against Bochum were world class, as was the semi-final away to Lyon. It was like watching us a year ago away to Barcelona: the intention was good, but they couldn't deliver. We simply took them apart. Louis has done a fantastic job, which will hopefully be crowned with three trophies. We're very hungry for trophies, and the players look like a team who want to succeed.' Van Gaal said, 'The first 25 minutes was the best football we have seen here in the Allianz Arena this season. These were unbelievably beautiful goals. I expected that Schalke was not going to win today; it's a very beautiful day. We're going to celebrate.' He was doused with champagne by his captain, Mark van Bommel, after the final whistle.

Bayern beat relegated Hertha Berlin 3–1 to win the German championship for a record 22nd time, Arjen Robben striking twice after Ivica Olić had put them in the lead in the 20th minute. In Germany, many football fans enjoy a love–hate relationship with Bayern and yet at the final whistle the country could not suppress a smile. Bayern finished on 70 points, 5 ahead of second-placed

Schalke. Mark van Bommel became the club's first foreign captain to lift the *Bundesliga* trophy in front of 75,000 spectators in the Olympic stadium, before he and his teammates chased coach Louis van Gaal around the pitch to pour beer on him. Earlier, van Gaal had expressed his dislike of the German 'victory beer shower' tradition and appealed to his players to refrain from dousing him. 'I told my players I didn't like it, although it's the least of my worries. I will have to adjust to the local folklore.' And just to be on the safe side he exchanged his designer suit for a tracksuit during the break, something that proved to be a wise move. Half the Bayern team chased a nervous van Gaal across the pitch. As he came out of hiding from behind one of the goals, Hamit Altintop grabbed a sleeve as Bastian Schweinsteiger and Daniel van Buyten tried to soak him with their tankards. Amazingly, the 58-year-old put in a burst of pace, sensing freedom, and sped away from the beer-spray, arms aloft. 'About five or six of them came after me. I did quite well and got only a little wet. But when I had dropped my guard a little, they came again.' Out of all people it was none other than countryman Mark van Bommel who managed to pour the full load of three litres right over his boss's head.

Van Gaal said afterwards, 'I think people will remember the Bayern team of the 2009–10 season. It is wonderful and it is just great that this crowd remained in their seats for the celebrations. We had the best attack, the best defence, and I think we played the most attractive football this season, and that is important for me. It is good to win and we managed to stay in our rhythm. I will party until very late tonight.' One of the spectators was the Inter coach José Mourinho. After the game he admitted that his trip to Germany to spy on Inter's fellow Champions League finalists was a waste of time. The Bavarians comfortably wrapped up the

Bundesliga title and the Portuguese's notepad was still all but blank at the final whistle. 'It was practically a friendly match, because Bayern were already champions and Hertha was already relegated. I saw the players and how they link up on the pitch, but it's best to study Bayern through videos to see what they did in their other Champions League games rather than what they did today.'

Van Gaal concluded, 'Every title is obviously incredible, especially when it happens in your first year. I achieved that at Barcelona, and again here. And I am also proud to be the first Dutch coach to win the *Bundesliga*. But as you well know, I haven't done this alone, but as the head of a large staff. I have been a champion with four different clubs in three countries, and each title has been special in its own way. We have become champions in a way that not many others have done previously. We play very attractive football, we're always looking to go on the attack and we always put the opposition under a lot of pressure. I have a great team. We always believed that we would do it together, and this is the result.'

Bayern had decided that the future was *Oranje*, and it brought them instant success. Bayern had been managed by a Dutch coach, captained by a Dutch captain and in Arjen Robben had a player who delivered 16 goals in just 24 matches. Bayern went up in many people's estimations thanks to van Gaal's success. Germany's most famous club had been good value for their 22nd *Bundesliga* title, playing a brand of exciting attacking football married with some real tactical maturity.

Bayern's chairman Karl-Heinz Rummenigge revealed on *Sport 1* television that van Gaal proved he was not kidding when he said he was a 'party animal'. He danced alongside his players in a nightclub until the wee hours: 'I was leaving [the party] at 4 a.m. and Louis wanted to take the players to a nightclub then,' Rummenigge said.

The Bayern players were given the day off training the next Sunday, but took part in a procession from the club's training ground to the city centre, where they showed off their silverware from the balcony of the city hall. More than 100,000 fans turned out to celebrate as they presented the *Bundesliga* trophy. To add to the celebratory atmosphere, beer brewer Paulaner offered 10,000 litres of free beer to the fans. Van Gaal and the players, kitted out in Bavarian dress including traditional *lederhosen*, appeared on the city hall balcony after a victory parade, with van Gaal dancing on the balcony with Munich mayor Christian Ude. 'We are not only the champions of München but also of Gelsenkirchen, of Bremen and of Hamburg,' said van Gaal. 'We are the best in Germany – and perhaps Europe.' As an aside, he also found time to note his own accomplishment: 'This trophy means a lot to me. There aren't many coaches in Europe who've been fortunate enough to win the league in three countries. I'm very proud of that.'

On the more prosaic side of things, Bayern would enjoy a financial windfall, even without winning another title. 'We are going to have the biggest turnover in the club's history,' Karl-Heinz Rummenigge said. 'Our profit will grow comfortably as well, and we'll be profitable for the 16th straight season.' Bayern had a turnover of 290 million euros in its previous financial year, placing them fourth behind Real Madrid, Barcelona and Manchester United. But unlike many other big European clubs, the Bavarians have no huge debts. Maintaining a frugal fiscal policy, while winning games, was in no small measure thanks to Louis van Gaal. He steadily introduced players who came through Bayern's youth programme. 'Van Gaal demonstrated great courage. I can't recall another Bayern coach who introduced young players on such a scale,' Rummenigge said.

In one of the most one-sided DFB Cup finals in memory, the *Bundesliga* champions swept away Werder Bremen 4–0, confirming their clear superiority in German football. It was Bayern's fifteenth German Cup title and completed their eighth domestic double.

With seemingly no instructions to take it easy before next week's game, Bayern players celebrated hard after the final whistle. 'My players are still not tired,' van Gaal said. 'When we win something, we have to celebrate. I don't know whether we'll train tomorrow, it depends on when I get to bed. On Wednesday I will start with preparation for [the Champions League final against] Inter Milan.' While Bayern was demolishing Werder, Inter squeezed 1–0 past Sienna to win their fifth *scudetto*.

'The league and cup double with Bayern is probably the most satisfying for me because the chemistry between the trainers, coaching staff and players is very, very good. My team has a bond and a trust in me that I have never experienced before.' Van Gaal even received praise from old rival Johan Cruyff, who wrote in his *Telegraaf* column that winning the league and cup double 'is and remains an extraordinary accomplishment, because you are dealing with two completely different competitions. One is for the long term. You need to take a deep breath and must especially be consistent. In the other you are not allowed, in a short period of time, to make any mistake because even one can be fatal. That requires a very different mentality. That means that [Bayern] performed optimally on two fronts, with each time a very different match approach, and that is a real achievement. It is clear that Bayern Munich and Louis van Gaal is a particularly good match. The management and players at the club were prepared to accept his way of thinking and operating, and that has resulted in a very strong co-operative effort.'

The Bayern players must have wished they could play at the Olympic Stadium every day. On two consecutive Saturdays, captain van Bommel lifted domestic silverware in the capital. Franz Beckenbauer, the doyen of Bayern, said in the Olympic Stadium: 'I found it out of this world, especially watching our exhibition performance in the second half. We hinted at it in the first half, but it's fantastic that they did not slacken off but went on to score even more goals. If someone had told me this would happen six months ago, I would have had him transferred to a mental hospital. It was a delight to watch this team.' Beckenbauer's judgement, by no means always so flattering to the club he joined 51 years ago, still counts for plenty. 'The game reflected a natural extension of our form in the second half of the season. Right now we are playing football of the highest quality, as our opponents have to admit,' said president Uli Hoeness. 'The team is a better footballing side than that of 2001. At the moment we are dominating the domestic opposition, which we didn't do then. Where we show our class is in our mental strength as well as our footballing skills. I am extremely proud of the team, but also of everyone in the club. Now we have won the double and we have nothing to lose in [the Champions League final in] Madrid. We will do all we can to achieve the impossible.'

CHAMPIONS LEAGUE

'It was a tactical masterclass from van Gaal.'

Franz Beckenbauer, after the Bayern–Lyon semi-final.

In 2001, Bayern Munich won the biggest prize in European football when they defeated Valencia 5–4 on penalties at the Giuseppe Meazza Stadium in Milan. After a nine-year hiatus, they looked almost certain to be facing an early exit from the 2009–10 Champions League, with the media on hand to finely analyse the frailties of the team and the failings of the coach. After a disappointing performance against Bordeaux, losing 2–0 at home, *Der Spiegel* produced an eloquent essay on '*FC Durchschnitt München*' ('Average Munich').

The *Spiegel* essayist offered a host of rhetorical questions for his readers: 'This is probably the worst realisation in Bavaria: in recent weeks and months, the star ensemble has declined to an average collection of kickers. Why this is so, neither the players nor the managers can say at the present moment. Is it the constant rotation of coach Louis van Gaal? Or a lack of understanding of the players of his complex system? Is it the new purchases that so far have failed to convince? The glut of strikers who miss their target, while there are gaps in other areas of the squad? Has the troubled preparation left its traces? Or does the Bayern squad simply not fit together? Uncertainty currently shows its many faces in the otherwise so self-confident *Mir san Mir* club.'

By the end of November, Bayern was languishing in third place in group A with just four points from four games: a win against Maccabi Haifa, a draw with Juventus and two defeats against Bordeaux. When a narrow second victory against Maccabi was secured, a parallel win by Bordeaux over Juventus meant that Bayern was still just about in the running. There was only one way through to the knockout stage, and that was to beat Juventus in Turin.

Subhankar Mondal summed it up nicely on *Goal.com*: 'He had been transported to the burial site and the rituals were ready to be performed. The grave had been dug and the wind at the cemetery was howling to welcome him to the "other side". The guests wore over-sized black dress, many were preoccupied reenacting the scenes from *Death at a Funeral* and some were preparing themselves to dance on his grave. Then came the shock, the Resurrection. The man who had dug his own grave rose from the dead with his lips twitched into a smile. After years in the wilderness, forgotten by most and vilified by those who bothered to remember him, Louis van Gaal had finally returned from the dead.'

It was the 4–1 defeat of Juventus in Turin that changed Bayern's season and reconfirmed van Gaal's stature. It was an all-round display built on attack that shred the *Bianconeri* into pieces and boosted the Bavarians' self-confidence and faith in their coach. Even before the match against Juventus, when everyone was debating who the next coach of Bayern should be, the 58-year-old maintained that he was not under pressure. Van Gaal has always been careful to see that his ultra-tough image remains intact. Eventually, earlier *Bundesliga* and Champions League defeats proved to be no more than blips in the onward progress of van Gaal's side.

The manner in which this success was accomplished was remarkable; all precisely according to the van Gaal blueprint. The great Bayern teams of the past were structured around hard-nosed defending, a gifted playmaker and strong centre-forwards. Lazy comparisons between the Oliver Kahn-led minimalists from 2001 and the flamboyant 2010 version swamped the German media. Yet it was an often-overlooked fact that Bayern had won Germany's last Champions League trophy with a sweeper system. The 2000–01 squad was anchored by Stefan Effenberg in midfield and Giovanni Elber up front. Swiss national team coach Ottmar Hitzfeld believed that the latest Bayern squad was playing better than his charges almost a decade ago: 'I think that they are technically better. We had some very good players – Elber, [Mehmet] Scholl and Effenberg were exceptional – but Robben and Ribéry can work absolute magic.'

The new Bayern was a well-organised yet playful and attack-minded incarnation of *Mir san Mir*: a lot of movement, quick cross-passing, combination play, prying and pressuring to find a way through. Van Gaal had shifted the emphasis, changing formations from a classic 4-4-2 to an extremely flexible 4-3-3. His idea is a modern version of the Dutch concept of 'total football' from the 1970s, but to realise this vision van Gaal had to make a number of bold – and risky – personnel decisions. The Turin game statistics were impressive: shots on goal – 22 to 7; corners – 11 to 2; possession – Bayern 60 per cent, Juventus 40 per cent; and that with Bayern as the away team.

Bayern started their last-16 Champions League match against Fiorentina as the favourite. The *Viola* put in a good performance and

Bayern eventually needed a last-minute goal from Miroslav Klose to pick up a 2–1 win in the first leg. Van Gaal observed, 'We've won, which is what matters. Fiorentina was extremely clever tactically, they changed their system, and we failed to find an answer. That's a shame. In the first half, we spent too much time running with the ball, and forgot to use the width of the pitch. Fiorentina created no chances but still scored. We conceded a goal from a corner for the first time in a long time, which was annoying. We finally put it in the net at the end, but it was clearly offside, so we've been a bit lucky. We're a goal ahead. It'll be difficult in Florence, but we have a fifty-fifty chance, or maybe just a little more than that.'

At the Artemio Franchi stadium, Bayern lost the second leg against Fiorentina, 3–2, but qualified on the away goals rule, 4–4 on aggregate. The Italians had been 3–1 ahead until Arjen Robben broke the home side's hearts with a stunning 30-yard strike. Cesare Prandelli was left to ponder how his ACF Fiorentina team had managed to win six out of its eight UEFA Champions League games and still get eliminated on away goals. Van Gaal later admitted that he had had a 'good feeling' about the game: 'I told the players at half-time that they needed to stay calm and have patience. I understand it is very difficult for the *Viola* to accept being knocked out this way and that the decisive goal was the one in the first leg that was offside. Under those circumstances [the strong winds], I saw a game with many individual errors and it became a difficult encounter. It wasn't easy for us, but we scored two wonderful goals and we are happy to be through. In the final 10 minutes we could have even taken advantage of the extra space to equalise. We always tried to play our football and that was our saving grace. But today we have also seen what we are still lacking. We have to improve on that. We can play a dominant game, but we did not do so over 90 minutes today, the way we should. But we are through, and in the end that's what counts.'

That set up a quarter-final tie against Manchester United. Not many Bayern or United fans needed to be reminded of what went on at Camp Nou in Barcelona in 1999 as Manchester came from behind in the dying stages of the final to record a 2–1 victory. Teddy Sheringham and Ole Gunnar Solskjaer netted in injury time to secure a remarkable victory. Each side had claimed a Champions League crown since – Bayern in 2001 and United in 2008. During Bayern's winning season, they had met United at the same stage in the competition; Paulo Sérgio scored the only goal of the game at the English club's base, Old Trafford, to give *Die Roten* the advantage heading back to Germany. Goals from Giovane Elber and Mehmet Scholl were answered by one from Ryan Giggs, but that was not enough to prevent the 1999 winners crashing out. Those will be the memories that Bayern was seeking to invoke and not the trauma and despair of Camp Nou: 'It was a big shock back then,' said Bayern chairman Karl-Heinz Rummenigge, who was vice president in 1999. 'Since the 1999 final, playing United has always been a big thrill. This duel has history.'

Sir Alex Ferguson and Louis van Gaal are two of the most experienced and decorated managers in Europe. Both have received high civil honours and share a penchant for pre-match psychology, not to mention a tendency to say what they think. Between them, they had managed teams in a combined total of 376 games in all European competitions but, remarkably, had pitted their tactical wits against each other only twice. Both of those occasions came in the Champions League group phase 12 years earlier, when the then Barcelona boss van Gaal proved Ferguson's equal during United's 1999 treble-winning season, the clubs slugging out two thrilling

3–3 draws. Awarded the Order of Oranje-Nassau in 1997 for his work at Ajax, two years before Ferguson was knighted, van Gaal was happy to shift all the pressure on United, saying Bayern were no longer at the same level as their opponents.

Van Gaal claimed, 'We are playing against a top-quality team and Bayern is not yet at that level. The difference is that United shows top quality on a consistent basis. We have shown that we can reach that level in specific games like we did against Juventus and Fiorentina earlier in the competition when no one in Europe gave us a chance. This is a huge challenge both for the players and for me. I know for sure that the organisation within United is very good. I am jealous of this organisation. If we had it at Bayern, we would be one step further on. These two games won't be as open as the games in 1998. That Barça team was a very different one. With Bayern, I play in a different style. He [Ferguson] plays a similar system to me, so there isn't much difference. But he has been in charge of United for 24 years; I've only been here 8 months.' Ferguson smiled when he heard the words of a rival who clearly enjoys psychological gamesmanship as much as he does and said, 'He's a very clever man – I don't pay attention to any of that.'

Manchester United was coming off a 7–2 aggregate defeat of AC Milan in the previous round, which was topped off by a 4–0 victory at home. So confidence and flamboyance were in plentiful supply as the English visited the Allianz Arena for the first leg of the quarter-final. Sir Alex Ferguson felt his team was playing its best football of the season following the return of Rio Ferdinand, Edwin van der Sar and Nemanja Vidić: 'There's a true saying, "Strong at the back, strong as a team". We looked fragile earlier this season, but we are looking very strong now.'

Bayern distinguished itself in Munich with a never-say-die attitude that produced a well-deserved victory after going behind – Franck Ribéry equalising off a deflected free kick in the 76th minute. It was a goal that had been coming, with Manchester United showing little creativity and Bayern growing in confidence by the minute, even despite the absence of Arjen Robben and Bastian Schweinsteiger. Before the game van Gaal had been unsure of Robben's involvement: 'The doctors need to take a good look at his calf to see what's wrong. If he can't make it, he is a player who we will greatly miss. We need a player like Robben, but if he is not 100 per cent fit he will not play.' He kept his word: Robben did not play and Bayern still won 2–1.

'We fully deserved to win,' van Gaal concluded. 'I was not happy with the first minute and the shock of conceding. We had to get back to the right mentality and that is hard. It's hard because ideally we didn't want Manchester United to score but they did that straight away. So I am proud of my players when they got back into the game with this mentality and in the first half we were already superior. We played excellent in the second half, created plenty of chances and never gave up right to the very end.' Olić's 92nd-minute strike gave Bayern a crucial one-goal lead to take into the second leg. Van Gaal praised Olić, although he also made sure to claim his own share of the credit for the winning goal: 'I think that Ivica Olić is always sharp and he also has the mentality to give everything and that is very good for a coach. I know that I can always count on him and I think that it was also clever of the coach to let him play on the right so he could come in and score with his left foot.'

At the press conference before the second leg in Manchester, van Gaal was asked about the previous rumours about him taking over at United when it seemed that Sir Alex Ferguson might retire at the end of the 2001–02 season. 'It would always have been an honour to replace him,' he declared. Ian Herbert wrote in the *Independent*, 'Whose honour it might have been – van Gaal's or United's – the Bayern Munich coach neglected to say. If you thought Ferguson, a knight of the British realm since 1999, was the ultimate high-and-mighty manager, then try Aloysius Paulus Maria van Gaal for size. The day after his Netherlands side beat Andorra 3–0 in 2001, he provided a first hint that he considered himself someone United would come looking for again. "I knew I was first on the list to succeed [Ferguson] last year," he said. "I don't have any contact with them now because I am coach of the national team but I can imagine that a club like Manchester United is still interested in Louis van Gaal." The use of the third-person form is always suspect in a sportsman, but van Gaal can afford it.'

Other British journalists were also on hand to say unfriendly things about the Bayern Munich coach. Duncan White of the *Daily Telegraph* introduced Manchester United fans to van Gaal as someone who is 'not a likeable man. He is arrogant, pedantic and players complain about his lack of emotional empathy. He is abrasive, remorseless and meticulous. And he is inevitably successful.' He got the last thing right, and at the end of the day the journalistic complaining did United little good. To add to Manchester United's concerns, leading scorer Wayne Rooney had limped off the field during the first leg of the tie, while for the second, Arjen Robben, Bayern's leading scorer, was back.

A maxim of the legendary Inter Milan coach, Helenio Herrera, was that 'touching the ball is good for the mind'. At the Allianz Arena, van Gaal's team had shocked Manchester United the Barcelona way, playing 'pass-show-receive' to make United look as impotent as they had against Barcelona in the previous year's final. Barcelona, followed by Bayern, had the best passing stats of the 2009–10 Champions League. In the table of who made the most potential scoring chances, it was Bayern followed by Barcelona. United could not believe Bayern would be so fluid on hostile turf. 'I'm sure they understand it'll be a different game when they visit Old Trafford,' said Rio Ferdinand. Edwin van der Sar added, 'We have the experience, and the quality, to go through.'

Van Gaal was van der Sar's manager when the goalkeeper broke through at Ajax in the mid-nineties, enjoying domestic and European glory with the Dutch side. The United goalkeeper wasn't always the cool and collected 'final barrier' he is today. In 1993, he was still in the process of learning the fine art of the *meevoetballende* goalkeeper that total football required (essentially, a keeper able to play good football and act almost like an additional sweeper). As he developed, he became an outstanding keeper, making numerous spectacular saves, and passed very accurately. Van der Sar believed van Gaal's arrival in Munich in 2009 was the root cause of Bayern's success: 'Everywhere he goes he brings his own concept. Sometimes it takes a little bit longer; it's not always immediate success. But he brings consistency to a club and the way the team plays. That takes a lot of work on the training pitch, but I think it's really paying dividends for Bayern. They had a slow start but he has seen them grow.'

Van der Sar felt he owed a lot to his fellow Dutchman, who signed him at Ajax and put him in the team ahead of then first-choice Stanley Menzo. 'Van Gaal is the biggest influence on my career. He picked me at Ajax ahead of someone who was playing in the national team. He gave me my chance and stuck by me. He was my coach with Ajax and the national team. So of course he is someone I have a great deal of respect for, and I know he will have

Bayern set up the right way to get a result to go through at Old Trafford. Van Gaal will know how to approach the second leg. It will be a challenge he will enjoy. The one thing we know about Bayern is that they will be mentally strong – as they were in the first leg after we scored first. It's a very German strength, of course. They are very fit and they have a belief in themselves that keeps them going right until the very end. And having van Gaal as their coach will have only added to their quality and belief because I know from experience he is a man who leaves nothing to chance.'

Even since their turnaround in Turin, Bayern had faced many challenging moments when the team's self-belief and courage were called into question. At Old Trafford, Bayern found themselves three goals down to a very different Manchester United side to the one that had so meekly faded in Munich the previous week. Van Gaal was understandably not happy. 'Before the game I saw Sir Alex Ferguson's line-up and knew that he had made a choice for aggression. So I said to my players that we also needed aggression but to play with control at the same time. For the first 20 minutes we showed no aggression and Manchester United played us off the pitch.' It would have been very tempting to panic, to quicken the tempo too soon after a 40-minute period in which Bayern barely had a kick and found themselves chasing shadows. Instead, Bayern preferred to play the waiting game, getting a first foothold in the game through Olić's vital, redemptive first-half strike. They bided their time showing an unshakeable confidence in their own ability, in their own system, their way of doing things, and ultimately, in van Gaal's philosophy.

As United scored three goals in the opening 41 minutes amid the tumultuous din of a heaving Old Trafford, Bayern buckled in the electrifying atmosphere. But United conceded twice to crash out on the away goals rule – the second, by former Chelsea winger Robben, came after Rooney had trudged off with more damage to his ankle and Brazilian full-back Rafael had been sent off. The game offered two significant lessons in coaching contrasts. As the Old Trafford crowd disappeared into the night, there was that nagging realisation that their team relied too heavily on Rooney. No matter how outstanding Robben had been on the Bayern side, van Gaal had not made the error Ferguson made, of becoming overly dependent on one player. The Bayern team was a unit. The second was a consequence of the first: whereas Ferguson was willing to risk the well-being of his forward, van Gaal notably did the opposite when Robben was not fully match-fit during the first game against Manchester. Ferguson complained, 'There were a couple of challenges on him [Rooney] and I don't think he got any protection from the referee.' Rooney or no Rooney, Bayern still went through, courtesy of a goal from Robben that van Gaal described as 'unbelievable'.

Van Gaal refused to enter a slanging match with Ferguson, who blamed Bayern for Rafael being sent off after 50 minutes when he tugged the shirt of Franck Ribéry. He accused Bayern players of putting excessive pressure on referee Nicola Rizzoli to show Rafael a second yellow card. 'There is no doubt about it,' Ferguson claimed. 'They were never getting through that tie. With 11 men, we had no problem. The young boy showed a bit of inexperience, but they got him sent off, everyone sprinted towards the referee – typical Germans. You cannot dispute that, they are like that.'

The reality was quite different. Despite great wing play from Nani and Valencia, even after the 30th minute, the middle of the park belonged to the strong and increasingly composed Bayern duo of Schweinsteiger and van Bommel. Bayern's midfield dynamism confused United defensively, and despite Nani adding a third with five minutes to spare in the first half, the game looked to be a less one-sided affair for the remaining minutes. Bayern were significantly better than United in the second half before Rafael's sending-off. Bayern's control of the game – 60:40 per cent advantage in possession, 457 (77 per cent) passes completed vs. United's 230 (66 per cent) – proved again that the men from Munich knew how to play football. Alex Ferguson forgot a football match takes 90 minutes. The truth was that the second goal would have arrived even without the sending off. Manchester United were too tired in the second half, and Bayern would have scored more if they needed to.

Ferguson's allegation was met with a swift rebuttal from van Gaal, who was unimpressed by his rival's complaints: 'I thought England was noted for fairness. I have been confronted with these comments. It is not what I call fair play. I do not share Sir Alex's opinion. Control is part of being a professional footballer. Every player must know his job. If you pick up one yellow card, a second means a sending-off. Every player should know that and it was a yellow card offence. It was the player who made the foul. As for United winning with 11, we will never know that, neither Sir Alex nor me, because this game will not be played again. It is easy to say these things after a loss. I told my players before the Schalke match that they needed to play with aggression and control but Hamit Altintop didn't show that and that's why he was sent off – and that is why their young player was sent off today.'

Van Gaal also had a notably different view of what constituted the essence of 'German-ness' to Ferguson: 'It's difficult to beat German teams. They don't play as attractively as, for example, you have it in the English league or in the Spanish league. But to break a German team is not very easy. We know that by playing them every week [in the *Bundesliga*]. [...] When I was coaching Holland, I used to always say that you have not beaten a German team, even if it is the 90th minute and you are ahead. We have many German players in our side and there are many foreigners who have played a long time in Germany. These players have learned a lot from German football and this extraordinary mentality of German footballers. That is also why I am here at Bayern Munich.'

Van Gaal praised his players for their composure and mental fortitude: 'Of course I'm proud. Given that we were 3–0 behind, it's incredible what we did in the second half. We had a good mentality to have played well tactically, and aggressively. We played like a great team.' Yet he was also critical of his team's inability to cope with pressure early in the game. 'We have to be ready from the first minute. I said this before the game.' Bayern started the second half looking much brighter and proceeded to completely control the flow of the game. Viewers could feel a goal coming, and sure enough, that goal came on 74 minutes. It was a gut-wrenching climax that left the British Premier League without a semi-final representative for the first time since 2003, and a Manchester United shattered after the biggest week of their season ended in huge disappointment.

Bayern seemed to have developed a curious appetite for adversity during this particular season: all the best performances came after they put themselves into perilous, desperate situations. It was a modus operandi that seemed to capture the imagination of the wider public including a sizeable number within the anti-Bayern constituency. 'Sympathy for Bayern throughout Germany,' read the headline of *Kölner Express*. Bayern had the bravery and audacity to be 3–0 down and still chase a game. As much as its tendency to start off poorly was a hindrance to its success, Bayern's blatant disregard for even the immediate past was what made the team so uniquely successful. Forget the scoreline, FC Hollywood would carry on, create its chances, and find ways to win matches: the more dramatic, the better.

By 2010, Bayern had contested 20 semi-finals in European competition, winning 9 and losing 11. To reach the final, they first had to dispose of Olympique Lyon. Before the match van Gaal admitted, 'I'd hoped to play Bordeaux next – after two defeats in the group stage I wanted revenge. I saw Lyon against Real Madrid and they were well-organised and a difficult team to beat.'

Lyon were forced to make their journey to Germany by road after the ash cloud caused by Icelandic volcano Eyjafjallajökull brought about the closure of much of Europe's airspace. Meanwhile, assistant Bayern coach Andries Jonker had to deputise for his boss both at the press conference and in the training session, with van Gaal absent due to a family funeral at home in Holland. The 47-year-old was well aware of the challenge facing his side at the Allianz Arena the following day: 'Lyon are a good team that beat Liverpool, Real Madrid and won consecutive titles at home. They defend aggressively and have strong dribblers.'

Bayern claimed a 1–0 first leg advantage at the Allianz Arena courtesy of Arjen Robben's long-range strike in the 69th minute, despite having Franck Ribéry dismissed in the first half. Ribéry saw red in the 37th minute after connecting heavily with the ankle of Argentine striker Lisandro López and was subsequently handed a three-match ban. Lyon, however, failed to make any inroads despite their numerical advantage and were reduced to 10 men themselves when Jérémy Toulalan received two yellow cards in quick succession early in the second half. Van Gaal said afterwards, ' I think that we showed Europe tonight how strong we are; we showed that by dominating with 10 men against 11. I did not think that we would win 1–0 with Ribéry getting a red card. We dominated. I think we created more chances when we played with 10 against 11. When we were then 10 against 10 I sent on Mario Gómez to score a goal faster. We created many chances but scored one goal. That is good.'

Arjen Robben's night didn't end with scoring the winning goal. In the 85th minute, he forced Lyon goalkeeper Hugo Lloris to make an excellent save at full stretch before, seconds later, finding himself substituted. He looked irritated and the 66,000 fans were bewildered as Robben walked off the pitch. When coach Louis van Gaal extended a congratulatory hand to his star attacker, Robben ignored it, and received a very public reprimand from his boss.

After the match, van Gaal explained, 'In three days we play Borussia Mönchengladbach and I have to make sure that we go there with all our players fit. So now we have won here, we did not concede a goal and we will go to Gladbach with Robben fit, Olić fit, and all my players fit.' Olić had also been substituted early in the second half to help keep him fresh for the final stretch of the season.

While his rationale was a plausible one, van Gaal only provided half of his reasoning to reporters. If there is one thing to know about Louis van Gaal, it is that he likes to be in control. Van Gaal's decision sent yet another clear message to his squad: during his reign, no player would be given preferential treatment, and respect for the team, coach and fans was to be paramount. When Robben was substituted, the underlying rationale was that not even Robben, perhaps the most in-form attacker in world football at the time, was bigger than Bayern under van Gaal: 'No player has a guarantee to play 90 minutes with me; he has to do his job. When he is not doing his [job] then he is out of the team. All the players have to know that.'

Arjen Robben felt he was playing 'the best football of my life'. The press agreed with Lyon daily *Le Progrès* dubbing him 'Bayern's Messi'. Certainly Robben's record for the 2009–10 season stood comparison with anyone: by the time of that notable encounter with his coach on the sidelines of Bayern–Lyon, he had 14 goals in 15 starts in the *Bundesliga*, 2 in 2 in the German Cup and 4 in 6 in the Champions League. In his last 19 games he has scored 16 goals. For a winger, that's hugely impressive. By comparison, he scored only 18 goals in 103 games for Chelsea and 12 in 2 seasons for Real Madrid.

Robben's goals weren't just any goals either. The one he scored against Schalke in the semi-final of the German Cup – where he picked it up on the halfway line, sprinted past two tackles on the right touchline, cut back inside another from the by-line and bent the ball into the top corner – was treated to a two-page spread in German newspaper *Bild*. A beautifully flighted goal against Fiorentina and the technically astonishing volley against Manchester United once again showed his footballing genius.

Robben had arrived at Chelsea in the same summer as José Mourinho six years earlier. The Dutchman had been a coup for Chelsea, yet Robben never quite delivered on his potential. Mourinho became frustrated with his insufferable fickleness – he refused to play through pain on several occasions. Sold to Real Madrid, he never quite managed to persuade the Bernabéu either that he was a true *galactico*. After two seasons he was on his way. He arrived at Bayern last with a total of €100 million in transfer fees to his name by the age of just 25: there was obviously something wayward about his talent. Then Robben was reunited with Louis van Gaal.

Van Gaal, prickly as he can be, coaxed the best out of his surly protégé. Robben benefited tremendously from his reunion with van

Gaal, who had originally coached him as an 18-year-old with the Holland Under-21 side. 'He hasn't changed much since then but I have,' said Robben. His previous coaches at Chelsea and Madrid were so obsessed with the next game that they had little time for one-on-one tuition with their players, but that's not how van Gaal operates. It was he who persuaded Robben to switch from being a central striker to a winger when he was involved with the Dutch national youth side. When van Gaal replaced him against Lyon with five minutes left, Robben got stroppy but van Gaal grabbed him, looked him in the eye and reminded him who was in charge. Robben immediately apologised for his behaviour on Dutch TV. Robben felt protected, indulged, wanted.

If van Gaal was managing Robben psychologically, there had also been a substantial improvement physiologically. Robben changed his diet and sought the help of Dick van Toorn, the venerable Dutch physiotherapist who had worked with Johan Cruyff. Together with club doctor Hans-Wilhelm Müller-Wohlfahrt, a way was discovered to manage Robben's unusual muscle fatigue and curb the regular injuries he seemed to pick up. The relationship between the Dutch and German medical specialists was later to deteriorate completely, at the expense of Robben and by extension Bayern. Commentators have argued that the episode sowed the seeds for the team's and the coach's decline a season later. But in these happier days the co-operation appeared fruitful, and the Arjen Robben Mourinho was to encounter in the final was a different Robben he met at Chelsea. Robben's utter brilliance and game-changing goals naturally captured the imagination in Bavaria and beyond. In the second game against Lyon, with Bayern 3–0 up and Robben desperate to score after seeing two of his shots saved by Hugo Lloris, van Gaal took him off again. This time, Robben smiled and shook van Gaal's hand. The message had got through.

One of the other big names in the Bayern team was in a slightly different place by this point. Franck Ribéry – or 'Ferraribéry' as he was known during his hugely successful period at Galatasaray – is small, wiry, fleet of foot and with an utter lack of pretension born of a tough childhood. There is even the facial scarring which goes with his turbulent early years, the result of a road accident in his parents' car when he was two years old which tore his cheeks and forehead to ribbons. They also called him 'Scarface' in Istanbul. There was surprise when his career took him to Munich in 2007 for €25 million. The joke has always been that Ribéry was not actually too sure where on the European map he was going, other than a place he associated with Karl-Heinz Rummenigge and Franz Beckenbauer.

By that April, Ribéry was reeling from a season ravaged by injury, transfer rumours and allegations of relations with an under-age prostitute. Bayern instructed their players not to respond to journalists' questions about the affair. Ironically, the one team that could stand to benefit from the allegations was Bayern. Eager to hold on to one of their marquee players, the Bavarian club's directors presented Ribéry with a luxury pen on his birthday earlier in April and said they hoped he would use it to sign a new contract.

Ribéry's somewhat contradictory statements about his future the previous summer saw him labelled a 'diva' and 'Mr Bullshit' in the press. His start to the season was then delayed by a series of nagging injuries including blisters, swollen toes, and tendinitis in his left knee, earning him the nicknames 'Krank Ribéry' and 'The French Patient'. Ribéry admitted to a lack of warmth in his relationship with van Gaal and the pair enjoyed frosty relations for a number of weeks until a breakthrough came; his coach rallied to Ribéry's cause in front of the press during the prostitution controversy: 'He was only spoken to as a witness.' In fact, in January 2014 all charges against Ribéry were dropped by the French courts.

The contrasting fortunes of Ribéry and Robben, of madness and triumph, monopolised the attention of many. But for those who looked beyond the headlines, there was another player looming large: Bastian Schweinsteiger. When Schweinsteiger wasn't playing stunning, inch-perfect cross-field passes, he was winning the ball back with expertly timed tackles. 'You only have to look at Schweinsteiger to understand why Bayern are suddenly close to a Champions League final,' wrote *Süddeutsche Zeitung*. 'When did Bayern last play with so much maturity and tactical structure?' Certainly, Louis van Gaal played a very important part in the ascent of the German international. In seven years at Bayern, Schweinsteiger was used to playing out wide on the right or as an attacking midfielder. But a few weeks into the season the Dutch manager moved him into his preferred role in defensive midfield.

Schweinsteiger relished the sense of responsibility, and it coincided with a serious growth-spurt in terms of his personal development. He consciously distanced himself from the teen-idol status and insisted on ditching nicknames like 'Schweini' and 'Basti': 'I started paying more attention to details like diet and relaxation periods,' he told *RAN Magazine*. 'I'm looking after my body more and feel the benefits.' Gone, too, were the days when he used to change his hair-style once a week or turn up wearing silver nail-polish (he had lost a bet): Schweinsteiger became a serious man. 'I think the manager's concept is simply very good,' he said with characteristic modesty.

Certainly van Gaal seemed to have the perfect answer for every tactical conundrum against Lyon, including a move that saw

Schweinsteiger help out as the central striker for a few minutes. 'I knew he would keep the ball very well,' was the manager's explanation for this unexpected ploy. An initially reluctant Joachim Löw, who wanted to continue with Schweinsteiger on the right of Germany's midfield, was won over. 'His Bayern performances have been both excellent and consistent in central midfield, that's why he'll play there for us at the World Cup as well,' said the national manager.

'President Uli Hoeness makes no secret in saying that Bayern wants to win the Champions League,' former England and Arsenal striker Tony Woodcock told *BBC Sport*. 'Bayern's strength is that they have people from a football background – Franz Beckenbauer, Uli Hoeness, Gerd Müller and Karl-Heinz Rummenigge – who've played the game at the highest level and know what they want. They really want to push the history of Bayern to the public, to Europe, to the world. They want success and they want to be top of the tree.' Woodcock, a veteran observer of German football since he signed for Cologne in 1979, recognised early that in van Gaal Bayern got the man to achieve that goal. 'Bayern is a top European club, one of the best-run clubs on and off the field that I've seen in professional football. And you need a big-time manager who can handle big-time players. He's come here with a very good reputation and he's doing it his way. The players can see that and feel that, and the players have to keep themselves in line.'

Bayern had to travel to the Stade Gerland a week later to finish the job, a stadium in which Lyon had lost only once in its Champions League campaign during the season and scored 15 goals there in six games. It turned out to be a 3–0 defeat for the French. For defender Daniel van Buyten, the hard work that Bayern had put in during the season had finally paid off: 'The score is important, maybe it's even severe, but we are simply reaping the fruits of all our work for months and months. It's a just reward. Tonight, we managed to take advantage of gaps. As soon as we opened the score it became much easier. We had a really bad start to the championship. We have not been affected so much by injuries, but we had to take time to adjust with new players and a new coach. It takes time and that's what we did with Louis van Gaal. The team found out more and more. We understood his instructions, his systems, and it paid off. We won several matches at the crucial moment, and with confidence, things were linked together naturally. I had already won the *Bundesliga*, but it is certain that we are close to living a great moment. We are in the final of the Champions League.'

In Europe, Bayern became an attacking, confident team under van Gaal. The team's success during the season was based around getting the best out of a selection of players who might have meandered elsewhere, or simply been considered less than the very top class. The best of Bayern was its right flank where Arjen Robben and Philipp Lahm provided as good a pairing as any around. Getting the best out of Robben was an achievement for van Gaal. He has great speed, technique and coolness in front of goal, but he might have drifted after leaving Real Madrid. At Bayern under van Gaal, his ability was fully expressed. Van Gaal achieved similar feats of talent-wringing elsewhere. The occasionally volatile Martin Demichelis and Daniel van Buyten became a first-choice Champions League final central-defensive pairing. Bastian Schweinsteiger was majestic against Lyon, his sure-footed talent realised more completely in central midfield. And of course Ivica Olić achieved a career high with a perfect hat-trick (right foot, left foot, head) in a Champions League semi-final. Under van Gaal, Olić seemed to be performing right at the peak of his potential as a striker.

The 4–0 aggregate win was the biggest winning margin in a Champions League semi-final since Juventus beat van Gaal's Ajax 6–2 in the 1996–97 competition. The margin of victory reflected Bayern's superiority over both legs and van Gaal was satisfied by his side's management of the tie. Despite Olić's headline-grabbing performance, the coach insisted the credit for the victory deserved to be shared among all his players: 'We had a great game, we were well positioned on the pitch, and if we play like this all the way it will be hard to beat us. Ivica Olić scored three goals, he pressed high on the pitch as well, which is important in our organisation. We can rely on him. Once again he scored three goals, but it is because he is the closest player to the goal. I'm sorry, but that's the way I think. The players now know what it's like to spend 10 months with van Gaal, they know it's not easy but they're happy now and so am I.' France is famous for its wines, but van Gaal did not hesitate to toast his greatest achievement with Bayern at that point with a glass of his favourite Rioja, from neighbouring Spain.

Lyon's Claude Puel conceded that Lyon had fallen to a stronger team. Despite having had their league game waived so they could rest up for the second leg of the tie – something van Gaal did not take kindly to – they were no match. 'We were fresh after six days off but it was not enough. I was impressed by Bayern. We have not met a team with such physical strength since the start of the competition. They controlled the ball and forced us to run a lot. You simply have to congratulate their team, which was fantastic in lots of areas. Their physicality, the quality of their play, their control of possession. They remained focused and strong until the last minute. They are a complete team. They are physically strong and never let their rhythm drop.'

With his side 1–0 down after the first leg, Puel had sent his men out in an attacking 4-2-3-1. Van Gaal said he had anticipated Lyon's change of approach. 'I expected Lyon would play in another way. I read the papers. They didn't play very well in Munich, so it's natural that a coach will change his team. I expected that they would play with a number 10 [Cesar Delgado]. My players were informed. We saw that our pressing in Munich was too much for them and we have also seen that today. Since our match against Juventus, we've always played really well in the Champions League. We defended very well, not just the defenders. I've always thought the team could make it to the final. They've done a great job. We played really well,' van Gaal commented.

Hoeness, Bayern's president, agreed. He is normally a fierce critic of managers and players alike when they fall below the club's high standards. But even he was gushing in his praise of van Gaal's team's performance against Lyon. 'The football we've witnessed was close to perfection. It's a long, long time since I've seen that from a Bayern team in an important match. We've found the right path to pursue, and it's leading us rapidly upwards.' Beckenbauer, Bayern's greatest ever player, called it 'a tactical masterclass' from van Gaal.

ALOYSIUS PAULUS MARIA VAN GAAL VS. JOSÉ MÁRIO DOS SANTOS FÉLIX MOURINHO

'This team can become even better.
We have not yet reached our full potential.'

Louis van Gaal

Patriotism made a return among German football fans on 22 May 2010. Club allegiances were forgotten in favour of a good, old-fashioned 'us versus them' spirit – a warm-up for the World Cup, starting three weeks later. Usually, it wouldn't be surprising that when the Champions League final came around, fans of German clubs other than Bayern and Italian clubs other than Inter would cheer for their countrymen to lose. While national pride may be important, club loyalties and local rivalries run far deeper. Inter fans, for example, famously took to the streets to celebrate after AC Milan blew a 3–0 half-time lead and lost the 2005 Champions League final on penalties to Liverpool.

But in 2010 the situation wasn't quite so clear cut. The Champions League final was about more than just who won: there was also the resulting effect on how many teams each country would have in the following competition. The number of entries each European nation gets into the Champions League each season is calculated through complicated mathematics based on each club's relative success. UEFA determines the number of teams each league can enter into the Champions League based on a formula called the UEFA coefficient, which awards points to each league for the performances of its teams in European tournaments in a rolling five-year period. The top three nations, which at the start of the 2009–10 season were England, Spain and Italy, could enter four clubs; the next three, Germany, France and Russia, were allowed three each. The margin between Italy and Germany's position was wafer-thin. Anything other than an Inter victory would swing the pendulum Germany's way, meaning *Serie A* would be down to three spots, while the *Bundesliga* would move up to four.

A further irony for the Italian fans to consider was that the Inter team started without a single Italian in the line-up; indeed, no Inter players had been named in the country's provisional World Cup squad. The Inter team was made up mainly of South Americans, with a sprinkling of Africans for good measure. By contrast, Germans played a major role in the Bayern team. That added to the sense that German football was feeling good about itself. Attendances were high and the domestic championship was competitive until the penultimate day.

Bayern made the unusual step of appealing to German fans for support in the final. The Bavarian side asked fans in an open letter signed by the players and van Gaal to put club loyalties aside as they attempted to win the European title for a fifth time: 'The Bayern fans and those football fans who normally view us in a neutral way should all be "Bayern". This is what we wish for. We will give everything we have at the Bernabéu stadium for Bayern but also for Germany. With a victory we will win back a fourth Champions League spot for the *Bundesliga*. We have a dream. Dream with us,' said the letter. Van Gaal was delighted by the generally positive response and said that, by playing the type of attacking football he demanded, Bayern's popularity, often limited in Germany to their Bavarian heartland, had grown: 'I try to play football for the fans and think that the image of Bayern has changed a bit this year because we play an attractive style. I am pleased the whole country is backing us. It is unbelievable that 70,000 Bayern fans are going to be watching the match on the big screen back in Munich at the Allianz Arena, and I hope we can give them something to have a party about.'

When it comes to football, the Dutch traditionally regard the Germans as their arch enemy. Such sentiments occasionally rise to the surface at international games. When I watched the Germany–South Korea semi-final match with Guus Hiddink's relatives in his home town of Varsseveld during World Cup 2002, such 'negative patriotism' was on full display. The Dutch supporters, in full support of the Hiddink-coached South Korea team, wore orange T-shirts emblazoned with the Korean flag, the World Cup logo and the statement '*Dies' mal brauchte man nur ein Holländer*'. This German phrase suggested, in a rather bold and overconfident past tense, that Guus Hiddink had single-handedly defeated the German side. This premature claim was not substantiated by the game's result.

Now that Dutch clubs no longer rank among the upper echelons at European level, the Netherlands' hopes are pinned on Dutch footballers and coaches making a name for themselves wherever and whenever they surface. In 2010, Louis van Gaal had become the most popular Dutchman in Germany since Rudi Carell, a celebrated Dutch TV presenter who became a mainstay of German television in the 1970s and 1980s. *Bild* wrote that the Dutchman scored high points in the categories of humour, charm, honesty and success. Van Gaal was pleased by the comparison: 'I think it is great that I am compared with Rudi Carell. It is the first time in my life that the media have approached me this positively. That was quite different in the Netherlands and Spain.' When Bayern under van Gaal went on their historic winning run to the final, the Dutch allied themselves firmly to the German side. Van Gaal commented on the amount of Dutch support received: 'Even from the Netherlands, I've received many emails from people who tell me they never thought they'd ever be cheering for a German team.'

After the Champions League final, UEFA president Michel Platini commented that the German fans did an outstanding job. He thanked the supporters of both Inter and Bayern for their contribution in making the Champions League final a memorable occasion: 'I would like to congratulate the supporters of the two clubs for creating a superb atmosphere, before, during and after the final. The way the Inter and Bayern fans conducted themselves was a credit to the game and its values, and the fair play and respect they displayed is worthy of the highest praise.'

Back at the start of the season Sir Alex Ferguson had texted José Mourinho about the Champions League final – 'Let's meet in Madrid in May.' Van Gaal put paid to that, but picked up the habit of texting his rival: 'After the semi-final I texted José: "You have one hurdle to go. I am already there. I will be waiting for you in Madrid." I absolutely love the fact that I am meeting a man who is my friend and who I admire for the work he is doing as a coach in Europe. It's nice for me that I am meeting José in the final, but it is also brilliant for the media. You're going to see the best press conferences you can wish for with us two.'

The two coaches knew each other well. In 1997, van Gaal went to Barcelona expecting to do the same again as he had done at Ajax. An up-and-coming Mourinho had expected to be moved out of the Camp Nou when van Gaal arrived, but the Dutchman recognised his potential and kept him on as his assistant for the next three years, during which they won *La Liga* twice and the *Copa del Rey* once. It was van Gaal who allowed the young coach to take charge of training sessions and handle the Catalan media in his place. Mourinho was full of praise for his former boss, saying, 'Louis was very important for me. With him I developed a very strong relationship as he gave me confidence. He gave me complete control in training sessions and I became, with him, a coach on the pitch.'

A former translator, Mourinho was assistant coach at Barça under Bobby Robson and van Gaal from 1996 to 2000: 'I owe to Bobby Robson because he gave me the chance to work in Barcelona. I owe to van Gaal because he wanted me to stay for three more years.' When Robson left the Catalan club, van Gaal took the ambitious Portuguese under his wing. Mourinho had other options, but a quiet word from the Dutchman convinced him his future was at the Camp Nou. Mourinho said, 'When I spoke with [van Gaal] about going back to Portugal to be an assistant at Benfica, he said, "No, don't go." He told me to tell the Benfica president [in 2000] that if he wants you to become assistant then you say no. If he wants you to be the manager then I'll take you to the airport and you go. Van Gaal is a very confident person, and at a time when a coach like me was young that was very important. He gave me the confidence to coach the team on the pitch. In friendly matches, in *Copa Catalunya* matches, he gave me the responsibility of being the coach. He told me, "I go to the stands, you take charge of the team," so he was very important in my development.'

Simon Kuper wrote in *Football Against the Enemy*, '[Barcelona is] a sort of psychological surrogate for the state they do not have.' And Mourinho understands exactly what they mean when Catalans say Barcelona is 'more than a club'. He also understands the fanaticism of Barcelona's intensely political rivalry with Real Madrid, the club of the Castilian elite and of the Francoistas. Before the Inter Milan–Barcelona semi-final he taunted the Catalans over how desperately they wanted to win the Champions League at the Bernabéu in Madrid, where the final would be held. 'To have a Catalan flag in the Bernabéu is an obsession,' he said. 'There's a difference. A dream is more pure than an obsession. A dream is about pride. The Inter players would be very proud to reach the final. For them they reached the dream. It's not a dream for Barcelona; it's anti-Madridism. I am not criticising. I am just speaking the truth.'

According to van Gaal, Barcelona would gladly have got rid of Mourinho, whom everyone from the president down had dismissively referred to as *El Traductor* (The Translator): 'I sometimes think I was the only guy at the club who believed in José,' van Gaal said. He saw more in Mourinho than Bobby Robson did, who, for all his qualities, was never able to make the leap of imagination that would allow him to define the Portuguese as anything more than a non-footballing asset. Robson put him in charge of the planning and preparations of his squad, something at which Mourinho excelled, preparing reports on opponents and structuring training. But it wasn't until van Gaal's arrival that he got much time to work on the pitch with the players.

As soon as he arrived at Barcelona, van Gaal had typically taken control of the entire organisational side of things. He did, however, delegate to his capable assistant. Suddenly Mourinho was getting his chance to work closely with Rivaldo, Xavi, Pep Guardiola, Patrick Kluivert and Luis Figo. It wasn't until his final year under van Gaal that he became restless. Mourinho remembers himself as 'an anguished assistant coach' who would drive home to his house in Sitges, mulling over decisions van Gaal had made, becoming 'harsh and overly critical' of his mentor. His ambition to have his own project was evident to those around him and the decision to leave Barcelona was made easy by the sacking of van Gaal and the departure of club president Josep Luíz Núñez.

'More than a specific detail, the important thing is that I remember the years we worked together,' Mourinho later said. 'We lived very close together – my home was 15 metres from his – and we worked 24 hours a day, 7 days a week. We had a very good relationship and he left a mark on me. I used to work like a beast, but I was happy to do so. I learned a lot from him. One of the main things was that if you want to get anywhere you have to work very hard. That has stayed with me.'

After a managerial career that saw him win the Champions League with Porto and numerous trophies at Chelsea, Mourinho had taken over at Inter in the summer of 2008 and was believed to be the world's highest-paid coach with a salary of €9.5 million. He was hailed in Italy for steering Inter into its first Champions League final since 1972. Asked about the Champions League final and about his former mentor, he said, 'I spoke with van Gaal a few minutes ago, but I have nothing to say about it. There will be a big hug before the match and a big hug after the match.'

Under a telling headline suggesting that, 'Louis van Gaal can finally silence translator José Mourinho,' Jason Cowley wrote in the *London Evening Standard*, 'Mourinho is an absurd, strutting egoist but also an astonishing coach: strategist, tactician, motivator. If he has an equal in world football it is none other than his old mentor, van Gaal. I have a small feeling that if anyone can stop him it is van Gaal, the obsessively note-taking Dutchman for whom Mourinho once humbly worked in a lowly role, writing detailed player summaries and coaching reports while refining his own master plan.' The final was the first time they had come against each other as managers: the time had come to see if the pupil had what it took to beat the master.

Both managers were very much systems men, sharing an almost evangelical belief that, by dint of tactical ingenuity, the manager is king. Van Gaal remained considerably more attack-minded than his Portuguese rival, permitting significantly greater scope for improvisation within the parameters of any tactical framework. Some suggested Mourinho's personnel management contained more 'emotional intelligence'. But the inclination of both towards very strong top-down management led some German media to describe the final encounter as 'God versus The Son of God'. 'He is a top coach and Bayern is a top club,' Mourinho said of van Gaal. 'Bayern is an example to many clubs, because the team didn't start well. Louis was in a difficult situation but the club kept confidence in him, let him do his work, and now he is in the Champions League final.'

The game had other fascinating narratives running through it, including the settling of a couple of old personal scores. Brazilian defender Lúcio had switched from the Allianz to the San Siro the previous summer, as van Gaal laid down the laws of team play, sending him into the open arms of Mourinho. Both teams, too, employed a Dutch midfielder discarded by Real Madrid. Both Wesley Sneijder and Arjen Robben had been told they were not good enough for

Real. Yet without their performances and their goals, neither Inter nor Bayern would have reached the final which, ironically, was to be played in Real's stadium. Robben, too, was itching to show his former coach that, far from being a spent force, he'd actually improved since the Portuguese sold him to Real Madrid during his time as Chelsea boss. Robben felt he and his friend Wesley Sneijder had been driven out of town by Real Madrid: 'We felt we were being forced out. We did not leave with the best of feelings about the club. Wesley was asked to come and join José at Inter, and I went to Bayern. We can't believe that we are now going to be back in the changing rooms of Madrid on the biggest night of our football careers. It is a massive feeling. I will make sure I will sit on my old seat in the Real dressing room. It is a dream. What I could not achieve at Chelsea, I have now achieved in my first season at Bayern.'

Mourinho is similar to van Gaal in certain ways. Both have a nomadic tendency, both have made their mark outside their homeland, both had a Champions League win to their name at the time of the 2010 final, and both have a superb record in finals and an unshakeable belief in themselves. Similarities, then, in their mental toughness and tactical genius. But there were noticeable differences, too. It would be too simplistic to say that van Gaal has been committed to attacking football his whole managerial life while an obsession with defence has characterised the Mourinho years, but there is an element of truth in such claims. In his six seasons with Ajax, van Gaal's team was top of the goal-scoring charts in five, while rarely occupying the same lofty position in terms of goals conceded. It was the same when he went to Barcelona for this three-year stint. Bayern scored 21 goals in the 2009–10 Champions League and conceded 13 until the final. Inter scored 15 and conceded 8. Therein was the difference in their philosophies.

Mourinho's Porto, Chelsea and Inter had all won titles while conceding fewer goals than everybody else, sometimes considerably fewer. Entertainment is not something Mourinho ever promised anyone. The *Nerazzurri* played a very defensive second leg at the Camp Nou against Barcelona to advance to the final, sparking a wild celebration from Mourinho at the full-time whistle, which elicited the comment of van Gaal that 'I would not have done what Mourinho did at the Camp Nou; I wouldn't have behaved in a provocative way. His analysis was good, even then [at Barcelona] you could see he understood football. But at that time he was very humble and it's great to see how he has evolved, he gradually became a personality. He trains to win, so do I, but I also choose to express good football. My way is more difficult.'

The stage was set for what was to become a historic Champions League final in Madrid: one of the two teams would go on to win the 'treble', a feat that thus far had been achieved just five times in the history of European football: winning the domestic title, domestic cup and Champions League in the same season. Two British teams – Celtic and Manchester United – two Dutch – PSV and Ajax – and one Spanish team – Barcelona – had been able to achieve this. An Italian or German side was about to join these illustrious ranks.

The final was billed as a technical, tactical battle, but it was individuals who decided the outcome. Youngster Thomas Müller, playing in front of substitute Mario Gómez, spurned two second-half openings for an equaliser, first when Júlio César saved with his feet just after the break, then when his volley was cleared by Esteban Cambiasso. English referee Howard Webb somehow missed Maicon handling in the penalty box. 'Just How Did You Miss That?' was the reaction of coach van Gaal according to the *Sun*. This decisive moment came when Arjen Robben's

16th-minute cross was blocked by the arm of the Brazilian. Webb did not give a penalty with the game still goalless, and Inter went on to win 2–0. Van Gaal believed it might have been Bayern's day if 'the referee had punished the hand ball'.

In an interesting exchange before the game, Phoenix Suns' basketball star Steve Nash annoyed José Mourinho with the following tweet: 'Inter's eleven for final: Butt, Yashin, Banks, Zoff, Maier, Tomaszewski, Zubizarreta, Schmeichel, Clemens, Higuita, Chilavert.' Van Gaal was less blunt after the game was over, but in effect agreed with Nash's observation. 'You must not forget that we chose a very difficult playing style. I think that it's the most attractive for the public. But we were simply not good enough and were never able to play our own game. You have to be in superb form against a team like Inter if you want to play an attacking game. The match went pretty much as I expected it to go. We dominated play, while Inter were waiting to hit us on the counter-attack. We did create chances, but when you don't take them then you lose the game. In a difficult game you need goals at the right time and Inter scored at the right time. We weren't on best form today. Defending is so much easier than attacking.

'However, let there be no doubt about it that Inter deserved their win. They put in a great performance and I'd like to congratulate them. I also want to congratulate José Mourinho. I'm very proud of what my players have achieved. The lads have learned a lot from this experience. Little details decided the match today and we missed the creativity of Franck Ribéry.' It was with some relief for the club after the match that Ribéry finally signed a new five-year contract.

Bayern had not been as attack-minded as it could have been, or should have been. Philipp Lahm admitted his team had paid the price for a lack of adventure in their defeat: 'We were too scared in the first half; we did not play bravely like we have done in the past few weeks. This is very bitter for us. We had so much resolve but we could not take it on to the pitch. We created a couple of chances but didn't take them. Our disappointment is huge. You don't play in a final like this every year.' Skipper Mark van Bommel was more philosophical about the defeat: 'Not the best team won, but the most effective team. Seizing those moments of opportunity is the key. That's not a criticism of Thomas [Müller]; he has scored so many goals this season. But situations like those decide such big matches. We don't score, they do – that was the difference.'

Still, van Gaal said he was proud of his team and proud too of the fact that, over the course of the Champions League campaign, Bayern and Barcelona proved to have the sharpest attacking instincts. In the final, UEFA's statisticians gave Inter only 34 per cent possession. Mourinho took so long to reach the post-match press briefing that there was no time to invite him to respond to that. What he did find the time to say was, 'It was a provocation in a football sense when van Gaal said before the match Inter are a defensive team. But I knew what he wanted and I wanted the same thing – to win. We played a beautiful final and we deserved to win, not just for this match but for the whole run to the final.' Beauty, of course, is in the eye of the beholder, and the Portuguese view of Inter's performance was not necessarily the majority view. Mourinho was nearer the mark when, in defending the absence of any Italians in the team until Marco Materazzi was sent on for the final minute, he spoke of 'a club with an Italian culture, proud to represent Italian football'. Bayern were denied by quintessential Italian football, whatever the personnel on the pitch may have been.

The biggest prize in European football was not to be a part of the Bayern trophy cabinet in 2010, but Uli Hoeness insisted his team had plenty to celebrate: 'Inter were just more experienced than us and we just lacked that bit of calm. Inter is a fantastic team who also knocked out Barcelona. They scored two goals from three chances while we did not take our biggest chance at the best possible moment – that was the difference. I am obviously disappointed and sad because when you reach a final you also want to win it, but we should not let this disappointment last for too long. We have played a magnificent season and had said before this game that nothing could be taken away from that. So we should not start to do that now. Our team has a great future ahead because it has so many young players. In 2011 the final will be in Wembley, and then in 2012 it will be in Munich, so there are lots of visions and aims for us. It is a long way to the final. There are 12 games and you could also get the luck of the draw or have a bad day. I would have to be a clairvoyant to say that we will do it again next year.'

THE VAN GAAL REVOLUTION AND THE 2010 WORLD CUP

'The future is looking bright in Germany.'
Bastian Schweinsteiger

According to former player Paul Breitner, Bayern Munich could not have reached the Champions League final for the first time in nine years without Louis van Gaal as coach. Breitner played in the first of Bayern's hat-trick of European Cup successes in 1974: 'Since a few months ago, I again am a real fan of Bayern. I suddenly enjoy going to the stadium again. Not just to see Bayern win, because that happens a lot anyway, but to enjoy the beautiful football. I have not seen Bayern play this well in about 5 or 10 years. [...] The reason we have been so successful is that after about 8, 10, 12 weeks, the team began to understand what [van Gaal] meant, his system, about winning the ball, controlling the ball, by having 60 to 70 per cent of possession throughout the 90 minutes. Our team is now playing completely different football than it did before. And it is playing completely different football compared to the other

17 teams in the *Bundesliga*. We are not playing like my old Bayern team of the 1970s. We are playing in a different way, more like Barcelona does today. It is attacking, it is attractive, the team goes looking for goals – there is no real comparison to the 1970s – it is a more modern approach. It is different now. Every player has had to learn a new style, a new way of football, but this took time. Louis van Gaal needed time to convince the team that his ideas of football are the right ideas. They would not be here without him.'

When you traced the roots of the successful teams at the 2010 World Cup, every clue pointed back to one man: Louis van Gaal. While credit was of course due to Joachim Löw, Bert van Marwijk and Vicente del Bosque, the Bayern coach was a strong influence behind three of the four semi-finalists: Germany, Holland and Spain.

Van Gaal had built upon the foundations established by Johan Cruyff: never pass onto a teammate's feet, but always a metre ahead of him to keep the ball moving. When the first man passes to the second man, the third man must already be moving into space ready for the second man's pass. In Catalonia, van Gaal promoted great passers such as Xavi and Andrés Iniesta, who now dominated Spain's midfield. Of the Spanish players featuring in the final, seven came through the ranks of Barcelona – Puyol, Piqué, Busquets, Xavi, Iniesta, Pedro and Fàbregas. The youth education programme set up at Camp Nou rivals the world-renowned system Cruyff and van Gaal helped to develop at Ajax, nine of whose alumni were in the Dutch squad – Stekelenburg, van der Wiel, Heitinga, De Jong, van der Vaart, Sneijder, Elia, Huntelaar and Babel. These players spent their youth absorbing Dutch ideology: football is about making passing 'triangles'. Boys at Barcelona are forever playing four against four, with two touches allowed. It is a game you win through passing and positioning. Football as chess, not football as wrestling.

At Euro 2008 Germany had reached the final, where Spain passed them off the park. Joachim Löw, Germany's coach, thought, 'I want a team like that.' A year later, van Gaal popped up as Bayern's manager, and taught his players a passing game. Bayern, the club that never cared much about how it won, as long as it won, began playing Dutch-Spanish football. Van Gaal turned Bayern's Bastian Schweinsteiger into a defensive midfielder, and stuck Thomas Müller in the first eleven. In the 2010 World Cup, Schweinsteiger and Müller starred for Germany. Their teammates in Munich, Arjen Robben and Mark van Bommel, starred for Holland. German, Dutch and Spanish football had crossbred so as to become almost indistinguishable. The Germans passed like Holland in disguise. The Dutch defended and counter-attacked like Germans used to. Spain played like Holland circa 2000. Experience and physique were secondary to whether you could pass at speed: Sneijder, Xavi, Iniesta, and Lahm are all 1.73m or smaller, but they understand passing. Most previews of the World Cup focused on the stars when instead they should have focused on passing cultures. At the end of the tournament, Ronaldo, Rooney and Messi were forgotten, while van Gaal, in absentia, was standing tall.

The last time Argentina were humiliated 4–0 in a World Cup quarter-final there were dark skies overhead and rain fell with the force of a monsoon. That game took place 36 years earlier in Gelsenkirchen. The match left observers with admiration for the Dutch victors, led by Johan Cruyff, playing total football. At World Cup 2010 in Cape Town the *Albiceleste* were humiliated 4–0 once more, albeit without rain, by another swift-moving football-playing team. Only this time the defeat was inflicted by the youngest German side in a World Cup finals since 1934. It had been a long time since Germany played such blistering attacking football, the team completing its metamorphosis into one of the most attractive sides in international football.

A day earlier, the Dutch were also busy stirring old memories as they came from behind to beat Brazil 2–1. Brazil's second-half collapse evoked numerous self-destructive performances by Holland while the fightback recalled spirited victories achieved by dull but indomitable Germans. In a funny way, the victory reminded the Dutch of their greatest nightmare, the 'Lost Final' of 1974 when they scored first and lost 2–1 to the Germans. The 2010 World Cup tournament made the Dutch both happy and troubled at the same time. They were euphoric that the *Oranje* was winning, but were uncomfortable about the style with which the outstanding string of victories was accomplished. They saw the German side and realised that they reminded them of the best of themselves.

On both sides of the Germany–Netherlands border a rapprochement had gradually replaced the poisonous football rivalry which followed 1974 and peaked in the late 1980s and early 1990s. An intriguing cross-pollination is now taking place. Germans are teaching the Dutch to win; the Dutch are teaching the Germans to play spatially aware, sophisticated attacking football. It was van Gaal who had converted Bastian Schweinsteiger from dysfunctional winger to the near-perfect creative defensive midfielder who made Germany tick. It was van Gaal who recognised Thomas Müller's potential and helped make him that year's World Cup sensation, winning the World Cup Golden Boot. Müller shared a tally of five goals with Wesley Sneijder, David Villa and Diego Forlán, but managed three assists while the others could hit just one. In all, eight of the Dutch national squad (Mark van Bommel, Khalid Boulahrouz, Edson Braafheid, Eljero Elia, Nigel de Jong, Joris

Mathijsen, Arjen Robben and Rafael van der Vaart) played or had played for German clubs. Mutual admiration was in fashion.

World Cup 2010 looked at one point like it might culminate in a Germany–Netherlands final, but this did not happen, courtesy of Spain. Did Joachim Löw lose his nerve? Those were the questions that immediately rose to the surface in the wake of the 1–0 Spanish victory over Germany. Germany had swept through the tournament – but for the minor road bump that was Serbia – and was, in the minds of many, favoured to not only get to the final but also win the tournament. It had the pedigree. It had the players. It had speed. It had power. It had forwards who could make goals, midfielders who could create scoring opportunities, and defenders who could deny them. They had Löw's lucky blue sweater and the predictions of an octopus named Paul (which they loved until he forecast a Spanish triumph). They loved, too, the fact that their team was not only winning but playing extremely well.

But Löw let them down. For reasons that are perplexing, to say the least, he sent a team out onto the Moses Mabhida Stadium pitch in Durban that was intent on defending, intent on stopping Spain from scoring, rather than trying to score itself. It was a curious decision. Germany had found the back of the net 13 times in its first 5 games and had conceded only 2. They had scored 4 goals in each of its 2 knockout-round victories. Argentina had been taken apart seam by seam in the quarter-finals by a German side that relished carrying the game to the opposition. Had Germany followed that path against Spain, the outcome might have been different.

Three months before the World Cup, van Gaal announced he was keen to succeed Joachim Löw as national coach: 'I dream of winning the World Cup with a team that can do it. Germany is one of them.' A Dutchman in charge of the German national team might seem a long shot but the 2010 World Cup squad was one with a strong van Gaal imprint. Full-back Lahm, Germany's only world-class defender, was of course always a shoo-in, regardless of his club's success. Klose and Gómez might not have had great seasons but still made the trip because their quality was not in question. But four further Bayern players wouldn't have been picked without van Gaal. Butt had only been a back-up for first-choice keeper Michael Rensing at Bayern at the beginning of the season, but van Gaal decided to install the 35-year-old as number one after a couple of games and Butt responded with solid performances. Schweinsteiger's nomination was perhaps never in doubt, but he, too, benefited tremendously from his club manager's input. Badstuber and Müller had started the season not expecting much playing time. Van Gaal's courageous decision to promote both of them to the senior squad in the summer and make them automatic starters was thoroughly vindicated. For Löw, their elevation was perfect: he had long looked for a reliable centre-back to partner Per Mertesacker and for a striker like Müller who could link well with the midfield or double-up as a midfielder if necessary.

Dutch national coach Bert van Marwijk admitted that he copied the style put in place at Barcelona by his fellow countryman: 'Van Gaal was the man who told the Barcelona players that unless they worked all the time they would not get to play. That style was taken on by Pep Guardiola, and look how they play today. I look at them and try to get my team to defend as a team the way Barcelona does.' Van Bommel always knew he would get a recall when Bert van Marwijk had been appointed two years previously – and not just because the new national coach was his father-in-law. Van Bommel was van Marwijk's mouthpiece on the field. He performed the same duty at Bayern, always chivvying and organising his younger teammates, ensuring they retained discipline and shape while going about his own deceptively simple work: trap, tackle, pass. Even when Giovanni van Bronckhorst wore the armband, van Bommel was captain in all but name.

The abundance of Bayern players within the German national squad posed a slight problem for Bayern's preparations for the following season – something that did not make van Gaal altogether happy, particularly as his team faced the 2009 *Bundesliga* winners Wolfsburg on the opening day of the 2010–11 season. 'Wolfsburg is one of the candidates for the title, but they don't have as many players at the World Cup as us. It's a disadvantage for us,' said van Gaal. Bayern's two Dutch stars, Arjen Robben and Mark van Bommel, were part of the highly effective Dutch team that made it all the way to the World Cup final, making van Gaal's pre-season preparations limited. In all, van Gaal had a full 11 World Cup 'absentees' to cope with. By contrast, Wolfsburg missed only Arne Friedrich. The Bayern coach had become a victim of his own success.

AUF
WIEDERSEHEN ...

'I am disappointed that van Gaal's spell at Bayern has
come to an end like this. He's done a lot for this club.'

Franz Beckenbauer

Many coaches have gone to Bayern and won titles. But not many
have done so with quite the headstrong panache van Gaal displayed
when he arrived in the summer of 2009. Big wins were nothing
new for Bayern, but winning in this twenty-first century style was.
The downside to Bayern's success was that the squad attracted
attention from national team coaches ahead of the 2010 World
Cup. Perhaps understandably, youngsters like Thomas Müller and
Holger Badstuber were unable to maintain their form. Certainly, it
is noticeable that Bayern often stumble in odd-numbered years –
the seasons immediately following big tournaments.

Bayern's second under Louis van Gaal was a shocking anti-
climax after the success of the first, with the team drifting in mid-
table for much of the season. By the seventh round of matches
it had descended to a precarious twelfth place, and barely a
day went by without a member of the club's executive board
issuing an energetic call to arms. The coach, however, remained
unflustered. 'There's no crisis at Bayern,' he insisted on ZDF's

Aktuelle Sportstudio show, adding he had warned in advance that Bayern would have problems at the start of the season. Full of characteristic self-confidence, van Gaal did not rule out staying on at Bayern beyond the tenure of his running contract, which had only just been extended to June 2012. While he would still like another shot at managing a national team, success remained his greatest motivating force: 'I want to win things. If there's no offer from a decent footballing country, I won't do it. And, if the club wants it, maybe I'll stay on at Bayern Munich.'

World Cup fatigue and a short pre-season were initially the diagnosis for Bayern's poor start to the season. At one point, van Gaal was left with a total of 15 fit players in the squad. By late October, he had to field another makeshift team, against Freiburg: 'I have been doing that for some time now and at some point it has to start bearing fruit. As the saying goes, practice makes perfect.' Wingers Arjen Robben and Franck Ribéry were suffering long-term injuries, while captain Mark van Bommel, defenders Diego Contento and Breno as well as midfielder David Alaba were also out. Striker Miroslav Klose was then added to the injury list, only a day after he recovered from another knock. Klose was set to spend more time on the sidelines after aggravating a thigh muscle injury during training: 'Miro really wanted to be on the bench against Freiburg. He trained and it went badly because he aggravated his thigh injury and will be out for at least two weeks. Obviously we went too fast. I made a mistake. It's the first time that I've listened to a player. At 32, you'd think that a player would know better, but a player always wants to play.'

The Arjen Robben injury saga was noteworthy and full of contradictions. The winger was injured for the entire first half of the season, and by the time he returned Bayern had effectively ceded the league title to Dortmund. In preparation for the World Cup, the Dutch had played a friendly against Hungary during which Robben suddenly gripped his hamstring after a backheel. Dick van Toorn was the wonder doctor who stepped in right before the tournament to offer his services to Robben and the KNVB. The normal time to recover from a hamstring injury is four to six weeks, but by early June Robben was back, with Van Toorn seemingly fixing it in just five days. The 78-year-old was a hero for a short time. Until Robben got back to Bayern, that is, and the German club claimed the Dutch medic had ruined Robben's hamstring. Robben couldn't believe he was starting the season with a heavy injury as Bayern doctor Müller-Wohlfahrt wanted him to believe: 'I really thought it was a bad joke. I felt good! I was ready to start practice and was standing literally with my boots in hand. I was in shock afterwards and totally gobsmacked.' Robben would go on to spend five months in recovery.

As Bayern prepared for another Champions League fixture with a makeshift squad dubbed 'Louis' remnants', the club were openly critical of the KNVB, threatening to take the matter to court if they didn't receive compensation for Robben's injury: 'We want to know by the end of the month whether an agreement is possible,' Bayern chairman Karl-Heinz Rummenigge said. 'If not, it becomes a legal question. And should it come to trial, it will have Bosman-like implications. In sporting terms we already have been disadvantaged. We have had to do without our best player from last season for five months.'

After months of argument, Rummenigge eventually announced that 'KNVB president Henk Kesler apologised specifically for the very rude tone he took against Dr Müller-Wohlfahrt.' Bayern agreed to play the Netherlands in a friendly on 22 May 2012 to compensate the German club for the lengthy loss of their key player: 'We are glad to have settled the issue. It is good for the football community that we have found a fair and satisfactory solution.' Bert van Oostveen, the CEO of the KNVB, said, 'We have accepted that we could not reach an agreement in general discussions, so it was best to settle our differences and to search for a viable solution for both sides. We have done that, we are satisfied with the result and we look forward to a great friendly match in Munich.'

Back in the Champions League, van Gaal watched his team throw away a victory against Roma, going from a 2–0 half-time lead to a 3–2 defeat: 'We played a great first half, we dominated, but then it was incredible how we brought Roma back into the match in the second half. [Roma coach Claudio] Ranieri changed his system from a 4-4-2 to a 4-3-3, but that wasn't the problem. The problem was that we lost too many balls and gave away too many chances to Roma. We've thrown away a game again, like we did against Mönchengladbach and Leverkusen and we have to find a way to stop doing that.' Dramatic second-half reversals became something of a Bayern hallmark during their season of misfortune. The game plan seemed to be going OK until the team's defence came under increased attack from opponents looking for goals. As a rule, Bayern's fragile defence could not withstand the pressure and caved in.

Even so, van Gaal was bright-eyed and bushy-tailed about Bayern's future prospects: 'It's fantastic what this beleaguered team has managed to achieve so far this season despite all the injury worries. We won the German Supercup, sit first in our Champions League group and we're still in the race to win the *DFB-Pokal*. We even still have a chance in the *Bundesliga*. The only problem we have at the moment is that Borussia Dortmund continue to perform well. I'm of the opinion that we are playing better football this term than we did last season. Things are only going to get better for us. Even Arjen Robben is on his way back again following his injury problems.'

Bayern honorary president Franz Beckenbauer did not subscribe to van Gaal's rosy view of reality: 'They make mistakes like in kindergarten. They are not good enough to win the league like this.' That came in the wake of criticism from Bayern's sporting director Christian Nerlinger, who suggested Bayern fans 'don't have to think about the championship'. Former Bayern goalkeeper Oliver Kahn told van Gaal not to take his club's warnings lightly: 'You hear that van Gaal is not such an easy character. Many things are accepted when you are successful, but if things don't go so well then certain types of behaviour are no longer tolerated. Van Gaal is pushing his luck. We should not forget that Bayern has always had big coaches who have been successful – he is not alone there. If a club is not pulling in the same direction at board level and at the coach's level, then this is extremely counter-productive.'

Equally worrisome for van Gaal was his difficult relationship with at least some of his players. Back at last from injury, Franck Ribéry kept having run-ins with his coach and comments given after the Roma match by van Gaal suggested that his relations with Ribéry were deteriorating still further. Van Gaal was asked how their relationship was and sarcastically replied, 'We talked at the hotel and it was love at first sight.' Van Gaal was rapped across the knuckles by Christian Nerlinger for that, who said, 'He sometimes provokes and you shouldn't always take everything he says seriously. But he is not giving the best impression of us at the moment and we have to work on changing this.'

Ribéry had made his comeback in a friendly match against Unterhaching, only to have van Gaal criticise his work rate: 'He did not put in any effort and showed no commitment. This is a shame. None of them put in much effort, but least of all Ribéry. He caused no confusion at all.' Ribéry was not impressed with his coach's comments after reading them in the press: 'It would have been better if he had said it direct to my face. I cannot say that I have a special relationship with him. I do my job and he does his. I give it my best, do everything to get fit again, but when the coach always speaks badly about you, when he keeps dragging you down, then it becomes difficult. I need his help, his trust. I would like more contact with him so there is more mutual appreciation. I have got to be able to talk with him and have fun with him. If I cannot do that, then it cannot work on the pitch either.'

Four months later, after it was announced that van Gaal would leave the club at the end of the season, Ribéry exhibited all the skills that had helped establish him as one of the most effective wingers in world football, during Bayern's 6–0 thrashing of Hamburg. Speaking candidly to *France Football*, the enigmatic player explained that he had not been enjoying his football under van Gaal. 'I have more fun on the field [in the absence of van Gaal],' Ribéry said. Asked whether the confirmation that van Gaal would step down as Bayern's coach in the summer had stimulated the team, the French star responded, 'I think so.'

Van Gaal had eschewed calls from fans, former players, media pundits and even the Bayern board to strengthen the squad in the summer. He preferred to work with players and improve their games, moulding them into his style of play. Young goalkeeper Thomas Kraft had received his backing and at the start of the season Diego Contento was hailed as the solution to the problems at left back. However, the most memorable vote of confidence was placed in a young Austrian, David Alaba, who due to injury has barely featured at that point. Van Gaal remarked, 'We don't need Sami Khedira, we have David Alaba.' But it was not the only van Gaal prediction that failed to bear fruit. Stung by his experiences of rotation at Barcelona, van Gaal wanted a settled side instead. However, a lack of fit and competent defenders meant a merry-go-round was in place at the back.

Van Gaal predicted that the likes of Toni Kroos, Breno and Holger Badstuber would make great strides forward this year. Badstuber, 'who is not a left-back but a centre-half', turned out to be the most consistent centre-back, followed interestingly by Anatoliy Tymoshchuk – a player over whom the coach had performed a rare volte-face. Breno, by contrast, suffered with injuries and was cruelly exposed by Raul in the defeat to Schalke 04. Kroos, meanwhile, was unable to recapture his form while on loan to Bayer Leverkusen, where he had lit up the *Bundesliga* with several stunning long-range strikes. To add to the confusion, he was used in a variety of roles including as one of the two controlling midfielders.

Another low moment in the season was when Mark van Bommel quit the club in dramatic fashion and revealed he had not even said goodbye to his coach: 'We shook hands, that's all,' said van Bommel about his farewell to van Gaal. Van Bommel was allowed to move to Milan during the winter break, despite his important role in the team. Van Gaal had reportedly planned to drop the team captain down the Bayern pecking order behind Toni Kroos and January signing Luiz Gustavo, but Rummenigge admitted Bayern's senior bosses were not happy to see van Bommel go. Van Bommel, meanwhile, made no secret that van Gaal was the reason he was leaving Bayern: 'Everyone knows what the matter is and I don't think I need to criticise the coach. I didn't actually want to leave, but it was a sporting decision; I have no problem at all with the club.' When he left, van Bommel thanked everyone at Bayern – from the groundsmen to the president – but no word for van Gaal.

Despite van Bommel's departure, Bayern seemed to be improving and van Gaal was full of praise after Bayern's 3–1 victory at Werder Bremen at the end of January: 'Credit to the team. We're in a Champions League place now and that's what we wanted. We scored three goals again too, unbelievable.' In fact, Bayern had scored 24 times in 6 consecutive competitive matches, taking the tally to 74 for the season in all competitions – more than any other *Bundesliga* club. The three points also saw Bayern jump to third in the table, the first time they had occupied a Champions League place all season. This being the case, Rummenigge once again defended his the controversial coach: 'He is exactly what we want. We can't reproach him, he has our trust. He's not always a fun guy, or fun to deal with. His extreme honesty and openness can lead to friction, but he is an excellent football teacher and coach.'

As usual, not everyone agreed. Former Bayern striker Luca Toni told German magazine *Sport Bild* about the time van Gaal proved to Bayern's superstars, including Dutchman Arjen Robben, Germany's Philipp Lahm and Bastian Schweinsteiger, how he was man enough to drop any of his players – and his trousers. 'I had never experienced someone like him before,' he recalled. 'I remember how he once tried to make it clear that he wasn't afraid to withdraw the so-called big names. He just dropped his trousers to show us that he had the balls to do so. Fortunately, I didn't sit front row so I didn't see anything. He's a crazy coach who doesn't know how to treat his players. Guys like him and Felix Magath are coaches from another generation and can't deal with the way players behave these days. Modern players want to communicate with their coach, but that's not possible with van Gaal. Everything goes the way he wants it to go.' At Bayern's match in Cologne the incident had not been forgotten. At various points during the game, FC Köln fans called upon van Gaal to drop his trousers. Bayern gave away its 2–0 advantage and lost 3–2. The headlines in the German papers read, 'Van Gaal loses his trousers again.'

A couple of weeks later Bayern suffered another defeat, this time beaten 3–1 by *Bundesliga* leaders Borussia Dortmund. This time, van Gaal's team was never really in the game. Dortmund were perfectly set up, and the Bayern midfield was overwhelmed. Nuri Şahin had an excellent match as he played his opposite number Bastian Schweinsteiger off the park, and the trio of Marcel Schmelzer, Sven Bender and Kevin Grosskreutz rendered Bayern's flying winger Arjen Robben redundant. There were obvious parallels with the Champions League final defeat against Inter the previous year. Bayern's wonderful possession stats (64 per cent) seemed pointless in the face of Dortmund's precise positional shifts at the back. *Süddeutsche Zeitung's* sports editor, Klaus Hoeltzenbein, summed it up nicely, saying, 'Bayern were like driftwood in a sea of yellow and black.' Blaming the defeat on individual errors, as van Gaal did, was problematic, he felt: 'A holistic system like the one presented by [Dortmund coach Jürgen] Klopp takes errors into account and includes safety measures. Van Gaal's purely offensive model is courageous, attractive but also risky and sometimes naïve because it doesn't pay enough attention to the opponents' abilities.' The win was so emphatic, so definitive, that Bayern officials and players were queuing up to congratulate the visitors for winning the championship 10 weeks early.

Misery was piled upon misery. In their next match, Bayern lost a German Cup game at home for the first time in 20 years, losing their semi-final to Schalke by a solitary goal. 'The disappointment is massive, because we've missed the chance to make a final today. If Bayern wins neither the league nor the cup, it rates as a poor season,' Bayern skipper Philipp Lahm was quoted as saying on the club's website. Having done the league and cup double the previous season, Bayern were now out of the cup and 16 points behind Dortmund in the league with 10 games left to play. Although Nerlinger said van Gaal's position was not up for discussion, van Gaal himself was all too aware of the situation as signs demanding 'Van Gaal out!' could be seen at Munich's Allianz Arena. 'I know that questions are asked when you lose two important games. That is always the case. I will just get on with my job, do as well as I can, and let the board of directors decide.'

A defeat or even a draw in the next league game, against Hannover, would have compromised Bayern's minimum expectations of playing in the Champions League next season. An unfamiliar tone of calm, resignation almost, crept into the communications of the usually flamboyant and confident manager: 'I know how things work at a top club. Sackings happen. I have not been sacked often. I have stayed with my clubs for a long time and I am proud and happy to be able to work with Bayern. If we win, then we will be third and we can still reach our goals and the world would look different again. Otherwise, I would be sorry for my colleagues here because I am near the end of my career anyway.' Van Gaal did not seem too worried about the prospect of losing his job, claiming to be 'receiving phone calls from other clubs all the time'. And he could not resist the temptation to resort to his favourite rhetorical device, speaking about himself in third person: 'It's not easy to fire van Gaal. The question who will follow is a very difficult one to answer.'

The unthinkable happened: Bayern lost 3–1 to Hannover, the first time in over 10 years that Bayern had suffered three consecutive defeats. Van Gaal's observation that 'We are all disappointed' was something of an understatement. 'The way we played today was the absolute low point of the season,' Rummenigge said afterwards. 'I am stricken – I'll make no secret of it. We're now in a situation which is very worrying for Bayern. We have to sleep on it and see how we proceed.' The defeat saw them slide to fifth in the league table. No Bayern manager could be forgiven for such a run, least of all van Gaal. 'If qualification for the Champions League is in danger, I get nervous. We have to act, not talk,' was all club president Hoeness would say on his way out of the stadium. Qualification for Europe's premier club competition was vital, and not only for financial reasons. Munich's Allianz Arena was the designated venue for the final in May 2012, and it would be unacceptable to the board for Bayern not to take part in the competition. Asked if this was the most difficult period in his professional career, van Gaal said, 'No, that was the second period at Barcelona.'

Van Gaal had started the season with considerable credit in his account. By March, the coffers looked empty and the media were certain how it would end. 'Last season Bayern and Louis van Gaal looked like a marriage made in heaven but now you feel that the divorce won't be long coming,' *Bundesliga* commentator Paul Chapman told *Deutsche Welle*. 'Last season, he tinkered with the team but he got everything right. This season he's been totally stubborn, gone his own way, and many things have gone wrong.' The *Frankfurter Allgemeine Zeitung* newspaper summed up the charge sheet, 'Van Gaal is dogmatic without a plan B ... Now that explanations for the weakness of Bayern's season [World Cup tiredness, Arjen Robben's injury] are no longer valid, he's at the centre of criticism. Why did he refuse to invest in defensive players in the summer? Why the constant positional changes? Why is he not interested in practising defensive dead-ball situations?' The positional changes in particular suggested an uncertainly on van Gaal's part: in the previous few weeks van Gaal had been moving players across the pitch like pawns on a chessboard. Several players had been playing out of position. Gustavo was not the only one to play in three different positions in one game.

Critics suggested van Gaal's reluctance to practise defence, his reliance on wingers Arjen Robben and Franck Ribéry and his insistence on possession made Bayern's game easy to read. Without 'Robbery's' presence, Bayern's attack was 'toothless, impotent and predictable', as one critic put it. Dortmund, Schalke and Hannover all exposed weaknesses in Bayern's shaky defence, frequently reshuffled under van Gaal and which was vulnerable to set pieces. For all Daniel van Buyten's and Martin Demichelis's physicality and brutal strength, the two players lacked football intelligence. Against weaker oppositions the two might overpower and outmuscle the attackers, but when they lined up against tactically astute managers and intelligent strikers their shortcomings were mercilessly exposed.

The day after the Hannover game, Louis van Gaal's future was the subject of a crisis meeting by the Bayern board. Bayern president, Uli Hoeness, the chief executive, Karl-Heinz Rummenigge, chief financial officer, Karl Hopfner, and the sporting director, Christian Nerlinger, took five and a half hours trying to find a solution to the club's conundrum. All short- and long-term measures were discussed and discarded as either impractical or undesirable. The best they could come up with was 'keep calm and carry on'. The next day it was announced that van Gaal would be allowed to stay in his job until the end of the season: 'He has certainly made mistakes,' the Bayern icon Franz Beckenbauer said, 'but he's also shown that he's a great coach. I prefer him to any emergency solutions.' The club didn't want to fire the coach due to a forthcoming Champions League game against Inter, and most German commentators seemed to agree that van Gaal was only allowed to stay on because the club could not find a new coach at such short notice. The official statement on the Bayern website read that van Gaal's contract was terminated due to 'a difference of opinion regarding the strategic direction of the club' but exactly what that 'strategic direction' was remained a mystery. For years Bayern had felt lacking in a sense of identity; van Gaal had managed to give them one, only for his vision to now be discarded.

Bastian Schweinsteiger spoke for the players when he said, 'We all want to be successful in the remaining weeks and to give [van Gaal] a fitting send-off. He has deserved it after the way we played last season when we won a lot. It is sad that we have not been getting the results recently and we are just going to have to make an extra effort since we need the points. I think it is a shame [that he is leaving] because I think that he fits in at Bayern. We are going to have to do all we can to win on Saturday. Nobody wants to play in the Europa League.' Alluding to van Gaal's decision to promote him from Bayern's second team to the first, Holger Badstuber said, 'I owe a lot to van Gaal. Without him I would not have been with the national team.' Nonetheless, Badstuber claimed that the coach had failed to strike a rapport with the players and suggested that van Gaal's demise at the Allianz Arena was partly due to his constant chopping and changing of the starting eleven: 'He didn't encourage us or inspire confidence. If you change a lot, especially in the defence, it is not beneficial or creates trust.'

Bayern's losing streak was broken by 6–0 defeat over Hamburg in their next game. Even so, a group of around 100 angry Bayern fans clashed with around 300 police officers after the match. The supporters chanted 'Executive committee out!' and 'We want to see the executive committee!' and were only prevented from rioting by the police. In the aftermath of the incident, the club's executive committee, led by chairman Rummenigge, met with a group of fans to listen to their concerns.

Van Gaal was understandably buoyed by the Hamburg win ahead of Bayern's next match: their Champions League last-16 clash at home to holders Inter Milan. The club were in a perfect position to avenge their defeat in the previous season's final: in the first leg in Italy, Bayern had come away with a 1–0 win thanks to Mario Gómez's late goal. Van Gaal had often criticised Gómez for his lack of finishing, but the softly-spoken son of Spanish immigrants was finally paying back some of the faith Bayern showed in him. The coach insisted his criticism of Gómez was misinterpreted in the German media: 'There is a misunderstanding on this subject. I always select the best possible team and, believe me, Mario plays much better this season than he did last year.' After Liverpool expressed an interest in taking Gómez on loan at the start of the season, Rummenigge had overruled van Gaal to keep the striker in Munich. 'I always believed in him,' agreed president Hoeness. 'We have waited a long time to see him play at this level for Bayern. It was pointless to think of him leaving.'

Another late goal, however, was to give Inter Milan a 3–2 win in the second leg and let the Champions League holders into the quarter-finals on the away goals rule. It was hard to take for Bayern, with the team at one stage leading 3–1 on aggregate and squandering at least two clear chances to put the result beyond doubt. Van Gaal was again angry with his team: 'We have already thrown away victory four or five times this season and we did it again today.' To rub salt into Bayern's wounds, Inter went on to lose their quarter-final to Schalke, the tenth-placed side in the *Bundesliga*, bulldozing them to a 5–2 aggregate defeat.

The criticisms of van Gaal continued. Clark Witney produced a scathing condemnation of van Gaal's management for *Goal.com*, under the title, 'Go now, Louis van Gaal – you can cause no more damage to Bayern': 'It takes tremendous constitution to overturn a 3–1 aggregate deficit. More so if it's done on the road, and in the final 30 minutes. From a Bayern perspective, the loss was a failure for the ages, one that was completely avoidable. Any international-quality side ought to be able to protect a 1–0 lead on their own home soil; history has proven such. But on Tuesday, Louis van Gaal became the second coach in Champions League history whose team failed to progress after first winning the away leg ...

'The result ultimately can be attributed to the ego that twice forced van Gaal out of Barcelona, and marred his return to Ajax. Glaring deficiencies stared him in the face in last year's final, yet he declined to request new centre-backs in the summer and in January ... He continues to neglect defence in training, and accordingly, his team defends with little more skill than a mid-table team from a lower league. Van Gaal chose to ignore his team's greatest deficiency. And on Tuesday, his Bayern got what it deserved.'

Louis van Gaal's reign at Bayern ended suddenly and ingloriously. Although he was due to quit at the end of the season, a dismal 1–1 draw at Nuremberg sealed his fate. The Bayern board held another emergency meeting after the match and took the decision to replace him immediately. A statement on the club's official website said the decision had been taken in the 'interests of the club as a whole'. It added that the draw meant Bayern had slipped back into fourth place in the *Bundesliga*, 'increasing the danger of the club failing to hit its minimum target for the season, the chance of qualifying for the UEFA Champions League'. To achieve that, Bayern needed to climb up to second to gain automatic qualification, or finish in third place to enter the final qualifying round. Rummenigge said that Bayern had been considering the decision to sack van Gaal for weeks: 'It is true we have taken a short-term decision but there has been dissatisfaction – I have to make this clear – for weeks. At the end of the day, it is the responsibility of the club to do everything we can to get third place. In terms of the decision, we simply didn't have an alternative.' Andries Jonker was placed in temporary charge until the end of the season.

One of van Gaal's controversial moves that had alienated his employers was dropping veteran goalkeeper Hans-Jörg Butt in favour of the young Thomas Kraft. It was Kraft's mistake – not the first since his promotion – that led to Nuremberg's equaliser. When the young keeper took his time with a clearance on the hour mark, he probably didn't realise that both his coach's job and his own position were on the line. He failed to clear the ball, Nuremberg scored and Bayern's bosses decided that they had had enough. Hoeness claimed van Gaal's decisions over Bayern's goalkeeping situation led to his exit: 'The whole crap started after the decision to replace Hans-Jörg in goal and replace him with Thomas Kraft. That led to complete unrest in the whole defence. The board repeatedly advised Louis van Gaal against doing that, but he went ahead regardless. He didn't learn anything from this subject. Success is one thing, fun another, but there has been no fun at this club for a long time, not amongst us [the board] and not with the players. And to say that he had the players behind him was a myth. Problems were created which were totally unnecessary and which have ripped the club to pieces. Louis van Gaal should consider what he has done.'

A more conciliatory figure, Franz Beckenbauer was moderate in his evaluation: 'The departure of van Gaal was inevitable. Unfortunately, we've been unable to keep our coach at the club until the end of the season after it became evident that he'd leave this summer. This could have worked out as we all wanted it to go. When you make the decision to say farewell to your coach, you should part company right away. I'm disappointed that van Gaal's spell at Bayern has come to an end like this. He's done a lot for this club. He won the double with Bayern and reached the Champions League final. He turned youngsters like Müller and Badstuber into the players they are now.'

On the surface, replacing van Gaal with his former assistant Andries Jonker for the last five games of the season didn't make much sense. But the move was necessary to clear the way to reinstate Butt in goal and avoid what Robben described as a 'horror scenario' – playing Europa League football the following season. Unfortunately for Munich, Robben was limited in how much he could help after being red-carded during the Nuremberg game for insulting the referee: 'I was just mad. I was frustrated and disappointed by the team and our performance. I should have let myself go in the changing room with my teammates and not on the pitch with the official. That was no example to set for fans or children. I accept full responsibility.'

So where did it all go so horribly wrong for one of the most successful teams in German football history? How much of the season's downward spiral was down to factors beyond van Gaal's control, and how much could he have prevented? Bayern made a disastrous start to the campaign and it was evident that the team was in need of some flair and conviction on the flanks. Arjen Robben and Franck Ribéry scored a phenomenal 30 goals between them the previous season from out wide, together with providing a further 18 assists. Robben had scored 23 of these goals, leading to the former Real Madrid man being named footballer of the year in Germany, only the fourth non-German to do so. The 2010–11 season was depressingly different, with both Robben and Ribéry missing the first half of the campaign with injuries. After nine games, Bayern had only scored eight league goals – the lowest tally in the entire *Bundesliga*.

It came as no surprise, then, that the team's performance improved considerably when both men returned. In mid-February, Robben netted twice as he combined with Ribéry to inspire Bayern's 4–0 win over Hoffenheim at the Allianz Arena, which moved Bayern up to third in the *Bundesliga*. 'Robbery' tore Hoffenheim to pieces and van Gaal insisted that the pair were Bayern's answer to Argentina's Messi and Spain's Xavi: 'With Robben and Ribéry, we have far more creativity,' he exuded. 'They are unbelievably important to Bayern, like Messi and Xavi for Barcelona or Ronaldo and [Mesut] Ozil for Real Madrid. We have waited six months for them to both be fit to play for us together again.' That 'waiting' certainly was part of the problem. Even so, the duo's skill and flamboyance were insufficient to sustain Bayern's upward movement because cracks elsewhere began to show. Questions arose about van Gaal's ability to motivate his players. Philipp Lahm and Bastian Schweinsteiger, to name but two, were far from their best all season.

Some alleged van Gaal's departure from the Allianz Arena was writing on the wall due to his rift with club president Hoeness. 'Mr Bayern' unleashed a tirade on van Gaal soon after the season's disappointing start, saying the coach was unable to take any advice. Not one to mince his words, the club president claimed the coach was difficult to talk to and a 'one-man show' – perhaps a strange choice of words to describe a tactician who had brought the club huge success in such a short period of time and was trying to get the undermanned team's campaign on track. Van Gaal responded, 'I am disappointed, very disappointed that my president says things like that about me. I always felt communication was one of my strong points.' Although the dispute was officially declared settled, the two men reportedly continued to have an icy relationship.

A lot was said about Bayern's defensive flaws. It seemed that every defender was underperforming. Mark van Bommel's January transfer to Milan left Bayern looking even more vulnerable at the back. In the six games after the defensive midfielder left the club, Bayern let in 11 goals. The team was middle-of-the-league in terms of goals conceded. Van Bommel might not have been everyone's cup of tea, but no one would dispute that he provided a welcome shield to any defence. Fans of the club argued an adequate replacement wasn't found: Andreas Ottl didn't have the quality of van Bommel, while the expensively acquired Luiz Gustavo found himself deployed at left-back, not the defensive midfield role which was his natural position.

It was puzzling that van Gaal decided not to strengthen key areas. Bayern's style was particularly dependent on its wingers, and Munich were unable to replace them adequately when they missed significant parts of the season. Van Gaal, too, could have used a top-quality defender. Money wasn't lacking, so why didn't van Gaal ask his bosses to loosen the purse strings? Part of the reason was his loyalty to two players he brought to the club: Edson Braafheid and Danijel Pranjić. Yet neither rewarded van Gaal for his faith. Braafheid quarrelled with the coach in the autumn and was shipped off to Hoffenheim, and Pranjić was average at best.

The other reason van Gaal decided to not to enter the transfer market was precisely the tendency that stood him in such good stead the previous season: his willingness to take a chance on young players. With Bayern's *Bundesliga* title hopes already looking remote in January, van Gaal decided to start planning for the medium term, allowing veterans Mark van Bommel and Martin Demichelis to go. His benching of keeper Hans-Jörg Butt in favour of Thomas Kraft was also part of this policy. As a means of opening up playing time for youngsters, especially ahead of the 2011–12 Champions League, this seemed a reasonable strategy. But it turned round and backfired terribly. Two mistakes by youngsters – a red card picked up by a 21-year-old defender and a botched save by a 22-year-old goalkeeper – doomed any chance of Munich salvaging the result during that fateful match in Hannover. It was the flip side of selecting youth to Müller and Badstuber's stand-out performances the previous season.

According to reports throughout the German media, van Gaal's treatment of veterans turned many of the team's key players, including Ribéry and Robben, against him. No one was thinking about the medium term any more in Munich. Rather than planning for what Bayern bosses had hoped would be a triumphant Champions League campaign ending in their own stadium, the team had to concentrate all its energy on just qualifying for the competition at all.

Earlier, van Gaal had informed the press that he intended to take a year out from football after leaving Bayern: 'I plan to have a sabbatical year starting in the summer. It is sad that I can't continue to work here but maybe it's better for the club that I am leaving. I came to Bayern because it's a top club. I love the culture, the fans, and they love me. That's why I am sad I cannot continue here.' Leading Inter 1–0 after the first-leg in Italy, van Gaal had one last chance to restore dignity this season: 'I want to leave the club with pride intact. I hope I can leave through the front door because we are talking about my honour.' Unfortunately for van Gaal, that did not happen.

VELVET REVOLUTION OR CIVIL WAR?

'This town ain't big enough for the two of us.'
Yosemite Sam to Bugs Bunny, in Bugs Bunny Rides Again.

After the ignominius end of his spell at Bayern Munich, Louis van Gaal said he was ready for a sabbatical. This year of leisure was regularly interrupted, at least for those beyond the tranquillity of the van Gaal household, by media announcements that he had been approached by clubs eager to sign him up. Juventus, Spartak Moscow, Vitesse, Feyenoord, Hamburg and Real Mallorca were all reported to have made enquiries, and van Gaal was even mentioned as the possible new national team coach of Argentina. Van Gaal, however, seemed happily unemployed and enjoying life on the sidelines. Then in September 2011 his life of freedom was interrupted by an intriguing episode involving van Gaal's long-standing rival, Johan Cruyff.

About a year earlier, Cruyff, the epitome of Ajax invincibility, had started a turnaround at the club he grew up at. In September 2010 he had sharply criticised the state of affairs at Ajax in his *De Telegraaf* column. Following lacklustre performances against a strong Real

Madrid and a weak Willem II, Cruyff expressed dismay under the headline, 'This is not Ajax any more': 'This Ajax is worse than the team Rinus Michels joined in 1965. It is a disaster everywhere – in finances, education, scouting, purchasing, and football.' He believed that the club was dominated by cronyism, and suggested that it would be better for everyone in the Ajax hierarchy to quit. The club, €22.7m in debt, was in need of a new start.

El Salvador returned. Cruyff was invited to take part in a discussion group to come up with ideas for a turnaround. Cruyff had never been someone shy to voice his opinions, especially when it concerned his footballing alma mater. So rather than have him shout from the sidelines, the powers-that-be wanted him safely between the four soundproof walls of the boardroom. Once ensconced at the club, Cruyff proceeded to set in motion what came to be known as the 'Velvet Revolution'. It wasn't a catchy name, except the revolution wasn't all that velvet. Cruyff and his fellow cohorts Frank de Boer and Dennis Bergkamp came up with a plan which included the hiring and firing at the club. Technical director Danny Blind, for one, they felt would have to go; in fact, his whole job had to go. Board member Uri Coronel expressed his displeasure over the new managerial style: 'high-handed' and 'dictatorial' were some of the kinder epithets he gave the manner in which Cruyff tried to make the board see things his way. Cruyff, disturbed by the resistance put up by the board, demanded it step down, which it did.

Coach Martin Jol was replaced by Frank de Boer, who went on to win Ajax's first *Eredivisie* title since 2004. With the first team in better shape, Cruyff's main focus was the once legendary youth academy. He introduced a new development model to be implemented by Wim Jonk and Dennis Bergkamp, with both appointed as heads of the academy over the summer. Cruyff himself took a seat on the board of commissioners beside Edgar Davids, Paul Römer, Marjan Olfers and chairman Steven ten Have, producing what was meant to be a balanced blend of two former players, a media specialist, a sports lawyer and a management consultant. Chief executive Rick van den Boog was dismissed. It was when Cruyff set about recruiting a new director to oversee the execution of his plans that the problems started.

Guus Hiddink was touted as a possible candidate, but he summed up the reasons he preferred to steer clear of the Amsterdam ArenA snake pit: 'I have seen an organisational model of the club and it frightened me how many commissions, councils and advisory boards Ajax has. I play some sport once a week with a couple of old friends who are involved in the club and there I witness the same pattern. They never agree; always things going on between the scenes, distrust and old feuds. They call it a big challenge, but I am 65 now and would like to enjoy the rest of my days in peace.'

On the pitch, Ajax had always benefited from the Amsterdam 'in-your-face' attitude. This unshakeable self-confidence had helped Ajax become one of the most successful clubs in the world and the best-supported in Holland. Off the pitch, however, this brash outspokenness could be toxic. There are a multitude of ex-players, mixed with players' agents, all of whom are more than willing to voice their opinions to the first microphone placed in front of them. In a way, Johan Cruyff and Louis van Gaal are exemplars of this do-not-take-no-for-an-answer bluster.

Cruyff suggested former winger Tscheu La Ling for the role. Ling seemed an unlikely candidate, as was quickly pointed out by Cruyff's fellow board members – he lacked managerial experience and had been out of football for well over two decades. Part of

Cruyff's peculiar attraction to Ling may have been that the Chinese-Dutch former winger shared his no-nonsense approach. One of Ling's claims to fame is that he was one of the few who had the gall to stand up to him. The 'Trivia' section on his Wikipedia entry contains this little gem: 'When Cruyff kept commenting on his billiard technique, Ling supposedly stated, "If you don't shut up, this cue will end up in your ass!"' As the search for a candidate went on, all five board members seemed to agree on Marco van Basten as a passable alternative, but his appointment fell through when Cruyff insisted on additional conditions that would limit van Basten's freedom, including an advisory committee consisting of Ling and Maarten Fontein. Negotiation was impossible. Cruyff was unrepentant, saying, 'If I want to appoint an advisory committee, I will do that.'

The Ajax board waited for Cruyff's next suggestion, which never came.

By November, Ajax had been chief executive-less since July – quite unusual for a business with a listing on the Amsterdam Stock Exchange. The board of commissioners had to act. The name they came up with came out of Ajax's own hat: Louis van Gaal. He was without a job and would not be afraid of the challenge.

Shortly before he was asked to become general director, van Gaal was invited by AZ to the away game against Ajax. In the ArenA dozens of people buttonholed the former Ajax hero: 'Employees, people of the members' council, honorary members … all were speaking about the chaos and the tumult, and saying that it was time for me to come back to help the club. Cruyff was commissioner and I didn't know exactly what was happening. But still I said that I was prepared to talk to the board of commissioners. The board told me the same things: no leadership, no communication, no structure, and certainly no co-operation in the workplace. I told the board of commissioners that as soon as the name van Gaal would be mentioned, Cruyff would literally do everything to stop that from happening.'

In order to appoint van Gaal, the Ajax hierarchy decided it needed a board meeting without Cruyff. The other members knew he would never agree to van Gaal and would leak the proposal immediately to his friend Jaap de Groot, sports editor at *De Telegraaf*, who could be trusted to mobilise Cruyff loyalists to opposition. A meeting was called when Cruyff was conveniently in Barcelona to celebrate his daughter Chantal's birthday. Van Gaal's name had not been on the agenda, only the usual innocuous heading 'Finding New Director', which had been a discussion point since the first gathering of the new commissioners. The Ajax board hired van Gaal without the foreknowledge of Cruyff – a piece of subterfuge that led to bitter and unsavoury squabbles between leading members of the Ajax hierarchy.

In the aftermath of 46 years of apartheid, South Africa needed a Truth and Reconciliation Commission to transition to a full and free democracy. Chile had its National Truth and Reconciliation Commission to come to grips with 18 years of Pinochet dictatorship. In Holland, apparently, warring factions at football clubs have a need for similar instruments of mediation; at least at Ajax they do. To improve the testy relationship between Cruyff and the four other commissioners, on 30 October a 'committee of reconciliation' had been called to life. Keje Molenaar, a member of the committee, considered the appointment of van Gaal to be an axe in the back of Cruyff. Molenaar invested much energy in the détente among the wrangling commissioners. He was quick to dispel the notion that attempts had been made to quell Cruyff's dissenting voice on the board: 'We are very happy to have Johan at Ajax. The story that we have asked him to leave the board of commissioners and become an advisor is untrue. Johan himself may decide and indicate what he wants to do.'

Ajax board chairman Ten Have insisted on having acted in the best interest of the club: 'Ajax can no longer allow itself to function this way. No special position was ever created for Cruyff. He is an extraordinary man, but nonetheless a member of the board. We gave Johan the opportunity. Four months, and no longer. During this time Cruyff proposed only one candidate: Tscheu La Ling. We did not consider him a suitable candidate. We have a crisis at Ajax. Something had to happen. In this case, it is a matter of "Louis van Gaal in" and not so much "out with Cruyff". At this point in time, van Gaal is more important for Ajax than Cruyff is.'

Cruyff, to put it mildly, was not amused: 'I do not know what I have to say. To start, I knew nothing, nothing, really. You think you are on the right road and then suddenly this happens. Legally, they all know how it works, but of course it stinks all around. Until Tuesday afternoon I was still in Amsterdam, and only then did I go back to Barcelona. It is very coincidental that the next day a meeting of the board is called. I could obviously not be there. The major shareholder must now decide what will happen. And that shareholder is Ajax itself. I would also like to know what all the coaches think. It is certainly clear that a lot of people have been taken for a ride, including myself.' He thought the van Gaal appointment did not fit his reform agenda. 'There was a plan presented to the club in March and we got the go-ahead to implement it and that is now being blocked. It's unacceptable. This should be the beginning of a new era when former players who are now coaches take the lead at Ajax.'

Edgar Davids had been the one to spearhead the effort to bring van Gaal back to Ajax. Not surprisingly, he came in for particularly strong Cruyff criticism. The former midfielder was being mentored as a youth coach by Wim Jonk, an adherent to the Cruyff style: 'So Davids wants to learn to be a coach according to my principles and is helped by Jonk, and in the meantime he signs another technical manager, who is not supported by me? Davids should know better! It's about Ajax, not about van Gaal or me. This way of operating is bad for the club. Davids approached him behind my back. They all knew, except for me! What does that tell you?' Wim Jonk responded immediately and emailed Davids to tell him that he was no longer welcome at the youth facilities of Ajax. A youth coach telling a board member not to come to the youth campus? Anywhere elsewhere in the world that might raise eyebrows, but not in Holland, not at Ajax.

As the Velvet Revolution was flaring into civil war, the odd thing was that the man at the centre of the controversy remained curiously invisible. Louis and Truus were on holiday in Asia as the battle was fought between Cruyff and his co-commissioners. Van Gaal's comments were sparse: 'What is happening right now at Ajax is terrible for the club. A situation such as this one occurring is just a great pity. It is out of the question that I become general director as long as Johan Cruyff is there; that is impossible. From my side, at least; from his side probably also.' Chairman Ten Have assured the doubters that, 'Louis immediately said he did not want to be a part of a game. Well, the four of us could give him that assurance. He added that he only wanted to do it on his terms. He did not demand strange and expensive things, just wanted firm and clear leadership. We are very happy with him. Louis is a club icon – a man who wants to work heart and soul to create the conditions for a bright future for Ajax. I think Louis loves Ajax a lot. He can calm things down, can turn circumstances to his favour, and can make Ajax great again.'

Nonetheless, part of the football-loving Netherlands was in dilemma – 'Trainer, yes, but an administrative function?' Former van Gaal agent Rob Cohen was not happy with the machinations of the board of commissioners, but fully supportive of the appointment itself. In fact, he had written a letter to Ajax a year earlier with the suggestion of making van Gaal general director, with Co Adriaanse as technical director. 'In the end, he signed at Bayern Munich. But it really is nice that it got to this point after all. This is how changeable things are in football. Only the way it was done wasn't decent. They should have informed Johan Cruyff, no matter what, even if he would not have agreed with the appointment of van Gaal. That would have been honest. This is only going to cause more shit. I think that the position of general director suits him very well. He is a football animal, completely honest and straightforward. I hope he will clean house at the club.' Cohen knew Cruyff well and built a close relationship with van Gaal. 'They really are so similar and they have the same vision. This eternal battle is really a pity. I would really like to get them back together at the table.'

The Ajax members' council asked the bickering commissioners, including Cruyff, to step down to end the bitter feud. The 24-man council chose to support neither side, saying they lost faith in any further co-operation among them. 'This board could not continue and therefore we made this choice,' members' council chairman Rob Been Jr said. 'Now we choose an interim board of three members, who will vote for the club at the shareholders meeting on 12 December and after that we will form a council of members, who will appoint a new board of commissioners. But none of the five members of the recent board will return as commissioner on the new board.' Cruyff obliged and said he would resign, if the other board members would do the same. But they didn't: 'The board will continue its work on behalf of Ajax and the stakeholders,' they announced in a written statement.

The Dutch media loved it, with the papers full of people wanting to add their two cents to the Shakespearean tragedy. On Twitter, too, it was the topic of the day. Sjaak Swart, aka Mr Ajax, said, 'Yesterday I didn't believe it, but now it is no longer a joke to me. But don't ask me. Louis van Gaal has some explaining to do.' Reporter Hugo Borst, never shy with words, and long-term item on the van Gaal blacklist, offered, 'Van Gaal is an asshole, but certainly a competent asshole. Perfect man for Ajax. Ten Have can be compared with Putin's better side. Four completed studies and a black belt in judo.' Stand-up comedians, politicians, journalists, ex-players, sports analysts, columnists and boardroom psychologists all offered their opinions. The situation became so serious that even Ajax's corporate sponsors had to take note. Adidas and shirt sponsor Aegon were both locked into long-term, multi-million euro sponsorship, but the in-fighting prompted outspoken comments from both: 'We're unhappy with the unrest within the club and we're concerned about the investments we have made,' admitted Ken Aerts, spokesman for Adidas. Similar sentiments were expressed by Aegon, with spokesman Jan Driessen admitting, 'This is not what we had in mind. We are extremely concerned.' By contrast, van Gaal's imminent return home was well received by investors. In the first minutes of trading after the news became public Ajax shares rose 3.9 per cent to €6.65. Trading volume was more than four times higher than usual – 2,000 shares compared with a daily average of 470.

The pundits and the ideologues in both camps have portrayed the stand-off as a problem of conflicting philosophies: Cruyff did not want to work with the notebook-wielding van Gaal, who himself would be unwilling to adopt someone else's technical blueprint for the development of Ajax and the club's young players. Cruyff said that 'Van Gaal has a good vision on football. But it's not mine. He wants to gel winning teams and has a militaristic way of working with his tactics. I don't. I want individuals to think for themselves and take the decision on the pitch that is best for the situation. He wants to control all these situations as a coach. I think he could make our first team successful. But we need more. We need to make the club successful, including the youth. And that means individual coaching and not straitjacket tactics. If Louis comes to Ajax, I won't be around for long. We think different about everything in life. I'm sorry, if this is what they want, it's over for me.'

Scholars to the rescue. Hille Engelsma, a professor of art theory and art history at the Hanzehogeschool in Groningen, suggested in the *Volkskrant* that an ideological marriage between van Gaal and Cruyff would produce no offspring. 'The football vision of Cruyff, as recorded in the March 2011 report "Toward Organised Chaos: On the Road to Success", is meant to bring tranquillity, continuity and progress in the long term. It seems logical to me that the new general director has some affinity with this; Louis van Gaal is not the one who comes to mind. He appears to value the game system more than the individual.' According to the art historian, the intuitive approach of Cruyff contrasts with van Gaal's more authoritarian and structured management style, as evidenced by Cruyff's commentary on the youth education programme that was in place at Ajax under van Gaal and Co Adriaanse. Cruyff said, 'I don't have anything against computers, but you judge football players intuitively and with your heart. On the basis of the criteria which are now in use at Ajax I would have failed the test. When I was 15, I could barely kick the ball 15 metres with my left, and with the right maybe 20 metres. I would not have been able to take a corner. Besides, I was physically weak and relatively slow. My two qualities were great technique and insight, which happen to be two things you can't measure with a computer.'

New head coach Frank de Boer wisely stayed above the fray. He thought that the differences in football ideologies were less than various commentators wanted the spellbound audience to believe: 'I will stay, no matter what. My future is with Ajax and I am here for Ajax. I'm not going to be involved with this battle. I respect both men and I wish they could work together. I'm sure they could, as I know their football vision is pretty similar.' When pressed who would have his preference, the man who brought him to Ajax or the man with whom he won the Champions League, De Boer tactfully responded, 'Don't ask me that. It's like asking which of my kids I prefer.'

Little is known about the precise cause of the enmity between van Gaal and Cruyff. It may be as simple as Cruyff once put it, 'We have a bad chemistry' – a conflict more of disposition than of views, more about character than management styles. The feud is long-standing, apparently irreparable and riddled with curious altercations. In 1989, for example, Cruyff hosted a Christmas dinner. Van Gaal was among the invited and enjoyed the night. Until the phone went. For Louis. It was his family, with the sad tidings that his sister had died. Van Gaal hastily left the house to be with his family. According to van Gaal's telling of the episode in his autobiography, Cruyff blamed him for not having had the character to properly thank him for the Christmas dinner before leaving. Cruyff refuted this: 'Nonsense. If van Gaal actually said this, he has Alzheimer's. Seriously, if someone thinks that of me, he lost the plot ... he probably lost the whole trilogy.'

The two first met when they were players at Ajax. Both are vocal, dominant, and cocky. You need to be when you play at Ajax, and you most definitely need to be when you want to be the playmaker. Cruyff was the pivot at Ajax, and Louis, four years his junior, was his understudy, biding his time to replace the master once he left. Van Gaal impressed in the youth system with his skills and vision but was too slow to succeed at the top. By the late 1980s Cruyff had already won the European Cup Winners' Cup as a coach with Ajax and was on his way to doing great things with Barcelona, while van Gaal was still finding his feet as assistant coach of AZ. When Cruyff left Ajax, he was adored by the fans. When Ajax head coach Beenhakker 'went home' to Real Madrid, Ajax pushed the young and self-confident van Gaal forward. It was van Gaal's second go at succeeding Cruyff and he wanted to make it count. Under his management Ajax went from ugly duckling to European royalty again. After winning national titles, the UEFA Cup and later the Champions League he eagerly told the media that 'Louis van Gaal was the most successful coach of Ajax.' Doubtless, Johan Cruyff did not agree with this characterisation.

Van Gaal's successes at Ajax coincided with Cruyff's at Barcelona. Sadly, but also typically, neither one could muster the courage to compliment or congratulate the other with his accomplishments. On the contrary, when Cruyff was asked in the mid-1990s which clubs other than Barcelona played good football he didn't mention Ajax – instead referring to Parma and Auxerre, teams that ousted Ajax from the European tournaments in earlier seasons. The intriguing similarities in their careers continued when the Cruyff reign at Barcelona ended, and, after Bobby Robson's one season, was replaced by van Gaal. Johan Cruyff had been Barcelona's longest-serving manager. With 11 trophies, he was also the club's most successful coach, until the arrival of his protégé Pep Guardiola. In his final two seasons, however, Cruyff failed to win any trophies, fell out with chairman Josep Lluís Núñez and was unceremoniously sacked. Embittered, he vowed never to coach again, an oath he suspended only 13 years later when he coached the Catalonia 'national football team' for some time. Louis van Gaal infused Barcelona with the footballing principles that Pep Guardiola's coaching would build on. But Cruyff never forgave van Gaal for taking the job he felt should be his, and criticised his rival's management of the team.

Around 2000, when Frank Rijkaard, also a Cruyff disciple, was head coach of the Dutch national team, Cruyff presented a development plan to the KNVB. When the federation picked van Gaal as Rijkaard's successor, van Gaal wiped Cruyff's plan off the table and presented his own, prescribing in fine detail how Dutch coaching should operate. After the Dutch bid for World Cup qualification ended in failure, van Gaal went and his masterplan went with him. Wherever and whenever Cruyff goes, van Gaal arrives. Or is it when and where van Gaal arrives, Cruyff goes?

After the appointment of van Gaal as technical director, Cruyff – along with 10 Ajax coaches – filed a lawsuit against Ajax NV (the name of the public company) and his four fellow commissioners. The injunction hearing at the court in the city of Haarlem was attended by pro-Cruyff Ajax youth trainers Wim Jonk, Marc Overmars and Jaap Stam. Board members Steven ten Have, Marjan Olfers,

Paul Römer and Edgar Davids claimed van Gaal's ratification was not dependent on Cruyff's approval. They insisted that van Gaal would have got the majority votes they needed despite Cruyff's disapproval. In December 2011 the court ruled against Cruyff by approving the appointment of van Gaal, but then suspended the appointment to gauge the confidence in the supervisory board of Ajax shareholders. Ajax NV and four commissioners appealed the judgement, but this procedure was lost in February 2012. In the judgement of the court, 'the appointment of managing and approving titular appointments is not valid because of serious flaws in the notification process'. The full supervisory board resigned. Ten Have and Römer vacated their seats on 13 April and soon thereafter were joined in their decision by commissioners Davids, Olfers and Cruyff. Cruyff continued his involvement with Ajax as an advisor.

The conclusion of this episode was that there was to be no Louis van Gaal at Ajax. After the dust settled, he gave a piece of his mind to the magazine *Elf Voetbal*: 'What I find most objectionable in the hoopla surrounding Ajax is that nobody took a stand against the threats to Ten Have and Sturkenboom [the interim general director until van Gaal was freed from contractual obligations at Bayern]. I didn't hear anything from *De Telegraaf*, from Cruyff, or even from the Ajax governing board. And that while their own president and director were threatened. That's really bad. This club badly needs structure, and that requires strong people. Cruyff always talks about the 14. But among them are some who are on the pitch just a few hours a week. Ajax is more than 14 coaches; it is an organisation that has more than 300 full-time employees. Another thing I noticed was that those implementing the Cruyff vision were all people who studied at the Johan Cruyff University [a sporting institute affiliated with the Hogeschool of Amsterdam]. We constantly hear that former players should run the show because they are smarter and more intelligent. But everything that has been put on paper has been done by people of the Johan Cruyff University. There is something not quite right, isn't there?

'People say that Ajax is now following the "Cruyff line". That's nonsense! There no more is a "Cruyff line" than there is a "van Gaal line". There is only an Ajax line and it has been in place for at least 25 years. I have contributed to that just as Cruyff has, with the difference that I was there longer. I have worked as coach at Ajax for nine years; Cruyff wasn't given that much time. The development of individual talent that is on everybody's lips now was discussed in the report that I wrote at Ajax in 2004. I would rather have become coach than general director. But I realised a director was badly needed at Ajax. Besides, I had been a director before and brought structure to the organisation. Cruyff was at Ajax now and I had no particular desire to start doing something with him. It wasn't my idea; I was asked. I'm not saying that the door is closed permanently. In my previous period at Ajax I once impulsively said, "I won't ever return until all the people who didn't lift a finger when I was fired as technical director are gone." Things now are up to Hennie Henrichs [chairman of the Ajax executive board], Cruyff and their cohorts. I wish them much success! We'll see what happens.'

Dutch football is not quite Middle East politics, though sometimes it provides as much room for practitioners of the fine art of conflict resolution. In the adverts for Benetton's colourful 2011 'Unhate Campaign', the pictures showed Barack Obama kissing Hu Jintao, Hugo Chávez kissing Obama and the Pope kissing an imam. Someone with access to Photoshop and too much time on his hands gave it a go with the Netherlands' duelling footballing rivals, and Internet visitors could see Johan landing a wet smooch on Louis. Unfortunately, with van Gaal and Cruyff not on speaking terms, any future collaboration between the two seems unlikely. Quite simply, Amsterdam is not big enough for both of them.

THE SECOND
COMING

'Van Gaal is the best.'

Johan Cruyff

The Dutch parliament has the idiosyncrasy of being home to a dozen or so political parties, whereas most developed nations do without such luxury and have to get by with a mere two or three. This situation roughly parallels the reality in many Dutch football teams where there are 12 distinct opinions on how to best play the game: those of the 11 players and the coach. Rarely was the celebration of such individual freedom and unbridled creativity on better display than at Euro 2012. Holland arrived in Poland and Ukraine as one of the favourites for the title, having finished runner-up to Spain at the 2010 World Cup in South Africa. The 10,000 or so fans who travelled to the team's base in Krakow, as well as those at the matches in Kharkiv, made quite an impact on the local communities, spreading the *Oranje* vibe wherever they roamed. Unfortunately, things just didn't work out on the pitch. Despite 28 attempts on goal against Denmark, somehow the team's opening game resulted in a 1–0 defeat. In the second match, Germany managed to exploit the lack of Dutch unity. The attack, midfield and defence seemed disjointed, almost mutually exclusive of one another. The team failed spectacularly. Holland did not get out of a Group B containing Germany, Denmark and Portugal, losing all three of its matches to finish at the bottom of the table.

Coach Bert van Marwijk confirmed his resignation soon after the tournament ended for Holland. The embarrassing disintegration of the national team prompted some soul-searching in the lowlands. Whoever succeeded van Marwijk, his first task would be to turn the team into a unit without room for excessive personal ambitions – such seemed the national consensus. The dramatic undoing of the team in Kharkiv showed that, more than anything, a new coach should be aware of which players were willing to put the national interest ahead of personal glory. In other words, there was need for a coach who would command respect, someone to whom even Rafael van der Vaart, Robin van Persie, Arjen Robben or Klaas-Jan Huntelaar – the so-called 'Big Four' – would submit themselves.

The shortlist of candidates included familiar names: Frank Rijkaard, Johan Cruyff, Louis van Gaal and Ronald Koeman. Given the the goal of creating unity, it surprised many that Louis van Gaal won the day, given the unfortunate conclusion of his first spell as national manager. Van Gaal had been unemployed since he was fired by Bayern in April 2011. During this coaching hiatus he had found the time to tour China and was impressed with what he saw in the country. He was also operated on five times to fix a dysfunctional hip. Despite this problem, the coach was fairly lean and in shape at 61. Fit enough for the national team, in any case. He had to set the record straight and prove that his ill-fated first tenure as *bondscoach* was an unfortunate glitch in his management CV. For their part, the team had a score to settle after Euro 2012. They were well suited, in other words.

KNVB [Dutch FA] director Bert van Oostveen was in no doubt van Gaal was the right man for the job: 'We are delighted to be working with each other. We looked for a coach with a wealth of experience and one who stood out on both a personal and professional level. Van Gaal has a proven track record nationally and internationally and we know him to be a devoted and very passionate coach. We were looking for someone of stature, with vision and a sense for innovation. You need that if you want to stay with the top of the world. Van Gaal was the first one we spoke with. We also looked for a people manager, someone who is known for his collegiality, and his personal and direct approach. You need that as well if you want to compete successfully. Finally, we wanted someone who knows the ropes and is willing to eagerly embrace the challenge. We quickly agreed on a common vision for the future and the basic assumptions. I am convinced that we are heading towards a beautiful and successful period.'

Van Gaal became manager in August 2012. The new *bondscoach* said, 'I have worked with the KNVB before and now I have been asked back. This is the challenge I have waited for.' Van Gaal is the proverbial comeback kid, a believer in second comings. He had returned as national manager just as he had done at Ajax, Barcelona and AZ: 'I came back to all my clubs. Only Bayern is left. I think it would be great if that too will still happen.' At his presentation in the KNVB press hall in Zeist, van Gaal put on his glasses and picked up a note: 'Of course, I have made a poem, which is something I know you all are waiting for. But unfortunately, the KNVB is not such an easy employer as Ajax. It's a pity, but I was not allowed to read any poetry.' He already had a clear conception of how the national team should play: 'But before I am going to speak about that, I am first going to consult with the players. I am not going to talk about the past Euro tournament [in public]. I am not judging from a distance. I do have some idea about what went wrong, but that, too, I would like to hear from the players themselves. Then we will quickly focus on the future. The KNVB wants us to make it to the semi-finals. That is a tall order, but we have to aim high. It will not be easy because at Euro 2012 we were out in the first round, and that was without Brazil and Argentina present.'

Van Gaal was joined by an Ajax-heavy support staff. He was assisted by Danny Blind, who much preferred working at the national team with van Gaal to continuing as interim technical director at Ajax without him. In *De Voetbal Trainer*, van Gaal explained his reasons for choosing Blind: 'When filling staff positions, I considered the tasks which the Dutch FA gave me. There are three: playing recognisable Dutch football according to the well-known principles of the Dutch school of football; youth has to be included; and the Dutch people have to again be able to identify with *Oranje*. It isn't, then, a surprise you end up with Danny Blind. As a top player and as team captain at Ajax he won just about anything a player can win. He has been youth trainer, assistant coach, head coach and technical director. Importantly, we have a common vision of football. That is a requirement for an assistant because otherwise there will be tensions at some point. You have to be able to jointly communicate one vision to the players. But also, importantly, we often have different opinions in matters of detail and I always need such opposition. "Yes men" are useless. On the basis of their expertise and sound arguments every staff member has to feel free to present a different viewpoint when he thinks it fits within the agreed upon framework and vision.'

In addition to Blind, van Gaal was also assisted by Patrick Kluivert: 'I know Patrick very well. He made his début at Ajax in

1994 with me; he played for me at Barcelona and also in the Dutch national team during my first period as coach there. I still am very happy with Patrick. The current generation of international players saw him play and he speaks their language. This is why Kluivert will be the coach in our staff who will communicate our vision to the players most of the time. In that area, we completely depend on Patrick. That was also a conscious choice related to the KNVB's assignment to rejuvenate the team.' Van Gaal chose further staff members he had worked with before: physical therapist Jos van Dijk and 'computer guru' Max Reckers, who took care of the video analysis; Ronald Spelbos was in charge of scouting, assisted by Edward Metgod; Hans Jorritsma stayed as team manager and Kees Jansma as media chief.

To make his already difficult task of resuscitating a team suffering from combat fatigue a bit more challenging, van Gaal also had to deal with some difficult matches, with little time to prepare for them. Media interest was huge: nearly 100 journalists were present at van Gaal's first press conference compared to 30 on average at the press conferences of Bert van Marwijk. Van Gaal's first match in charge saw Holland face Belgium in a packed Koning Boudewijn Stadium in Brussels. The entire Belgian population considered the friendly against the *diknekken* – the 'fat necks' from the north – as the match of the year. The stadium was sold out months earlier, as if it were a decisive World Cup qualification game.

The van Gaal trademark became immediately visible. The coach made clear in no uncertain terms that on his watch no one would be guaranteed a place, and that he would be the one calling the shots: 'In the Dutch national team you no longer have a *tienrittenkaart* [a 'ten-rides-ticket', a commonly-used type of ticket on Dutch transportation]. You will be evaluated every time, and I am the one making the decisions. We will be judged on the 10 [qualification] games we have. So I will try to field the best eleven whenever the team plays.' Van Gaal did not get off to the start he hoped for, however, as his team was humbled 4–2 by a revitalised Belgium: 'Despite a poor first-half performance in ball possession, we created six chances. In the second half we started well with a well-executed building game. The personal foul [of Nigel de Jong] was crucial as we were in control. Not only did we concede the equaliser but we also allowed Belgium back in the match. You can't win this way. We made so many mistakes during the last half hour. Then everything comes to a halt. In the beginning of the second half I saw the kind of play that we want to play. Is it strange that we played with many inexperienced boys at that time? [Ricardo van Rhijn, Nick Viergever, Stefan de Vrij and Martins Indi in defence.] Yes, perhaps it is. I have seen good and bad things. I can do something with that. I don't have much time because in three weeks we already play against Turkey. That's the real deal. Then we have to make a stand.'

A key touchstone for selection would be player fitness. Physical vitality was the required minimum, but van Gaal wanted more: 'When I speak of fitness, I don't mean just physical fitness. Mental fitness is at least as important. Players who are preoccupied with other things don't meet this criterion. During my first time as national coach I occasionally selected a player to let him build confidence. You can do that as club manager, but not as national coach. With *Oranje* the result is what matters every time, and at this level you can only attain your goal with 100 per cent match-fit players. No player is indispensable for a team, unless your name happens to be Messi. We don't have a player of that magnitude yet, no matter how talented some of the players may be. Maybe one of them will reach the level of Messi someday, but that is not the case right now. That is why you will have to be in top shape when you report for duty at the national team. We don't reserve time and space for players who are recovering from injury during match preparation time at the national team, just because they want to be in the group so badly.'

Van Gaal recognised that many players lacked rhythm and form. Consequently, he decided that he would not be relying on the services of veterans Rafael van der Vaart, Nigel de Jong, Gregory van der Wiel and Ibrahim Afellay. The foursome, with 240 international appearances between them, had played little during the pre-season because of various transfer sagas: 'They aren't fit. A transfer to a new club is no small affair,' judged van Gaal. Two days before the Turkey game, a radio-controlled octocopter had been spotted buzzing above the Dutch training session at the Amsterdam ArenA, a somewhat brazen attempt to film what Louis van Gaal had up his sleeve for the forthcoming match. The sight of it crashing onto the roof of the stadium seemed a satisfactory ending to this bizarre incident. The coach drily observed, 'We just have to deal with it and not allow it to affect us. We are eager to train behind closed doors, but that camera intended to work out the line-up so they can publish it in the newspaper – then the Turkey coach would also know. At Barcelona they filmed our sessions from nearby apartments – it is not how it should be, but I will not lose any sleep over it.'

The identity of the eleven facing Turkey in Amsterdam was a secret to those outside the camp, but many within it knew their role early: 'I am a coach who explains everything. I think it is important that the players are able to focus, so it is better for them to know already. If the Turkish team finds out about the line-up beforehand, so be it. The KNVB gave me a clear mission to play "Dutch school" football and with the quality of this squad that must be possible.'

Van Gaal said he preferred Klaas-Jan Huntelaar to Robin van Persie as a centre-forward against Turkey, yet added this caveat, 'That can change after one match because the team is more important than 11 Huntelaars or 11 van Persies. The competition [between players] is important. When a team already is set in stone, you lose that aspect.'

Louis van Gaal remained true to this vision. He ignored reputations and selected players who were, in his judgement, in best shape. Maarten Stekelenburg, Joris Mathijsen and Klaas-Jan Huntelaar had to be satisfied with a seat on the bench. Van Gaal surprised by preferring keeper Tim Krul, who made up the defence with novice Daryl Janmaat, Everton's Johnny Heitinga, and the inexperienced Bruno Martins Indi and Jetro Willems. Wesley Sneijder found himself back in midfield with Kevin Strootman and newcomer Jordy Clasie. The forward line consisted of Arjen Robben, Luciano Narsingh and Robin van Persie, who, after just one game, was again preferred to Huntelaar. Van Gaal understood that he was taking his chances with so much untried talent, but emphasised that the national team had lost four games in a row while relying on its trusted, original formation.

Van Gaal's guts paid dividends and Holland defeated Turkey 2–0. Even so, the head coach was not happy with the performance of some of his young players. Clasie and Janmaat were singled out for criticism, while only a significant improvement after half-time spared Martins Indi and Willems: 'Janmaat was not Janmaat. Clasie can offer a lot going forward, but he did not. That's why I changed them after the break. In the first half I was also dissatisfied with Martins Indi and Willems, but in the second half they improved handsomely. That is very impressive at that age and says a lot about those guys.' Van Gaal was pleased with a result, which was a marked improvement on the beginning of his last qualification campaign at the helm: 'Then we started badly in the ArenA with 2–2 against Ireland. Now we have a good beginning. That's wonderful. It is very important that we have won the first game; otherwise, you are immediately behind the pace. I think the public enjoyed it, you could see that from their reactions. We had many more chances than the Turks.' For all the young Dutch league players in the side, it was Arjen Robben, Robin van Persie and Wesley Sneijder who, truth be told, made the difference. Van Persie in particular fired a beautiful opening goal and offered some great movement up front.

Willem van Hanegem wrote in his column in the *Algemeen Dagblad*, 'I am mostly optimistic when it comes to the national team. I thoroughly enjoyed what I saw against Turkey. First of all, there was the result. Louis van Gaal was right to emphasise that after the match. You shouldn't allow yourself to be preoccupied with the scoresheet too often, but in my opinion that is warranted at the start of a qualification series. After a win the coach gets a reprieve to pursue his established course a bit further. You know how it is: If the team loses, all the professional critics will be complaining in unison, especially when it's van Gaal. He does not get a lot of credit from a number of people who are paid to analyse football in TV programmes. It is a bit nauseating at times, but that's just the way it is. In the match against Turkey we saw the return of the panache we lost last summer. That is, besides the 2–0 score, the biggest result on the night. Things are fun again; the chagrin is gone. That is not intended as criticism of coach Bert van Marwijk. He accomplished some good things with *Oranje*. But someone else was needed to shake things up a bit. Louis can be trusted to do exactly that, as we witnessed.'

The *bondscoach* was even more pleased with the team's next result, a 4–1 victory over Hungary in Budapest: 'In an international game, 4–1 is a fantastic result. In the second half Hungary played in a very disorganised manner, and we should really have used that better. We didn't do that against Turkey either. Although we made more goals this time, we missed too many chances. My substitutes worked out nicely, if I may say so.' Stekelenburg was impressive in Budapest – quite an accomplishment according to van Gaal: 'That boy had to process a real disappointment. But immediately after Krul couldn't go on, I could tell Stekelenburg that he would be in goal. He as well as Mathijsen conducted himself as a top sportsman. That is how it should be, but unfortunately it isn't always that way!'

Once again, it was striking that there were no less than seven *Eredivisie* players in the team. Only Maarten Stekelenburg (AS Roma), Ron Vlaar (Aston Villa), Wesley Sneijder (Inter Milan) and Robin van Persie (Manchester United) ply their trade outside of the Netherlands. Van Gaal said, 'The *Eredivisie* is of a tactically high level, and technically not bad. In this period what is most important is the team spirit. The confidence you give to your players matters most. It is all about experience. You can also have that when you are 16 or 18. I let Seedorf start when he was 16; Iniesta was 17; Xavi 18. As a club coach you can take such risks more easily. For a national coach it is much more difficult. It is a risk. When things go wrong, my head will be chopped off. Six points out of two matches, six goals for and one against. That is excellent.'

KNVB director Bert van Oostveen was happy with the new *joie de vivre* in the national team: 'I see what everyone sees: we again have a team that exudes the joy of playing football. Like everyone else I was curious to see how the start of this new term would turn out. Beware of euphoria, but I am very satisfied when, apart from the game result, we see so much vitality. This is a work in progress and is in good hands with Louis van Gaal, a man who well knows how to guide young players. The federation coach has his own selection policies, and it will stay that way. It is not the task of the KNVB to say: Johnny can play on the national team, and Jacky can't. In the preparation for this qualification sequence and in negotiations with van Gaal we did speak about the goals and style of play of the team. At the FA we wanted to see a return to the Dutch school of football. Based on that, the coach selects whomever he wants. We are happy with the way things are going. Look at the responses of the fans, of the media, and on the social networks.'

In the run-up to the – as always, charged – friendly against Germany, interest from Holland's next-door neighbours in the 'Tulip General' was so overwhelming that the KNVB organised a special press conference for the visiting media. The Germans find him in many ways the personification of Dutchness, while Dutchmen ascribe to van Gaal certain German characteristics. Dutch football historian Matty Verkamman once referred to him in jest as 'Ludwig von Gaal'. Van Gaal enjoyed pointing out that his inheritance was still visible in Germany, both at Bayern and in the national team. The so-called 4-2-3-1 concept is holding: 'They are still playing my system. Other clubs in Germany also have adopted that system, like Schalke 04 and Dortmund. The German national team started playing this way under Löw, so that is his accomplishment. They play attractive football, which is not something you can say of many other countries.' The match ended as a scoreless draw.

The bench is not only the location from which van Gaal directs team affairs; it is also one of his greatest weapons. In the friendly match against Italy in February, in an attempt to encourage competition, van Gaal fielded 10 players who had not been part of the starting eleven at the beginning of Euro 2012. Only van Persie retained his place. In doing so, van Gaal demonstrated his ambition of being able to count on an expanded squad of 30 players. A new golden rule was established that all players had to do their utmost in their domestic leagues at the weekend to stand a chance of being picked for the national team. In the almost unprecedented youthful formation, the team almost caused an upset. After ill-fated attempts in 11 previous matches, the Dutch seemed as though they would finally defeat Italy. However, the Italians managed to equalise in injury time – 1–1.

The national team travelled to Indonesia for a friendly game in Djakarta and played against China in Beijing four days later. Van Gaal said, 'Of course we are going there to earn money. But we are also going because we will be playing under similar circumstances in Brazil. It will be hot, sunny and humid in Asia, just as in Brazil during the World Cup. We will be able to find out how the players respond to each other in such conditions. Everybody wants to go. Almost nobody has been in Indonesia, so this will also be a new experience for the boys. We are also going for the development of Dutch football, especially amateur sports and the youth. Because of the economic downturn there are fewer sponsors. This way we find the right balance.' Holland earned more than 1 million euros in Indonesia and China.

It was the first Dutch game against post-colonial Indonesia. In 1938 the Dutch national eleven defeated the team of the Dutch East Indies 9–2. Upon the arrival in Djakarta the contemporary Dutch team were welcomed as heroes. Fans held up shirts emblazoned with the names of van Persie and Robben and wanted to be photographed with Louis van Gaal. A bumper crowd of over 80,000 watched Holland cut a silky swathe through the Indonesian side and record a convincing 3–0 success. Robin van Persie captained the *Oranje* for the first time: 'The coach asked me on Monday if I wanted to be captain. I said yes because it is such a great honour for me. It was not always an easy match. There was not a lot of air and it was really hot out there. We played in our own style, with an eye on the future, and all in all did pretty well,' van Persie said.

The Dutch team is never far from drama, and the rollercoaster ride of veteran Wesley Sneijder became something of a national spectacle. At 5ft 7in the attacking midfielder is certainly not of imposing stature, but what he lacks in size he makes up with expertise. He is agile, strong on the ball, and his passing range is enhanced by his ambidexterity. In addition, he has an uncanny ability to score from free kicks. Nonetheless, van Gaal was unrelenting and explained why the 29-year-old ex-captain had not been selected for a friendly game against Portugal: 'Things are not automatic, even for Sneijder. The reason he isn't on the team is that, first, he has to focus on getting fit, then he has to concentrate on getting back to form, and then I am going to compare him to what else I've got. He is not off my radar, but he does have to prove himself.'

From his side, the 93-times capped player had 'hoped for a little more credit' from his coach. Sneijder said that he'd have rather heard from van Gaal personally whether or not he had been selected. Van Gaal did not take too well to that comment: 'I spoke with him in Turkey, Hoenderloo [the Dutch team's training facility], Indonesia and China. If he still doesn't understand then that is the end of the road. He shouldn't have leaked that one sentence to the press because experienced players know what will happen when you do that. I don't like it; now I have to constantly react to this situation. That is not good. Players have to talk about their club at their club, and about the Dutch national team at the Dutch national team. That is our rule. If you are not fit, you can forget it. Wesley is on the way back, but to be really fit you need seven weeks. When we are in possession he is pretty sharp, but when we lose the ball it could be better.' The coach's door remained open, however: 'You can't ignore a fit Sneijder who is also in good form.'

On a balmy summer night in Faro, Holland seemed on their way to only their second victory in 12 meetings with Portugal. The last time they'd beaten Portugal was 1991. Defending a 1–0 lead for most of game, Holland still came up short when Cristiano Ronaldo equalised Kevin Strootman's early goal in the 87th minute. After the match van Gaal said, 'If you don't lose against Germany, Italy and Portugal, you are doing well. Still, I found this the least of those games. After the break we played poorly in possession. We could not hold on to the ball, and you could see tiredness with some of the boys. Perhaps we played better last year [when losing 4–2] against Belgium.' Arjen Robben agreed with much of van Gaal's assessment: 'This was a real test. We are certainly making headway. We have to, because at the World Cup we will be encountering opponents of Portugal's calibre.'

Louis van Gaal felt he was on course to achieve his desired end result: a full squad of fit players, able to play with each other in varying but thoroughly unified team formations. Whether or not there would be space in the final squad for veterans such as Maarten Stekelenburg, Gregory van der Wiel, Joris Mathijsen and John Heitinga, only time would tell. But Nigel de Jong was given another opportunity to prove that he was the needed controlling midfielder, or 'number 6' in van Gaal parlance: 'We are going to look how we have to play. One type number 6 is different from another type number 6. That has nothing to do with individual qualities but everything with the type of player. We will look at what is needed against a particular kind of opponent.'

In September 2013, the Netherlands travelled to Estonia for a tricky qualifying match. Van Gaal still remembered the memorable Estonia–Holland qualification match of 2001 – 'we won' (4–2) – though the coach was happy to see that the brown potholed pitch of back then had been transformed into a smooth green playing surface. Guest of honour at the Dutch training camp was Jari Litmanen, the former Ajax star now living in Estonia. Van Gaal still referred to the hardworking Finnish midfielder as his 'ideal number 10' as he tried to explain to Rafael van der Vaart, Wesley Sneijder and Adam Maher how an attacking midfielder ought to operate in a van Gaal-managed team. The match ended in a draw and van Gaal was not happy with the Dutch performance: 'If you play 2–2 against Estonia, you cannot be satisfied. Especially when you are ahead 1–0 after a few minutes and create so many chances.'

Van Gaal had predicted that, according to his 'whole person principle', Konstantin Vassiljev would be the man to watch. A few days prior to the match, the Estonian had become the proud father of a baby girl. Van Gaal was proved right: buoyed by the bliss of new parenthood, the energised midfielder scored twice, leaving Holland trailing for most of the second half: 'We were running to catch up. We had pulled everything out of the closet. It is an accomplishment that we could still generate the spirit. I substituted completely for attack; in the end, we only played with three players in the back. They did give everything. I am disappointed, not angry.' Deep into injury time, captain Robin van Persie spared Dutch blushes by engineering a penalty and converting it successfully. It was the first time the Dutch had failed to win a World Cup qualification game for eight years. After 14 wins in a row, the Dutch lost the chance to set a new world record, failing to bypass Germany's record of 16 games.

With Romania losing 2–0 at home Turkey, Holland's 2–0 defeat of Andorra saw them qualify for Brazil as group winners with two games to spare. After the match, Louis van Gaal was all smiles: 'We did a good job and have a place in the World Cup. We have to look back at the past. After the Euro tournament I had to pick up the squad and create a new team with young players. That is always difficult, certainly as it was not a good Euro tournament, which meant I had to deal with disappointed players. When you are the first team in Europe to qualify with a goal difference of plus 20 then you have done very well.'

Dutch FA boss Bert van Oostveen was also pleased: 'I congratulated everyone. The KNVB is very proud of the *bondscoach*, the staff and the players. I received many text messages from football board members all over Europe. Our team has performed terrifically, everybody thinks. I even sense some jealousy because we can already start making preparations. It gives you a little more time. On the other hand, much has already been arranged. We have our training camp in Rio. A physical therapist and a climate expert are making all the necessary arrangements there.'

Getting into World Cup mood, Louis van Gaal announced the team selection for the final qualification games, against Hungary and Turkey, wearing a flashy tie with Brazilian flags: 'I got that tie from the president of Visa. I gave a lecture for the *Stichting Spieren voor Spieren* [Muscles for Muscles Foundation] at his company, and he thought this might help me get across to our friends of the media what a great accomplishment it is that we are the first country to qualify for the World Cup. I agreed that was a pretty good idea.' Qualification might already have been achieved, but the match against Hungary in the Amsterdam ArenA was still witnessed by a capacity crowd. It was a memorable night for the Dutch, as they won 8–1. A toe injury had almost kept Robin van Persie from playing, but play he did and a hat-trick earned him the status of the Netherlands' all-time leading scorer. His tally of 41 in 80 appearances passed Patrick Kluivert's record and there were poignant sideline celebrations with the assistant coach. The crowd were enraptured by the performance and van Gaal was happy too: 'I have seen great moments. But what I enjoyed most was that everyone was prepared to play a full 90 minutes pressing. I am proud of that. The effort and the willingness was enormous. It's a difficult process to squeeze right from the start and then to sustain it. We were never able to do that yet. Against Romania at home, we managed 75 minutes at best. But now – 90 minutes. That's the way you make steps in the process towards Brazil.' On van Persie's record-breaking night, van Gaal had this to say: 'It's a great achievement, but ultimately is all about the way the team puts him in contention.'

Even Johan Cruyff was appreciative of how Holland were playing. Prior to the match, Cruyff had criticised the tendency of Dutch club teams to rotate the ball for a long time before pressing forwards. Van Gaal's selection choices indicated that the national team coach concurred. Instead of fielding Stefan de Vrij and Bruno Martins Indi he picked more attack-minded central defenders Jeffrey Bruma and Ron Vlaar, who rapidly passed to available midfielders or strikers. Van Gaal said, 'I think that Johan could see that the ball was played to the front all the time. We always found Strootman, van Persie or van der Vaart.'

Willem van Hanegem, who had only recently claimed that van Gaal had 'lost his mind' for asserting that *Eredivisie* quality could be compared to Italy's *Serie A*, was effusive in his praise of the Hungary game: 'When we don't have to perform, we usually aren't at our best. And then there was that game against the Hungarians. What a fantastic match that was! Credit is due: Louis van Gaal steadily worked his way towards this kind of performance. He rapidly processed the joy of World Cup qualification and put new pressure on his team. The coach singled out three confirmed key players – van Persie, Robben and Strootman. Everyone else has to keep fighting for a spot. That approach of van Gaal's worked very well against Hungary, so I salute him. It's a job well done because it is difficult to keep a group that has already secured a place at the World Cup finals on edge up to the threshold of the tournament. This 8–1 is a powerful statement – team-wise and individually.'

For the final qualification match, against Turkey, van Gaal changed his team in no less than five places. Turkey had everything to play for, knowing they had to win to end in second place in the group and qualify. Dirk Kuyt, who had moved from Liverpool to Istanbul club Fenerbahce in 2012, gave an insider's view of what to expect: 'The country will stand on its head. They'll do anything to make it to the play-offs. There will be some animosity in the air, but I think that will be a useful experience for our team.' He also expected that during the night before the game it would be anything but peaceful around the players' hotel: 'I don't think they'll let us get much sleep.' Even hours before kick-off there was a great atmosphere in the Sükrü Saracoglu Stadium. But within eight minutes Arjen Robben caused the Turkish din to subside. He curled a free kick from the right side past goalie Volkan Demirel into the far corner. Right after the break, the Dutch shattered whatever was left of the Turkish dreams when Dirk Kuyt passed to Wesley Sneijder, who made it 2–0. The two 'Turkish Dutch' (Sneijder was a Galatasaray player) didn't celebrate their goal and walked back with heads bowed, a display of respect which was appreciated by Turkish fans and media alike.

Holland finished with 28 points from 10 qualification games, scoring 34 and conceding just 5. It was an excellent result for a team that was falling to pieces little over a year earlier. Despite having already qualified, the two concluding matches had been played with conviction, against teams who had everything to lose. Holland rarely performed this way when they had nothing to play for. This was Louis van Gaal's accomplishment.

Van Gaal used his next two friendly games, at differing times and against non-European opponents, to simulate some of the conditions his team might be encountering in Brazil. The match against Japan was played at 1:15 p.m., with van Gaal explaining, 'I hear *Eredivisie* coaches complain about early afternoon matches, saying this does not give them enough time to get the players ready in warm-up. We can gain some experience this way, in light of the World Cup.'

The match would also be played without Robin van Persie: after a very draining first quarter of the season, the illustrious team captain was recovering at home in England. Van Gaal explained, 'After the Sunday match against Arsenal, van Persie called me and in mutual agreement we decided that he takes a break. This guy goes on and on, and because of that he really is a little frayed at the edges. Even if we would have had to play an important qualification match, I think he wouldn't have been called. What he needs most right now is rest. The boys will have to get used to the forward line being different. It will be nice to see how they will deal with that.'

Van Gaal's pre-match press conference drew a few dozen Japanese journalists and even more photographers. He obviously felt more comfortable with the deferential Asian representatives of the fourth estate than with the pig-headed European variety. Van Gaal complimented one Japanese reporter who noted that there are so many talented central defenders in Holland: 'I completely agree with you. Perhaps you could speak with some of your Dutch colleagues; they have a different view.' But he added the following caveat: 'What matters is that they execute our vision. Experience does not always mean much. You may be 30 and have participated in two World Cups, but maybe you only have experience in doing something wrong. You don't unlearn that at such a late stage. In that respect, an 18-year-old boy may have more experience of the type we are looking for.' The match ended in a 2–2 draw, leaving van Gaal unhappy: 'My strongest impressions are of the second half. We brought Japan back into the game. When you conclude the first half with a 2–0 advantage, you know that after the break you can play the same way. But then you help Japan back into the saddle, and they didn't get out again … The Japanese were able to go on for 90 minutes. But we could only play 90 minutes pressing against Hungary. How is it possible that my players aren't fit this season? I don't know, but I am dependent on the club coaches. In the run-up to the World Cup I may have three or four weeks. I do not know if that is enough or not.'

Continuing the World Cup preparations, the Dutch then played a friendly at the Amsterdam ArenA against Colombia. Guus Hiddink, in line to succeed van Gaal as national team coach after the World Cup, was a spectator at the match and was full of praise. 'I love such games; this is what I want to see. Go for broke. *Oranje* showed a real will to survive.' The match ended 0–0, with Jeremain Lens hoodwinked into committing a dumb foul and dismissed with a red card: 'It makes you wonder how many learning moments I need,' the gullible striker confessed. Van Gaal, however, was proud and very pleased with the 0–0 game: 'With 11 players we already were better, and with 10 we stayed in contention really well. I have seen a great game; perhaps the best one under my leadership. We battled to stay in the match. It was a top game. That red card of Lens was unjustified. That was more a yellow. Yet Lens should have controlled himself. That is also part of your profession. That other Colombian guy wanted to kick van der Vaart out of the match. Those things can happen in a real match. I am happy with such an opponent and proud of my team. I am going to drink a glass of wine to celebrate.'

Acclaim for the new van Gaal's performance also came from unexpected quarters. Johan Cruyff thought that Louis van Gaal was the man of the hour at the national team. Well, he did not say that in so many words. On the fourteenth anniversary of the Cruyff University he participated as a guest of honour in a 'yes-no' game, as was popularised on the Dutch TV show *Barend & Van Dorp*. To the question whether van Gaal was the best manager for the Dutch team, Cruyff replied, 'Yes'.

VAN GAAL 2.0

'There are times when I don't really think about Louis, but the other day a book, *Louis van Gaal – the Man and His Method*, fell on my desk. Van Gaal won't be pleased with these three hundred pages of information about him. He wants to carefully vet such publications, but author Maarten Meijer, who already wrote two books about Guus Hiddink and one about Dick Advocaat, did not involve Louis. His book bulges with fascinating van Gaal intelligence. While reading, you can't help but once again be drawn to the man. I enjoyed reading the book about Louis and am completely ready for his comeback.'

Johan Derksen, editor of Voetbal International.

'I am surprised.' That was Marco van Basten's reaction when he heard that Louis van Gaal had become national coach for a second time: 'But I think he is a good choice. He is an experienced coach. I am curious to see how he will manage.' When van Basten managed the national side from 2004 to 2008, van Gaal had repeatedly criticised his younger colleague's performance. This was not appreciated by the *Coaches Betaald Voetbal* (CBV), the Dutch body of professional coaches. The organisation censured van Gaal for these very public evaluations, who cancelled his membership in response.

Ronald Koeman, who had also been on the KNVB shortlist, expressed a similar sentiment. The Feyenoord trainer, who repeatedly had run-ins with van Gaal at Ajax, said to online sports magazine *NU-Sport*, 'I find the choice of the KNVB surprising. I was not available and that was true for other coaches as well. He was sixth choice, I believe. Please add "joke" to that; otherwise, that one sentence will be completely pulled out of context tomorrow!' Johan Cruyff, unsurprisingly, had not been overly enthusiastic about van Gaal's appointment: 'I can't escape the impression that decisions, which are essential for Dutch football, have been taken very rapidly by KNVB director Oostveen. Whether that is a good or bad decision will now depend on coincidences. It should not be that way. Let's hope that van Gaal will use the opportunity to settle scores in a sportsmanlike manner, and that he will also bring back the spirit to Dutch football we once had. That is, to play audacious and innovative football. Other than that, I don't want to look ahead, concerning van Gaal.'

More enthusiastic endorsements had come from other quarters. Ruud Gullit, Ronald and Frank de Boer all expressed their delight and wished the new Holland boss well via Twitter. 'Louis is the best we have,' was the response of PSV coach Dick Advocaat. 'They could not have made a better choice. That man has won just about everything. Which prizes doesn't he have to his name? He has a proven record in all areas, bar none.' The supporters' association of the national team was also happy with the appointment. Despite the unhappy ending of van Gaal's first period in charge of the team, members of the organisation have good memories of the time. Board member Theo Pauw explained, 'So far, he is the only *bondscoach* who participated in our activities. Of course, the supporters back up any coach as a matter of principle, but van Gaal is genuinely popular among the fans.'

Van Gaal intentionally did not consult his predecessor when taking the job: 'I want to make an unprejudiced start. The chemistry between players and staff depends on the people who happen to be present at a particular time. I am a very different person from Bert van Marwijk and almost all the members of my staff are new as well.' He wanted to hear the views of the players, and after his first training session with the national team set up a meeting at the *Huis ter Duin* hotel in Noordwijk, a regular haunt of Dutch national football teams, past and present. 'It was a beautiful room with a wood fire,' explained van Gaal. 'I had asked that they adjust the lighting. The chairs of the players were placed in a semi-circle, so that everybody could face each other.'

Noordwijk was not new to such Knights-of-the-Round-Table-type gatherings. In 1998, under the governance of then coach Guus Hiddink, team manager Hans Jorritsma had composed a code of conduct for members of the Dutch team. Players such as Giovanni van Bronckhorst, Phillip Cocu and Frank de Boer were required to sign the document, which was replete with rules and regulations about playing style, interaction with the media, behaviour in hotels and so on. To some it may have seemed a little over the top, but after the disastrous Euro '96 campaign it was necessary.

In my book, *Guus Hiddink – Portrait of a Supercoach*, I noted, 'After that tempestuous summer of 1996, Hiddink formulated a sort of Ten Commandments-type covenant for national team members: a code of conduct that later came to be known as the *Handvest van Noordwijk*, the "Noordwijk Manifesto". By submitting themselves to these rules, players formally committed themselves to achieving a common team goal despite having to possibly make personal sacrifices along the way. It was an insurance against another failure at a major tournament, caused by egocentrism and disunity.'

Van Gaal wisely took a leaf out of Hiddink's book when he starting preparing for the 2014 qualifying campaign. The coach stayed mum on the actual content of the fireside team talk, in which 13 players participated: 'After the European tournament it was clear there were a lot of unresolved issues. A lot of it had been broadly publicised. Everyone could read, see and hear how the relationships between certain players had been spoiled. I opened our gathering with images from a 2010 TV broadcast that summarised all that went wrong during Euro '96 under Guus Hiddink, and what he did afterwards to lead the national team into a fantastic World Cup in 1998. New rules and clear agreements about how to interact with one another played a big role in that revival. Interestingly, Patrick Kluivert appears in that programme, and he was sitting in the room with us. Then we showed fragments of the successful World Cup in South Africa and an interview with Wesley Sneijder just before Euro 2012. He said that a Dutch national team with so much quality couldn't settle for anything less than the championship. Then I asked, "So how is it possible that things went so differently?" That turned into a conversation of two hours, but I will not say anything more about it.'

At the conclusion of that discussion, van Gaal presented the players with his own manifesto: 'That naturally connected with the start of the gathering, the documentary about 1996 and 1998. Of course I had discussed the rules in advance with the other staff members. They had added some things and omitted a few others. In the end, we were able to present a version that every staff member was more or less in agreement with. These rules were also backed up with visual imagery. The discussion of the agreements about the use of headphones, for example, was preceded by the YouTube video '*Headphones* of [Belgian cable-TV football channel] Sporting Telenet, which ridicules the use of headphones by top athletes. The intention is that we check up on each other and correct anyone who doesn't abide by the agreements, whether this is a player or a staff member.'

'Relaxed and diplomatic' seemed one possible characterisation of van Gaal's demeanour on becoming national coach for the second time. Perhaps he had really changed, 133 international games after his memorable departure at the conclusion of his first stint as manager? Not so, was the immediate verdict of several press pundits-cum-amateur psychologists. Reporter Wilfred Genee told his readers in his *AD Sportwereld* column, 'He had waited for nearly 11 years for this moment, after he had said farewell in that ridiculous press conference [at Dutch FA headquarters] in Zeist – a press conference at which everyone was blamed for the failure of *Oranje* [to make it to the World Cup 2002 finals] except van Gaal himself. Eleven years later, there still was no indication that he felt responsible in any way. Nothing changed; nothing learned. Brazil is still a long way away. Again, we have a technical staff that adores him. Louis van Gaal typically surrounds himself with people who are not keen to criticise his management style. We again hear from those people who claim that van Gaal is such a kind man in daily life. Why don't we ever get to see any of that in public?'

From Germany came a slightly more measured assessment, by Rafael Buschmann, in *Der Spiegel*: '"I have not changed," [van Gaal] says before the match against the German national team. In this regard, the 61-year-old remains true to himself: Van Gaal sees the world only through his own eyes. Therefore, it was hardly surprising that the Champions League winner was at odds with the bigwigs of German football in recent weeks. Hardest hit was Uli Hoeness, the president of Bayern. For a coach, so went the message, working with

Hoeness was hardly possible. Even Germany coach Joachim Löw got the following broadside: "Great coaches must also win titles. Löw has not yet won much." Judging van Gaal by his comments, it is clear: no, he has not actually changed. His mood is just good for the moment because the Dutch team plays successfully.'

Van Gaal claimed he established the groundwork at Bayern for the club's subsequent 2012 and 2013 successes: 'I started with the system. Jupp Heynckes adopted it and Pep Guardiola adheres to the philosophy of van Gaal.' Not surprisingly, Uli Hoeness ridiculed van Gaal's sketch of recent Bayern history: 'Only Louis van Gaal can come up with something like that. Before the world existed, there was Louis. If you see things from such a perspective, you don't really know how the world works. Van Gaal cleared out the bad inheritance of his predecessor Jürgen Klinsmann for us. In doing so he partially contributed to the current development of Bayern Munich. But he cannot claim responsibility for our current success beyond that, and neither for the appointment of Guardiola. Because of his behaviour almost nobody in the world considers him a likable man, even though he has been a successful coach. Take as an example what has been happening at Ajax: letting yourself be appointed as director and then having to appear in court four weeks later. That only happens to van Gaal.' Van Gaal's claims, however, may not be as outrageous as they seemed to Hoeness. In the 22 years that van Gaal has been in management, he has won an incredible 19 trophies with the teams he has managed. But some of his achievements in football are less immediately obvious, such as his impact on Guardiola and the Barcelona of 2008–2012 that he would create. In Guillem Balague's *Pep Guardiola – Another Way of Winning*, van Gaal shares praise with the initial instigator of Barcelona's great ascent under Guardiola, Johan Cruyff. Guardiola experienced first hand how two great architects of Dutch football employed a philosophy that would eventually propel the Catalan club to unprecedented heights. Cruyff initiated the process of playing football that would define Barcelona, while Guardiola would become the man to perfect it. The van Gaal years of 1997–2000 act as a fascinating conduit between the artistic intent of Cruyff and the winning style of Guardiola. Van Gaal built on Cruyff's legacy at Barcelona, but with a detrimental determination to never be questioned over his methods. What he did was not necessarily wrong, but it was wrong for Barcelona, a point that became clear when Guardiola adapted van Gaal's stern approach when he himself took control. Guardiola, far from distancing himself from van Gaal's style, finessed with a local touch that allowed him to prosper. Guardiola's move to van Gaal's old club Bayern was predictable. Guardiola has flourished in Munich and the hard work of van Gaal and Heynckes before him offered him the perfect foundation on which to do so.

In November 2012, in the 4–0 away win against Levante, Barcelona reached a considerable milestone. When Dani Alves became injured and was replaced by Xavi Hernandez, Barcelona played with an entire team of players originating from its own youth system. At the conclusion of the game, Xavi strikingly singled out Louis van Gaal for praise: 'During his time at Barcelona he always said that the club should strive to build a team with players only from its own schooling. Now we have achieved that goal. That is a surprising and extraordinary accomplishment. Van Gaal has established the basis for that. I would like to take this opportunity to thank him for that.'

From a certain perspective, Louis van Gaal can be seen as the poster boy for the old-school, omnipotent, teacher-knows-best style of management. In this enlightened day and age, such ways are penalised, even if they appear to work. But the real problem may just be that van Gaal does not fit the current stereotype of the charismatic, smooth-talking football manager, which the media seem to be so fond of. He is out of style, and politically incorrect besides.

Columnist Sjoerd Mossou illustrates this point in *Algemeen Dagblad*, with some irony:

'It is hopelessly out of style to consider our national team coach merely a surprising and intriguing personality, who adds some colour to the world of football. Praising van Gaal for his courage, his originality and his peculiar view of football – that is something very retro, from the 1990s or so. Quite a few people think that Louis van Gaal is asking for trouble, and they've got a point. It is unmistakably true that van Gaal lacks a few vital social skills, or lacks the character to bend to whichever way the wind blows. That apparently qualifies him as someone who can be labelled "insane" assuming that one is willing to leave out everything else. For someone with a highly complex personality like Louis van Gaal, "insane" seems convenient shorthand, a useful summary. Besides, it has a potent ring to it. The other day, football pundit Johan Derksen said on national TV that Louis van Gaal is not only a "lunatic" but a "dangerous lunatic". He had come to this conclusion by observing the way the national team coach moved his mouth, or something like that. Derksen proclaimed all of this without a hint of irony. I have attached various labels to Louis van Gaal at different times but "dangerous" has never been one of them.'

Mossou's colleague, Bert Nederhof, wrote about the 'different faces of Louis van Gaal' in *Voetbal International*: 'Like others, I have some special experiences interviewing Louis van Gaal. Our first interaction took place in the early 1980s. Back then he was teacher of PE at the Don Bosco School in Amsterdam. We had made an appointment to meet at the school for an interview. To my surprise, after I asked my first question, van Gaal immediately responded with a question of his own. This applied to all my other questions as well. Consequently, our meeting did not turn into an interview, but a discussion. I had no problem with that because I had a good story in which Louis was quoted as making some striking statements. I was struck that during our conversation some students of his came by, among whom were some teenagers from the Ajax F-side, all showing a lot of respect for their teacher. Even then, van Gaal was a real leader who inspired awe among his pupils.

'In 2005 I tried to create a portrait of the man behind the manager in the series *Life Without Football*. Almost everyone who has been closely involved with van Gaal speaks about a warm and accessible man, who genuinely commiserates with the suffering of people he directly works with. Louis was willing to support my inquiry and in that process made some surprising remarks. For instance, in response to my question "cried most recently when …", he said, "When my wife died in 1994." Van Gaal became visibly emotional and thus showed his human side. As a consequence, he became much more likeable. Why can't he be a little more vulnerable during his TV and radio interviews? That would result in a much better image with all those who love football – a human being, rather than a coach who is constantly getting into arguments with journalists.' Maybe van Gaal has quietly taken such well-intentioned advice to heart.

Before the party even started, Louis van Gaal announced he would step down immediately after the 2014 World Cup. 'I took over as national coach with the ambition of going to a World Cup or a European Championship. I have never done this before and I am doing everything to make sure I can achieve it. After that I will leave. I constantly have to borrow other coaches' players and

I don't enjoy that. What I love is being with my players every day and working with them on the pitch.' Bert van Oostveen wasn't surprised that van Gaal considered the qualification series a sacrifice for the global stage in Brazil. 'If you know Louis van Gaal a little, then you will understand that it is difficult for him not to have control over a team. He does not like being dependent. But we primarily judge what is happening between the lines. Van Gaal is in the process of building a new Dutch national team for the World Cup. He managed to qualify with nine wins and one draw. That he does not always come across well in the media sometimes isn't nice for the KNVB and our image. On the other hand, it is often exaggerated by others to score points.' Van Gaal confessed to seriously thinking about ending his coaching career altogether after the World Cup: 'Except when a nice club from the Premier League expresses interest. I would consider that together with my Truusje.'

Another Dutch journalist, Willem Vissers, wrote a dissenting opinion in the *Volkskrant*: 'This is a message of the just recently established committee "Louis Must Stay". With Louis at the helm we can again believe that the 2014 World Cup will have a pleasantly orange hue. He is a quintessential team worker, and football is, despite all the Ronaldos and the Zlatans of this world, a team sport. Louis is positive, he makes players better, he selects and tries out new players, he believes in youth, he is not cynical, he works in a structured manner, he is never dull, and nowadays he even seems able to handle a little bit of criticism. He still gets angry, but not as angry as in the past. He is a little full of himself, but who cares? That also makes things more entertaining. He is genuinely proud when his players donate €50,000 to the victims of a typhoon in the Philippines. He, the family man, is sincerely happy when the girlfriend of a new player in his selection gives birth to a child, and when that player (Patrick van Aanholt) is back at training the next day, flying high with happiness. Louis' eyes are shining at such moments. We aren't quite done with Louis. Yes, you may be done, but the committee isn't. Forgive him his quirks, please. We all have them. There is no one who can lift us up the way Louis can. That's why Louis must stay, until 2016. The committee "Louis Must Stay" thanks you for your attention. End of message.' The wish of the committee, however, was not fulfilled: Guus Hiddink, it was announced, would replace Louis van Gaal after the World Cup ended. As for van Gaal, his hope for interest from a 'nice club' in the Premier League was about to come true.

THE CROWNING JEWEL – MANCHESTER UNITED

'He is a great football manager and I am happy he
joins me in the same country and the Premier League.
But more important than that, he's a great guy,
a great man, and I wish him well.'

José Mourinho

Louis van Gaal's luxury penthouse in Amsterdam is up for rent. The place is on offer on the website *Bekende Buren* for €3,000 per month, which gets you 1,335 square feet of space, five rooms, two bathrooms, a Jacuzzi and a nice view of the 'IJ', the bay that makes the north-central section of town so desirable. Amsterdam was intrigued: did this mean one of the city's favourite sons was really moving to England? For weeks, people on both sides of the North Sea were held in suspense by drawn-out negotiations between Manchester United and the coach of the Dutch national football team. The Dutch FA wasn't happy with what it considered to be a distraction on the eve the World Cup. Van Gaal indicated that it would have been nice if things had moved along 'a little quicker'.

As the rumours kept coming, the British media caught up with van Gaal at his holiday home at Vale Do Lobo – a 500-hectare luxury resort on Portugal's Algarve coast with hundreds of villas, 15 restaurants, two golf courses, a supermarket and a nightclub. Van Gaal prefers staying at the villa he owns there to spending time under the gloomy Amsterdam skies. The place is at the top end of the price scale, with a large balcony offering a sea view. It also overlooks the first green of the Ocean Golf Course, where the coach plays whenever he can. As Manchester United were casting their net to find their next manager, van Gaal was leisurely fishing his golf ball out of the water after a poor tee shot. The visiting journalists left Portugal with the thrilling news that the coach was wearing a pink shirt. Van Gaal talks when he wants to; that day he didn't.

Ed Woodward, United's executive vice-chairman, eventually confirmed what had long been expected. In a statement from the club he said, 'In Louis van Gaal we have secured the services of one of the outstanding managers in the game today. He has achieved many things in his career to date and Old Trafford provides him with a fitting stage on which to write new chapters in the Manchester United story. Everyone is very excited about this new phase in the club's history. His track record of success in winning leagues and cups across Europe throughout his career makes him the perfect choice for us. People know him as a larger than life character but I have also been extremely impressed by his intelligence, thoughtful approach to the role and his diligence. I'm looking forward to working with him.' Former United midfielder David Beckham, who came through the ranks as part of the famous 'Class of 92', offered his own endorsement: 'He has got a history of working with young players, bringing players through academy systems at places like Ajax. As a Manchester United fan and for Manchester

United as a club, to have someone like this with his pedigree can only be great. He has worked with some of the biggest and best players in the world.'

Early congratulations came from one of Manchester United's biggest rivals. Old van Gaal friend and colleague José Mourinho, now Chelsea manager, was one of the first in line. 'José was very quick,' said van Gaal. 'He immediately sent a text. He said he was was a bit jealous of my list. He even included AZ. That was beautiful.' Others on that list were of course Ajax, Barcelona and Bayern Munich. Van Gaal is clearly intent on equalling Mourinho's accomplishment of winning both *La Liga* and Premier League titles. Van had achieved the former with Barcelona and now hoped to do the latter with Manchester United.

Not all close to van Gaal's heart were as enthusiastic about his new role. If things had been up to his wife, van Gaal would have discontinued his activities in top football after the conclusion of the World Cup: 'Truus wanted me to retire. I wanted to go to England. Fortunately, it turned out to be England.' Van Gaal's eldest daughter tweeted, 'Dear MU fans, Thank you for the warm welcome. But to be clear, I will not pass any messages to my father.'

The scenario of a larger-than-life figure overshadowing those who come after him has proven to be problematic in football. The announcement that Manchester United manager Sir Alex Ferguson was retiring was worldwide news. Sir Alex's decision, after 26 years in charge, meant he relinquished his title as Europe's longest-serving coach after the final game of the Premier League campaign, his 1,500th in charge of Manchester. (That honour passed to Portadown FC coach Ronnie McFall, who was appointed six weeks after Ferguson took charge at Old Trafford. But with due respect to Northern Irish football – it is not the Premier League.)

The history of Manchester United over the last few decades is somewhat of an anomaly in the world of professional football. Unlike employees at other types of companies, those working in football are accustomed to very short periods of employment. Both players and managers generally move from club to club at very irregular intervals, often after three or two years, or even less. In the UK, tenures tend to be somewhat longer than on the continent. The two and a half decades of Sir Alex Ferguson's tenure are extraordinary not only because of their sheer length but also because of the outstanding results they yielded. His managerial journey produced two UEFA Champions League titles, the European Cup Winners' Cup, UEFA Super Cup, 13 Premier League crowns, five FA Cups and four League Cups. It would be a hard act to follow for anyone. It was an overwhelming challenge for his fellow countryman David Moyes, who had the misfortune of being elected Ferguson's successor.

When Alex Ferguson gave an emotional farewell address to Old Trafford there was a mix of celebration and apprehension in the air – 'What is next?' Twelve league defeats later, that was painfully clear. The spirit that built up over a quarter of a century was obliterated within a season. It is probably unfair to lay all the blame for the dramatic undoing of Manchester United at the feet of Moyes. Alex Ferguson had been the glue that held an ailing side together, and without the supervision of the tough Scotsman it came apart at the seams. United quickly admitted that the Moyes experiment had been the wretched failure of a good man and a decent manager floundering out of his depth.

The Dutch coach Raymond Verheijen, who worked with van Gaal as part of the national setup, was a steady critic of United's decision to install Moyes. Now a consultant with the World Football

Academy, Verheijen had worked alongside the late Gary Speed for Wales and knew the British game well. He thought United's hierarchy were rather naïve to bring in Moyes from Everton: 'You really wonder if the people who are responsible at Manchester United were actually doing their homework. I don't think it is so much the problem and responsibility of David Moyes. But if the people at United had done their homework they would never have appointed Moyes, they would have appointed someone else. When you are managing Man United you need different tactical qualities to when you are an underdog like Everton. It has to do with tactical flexibility.'

Out went Moyes, in came van Gaal. The Dutch media were enjoying themselves with comparisons between the press releases announcing the respective appointments. When Moyes was introduced, Manchester United conveyed his state of service in one succinct sentence about his time with Everton and Preston North End. When it was van Gaal's turn, the United PR department needed half of an A4 sheet to communicate his essential CV – his main successes and clubs managed. The contrast – one press release next to the other – became an instant Twitter hit.

By disposition, Louis van Gaal is a whole lot more like Sir Alex Ferguson than David Moyes is: a confident, skilful, eagle-eyed disciplinarian. He will not be daunted by the thought of having the revered Scotsman, who is 10 years his senior, evaluate his management performance on a regular basis. Ferguson has a premium seat at every United home game, and his opinions understandably continue to have weight at the club. Van Gaal commented, 'I doubtlessly will have a drink with him. We did so occasionally in the past as well. We get along quite well. In fact, I came close to being his successor once before, more than 10 years ago. This was before the World Cup of 2002. I was in contact with Manchester United through [then chief executive] Peter Kenyon. I was told that Alex Ferguson was going to retire. The moment he'd go, I'd succeed him. But, in the end, Ferguson didn't want to quit. I put a lot more pressure on myself than anyone else would ever be able to leverage on me. So I don't expect a problem with anyone, including Ferguson.' The tough-talking Dutchman will impose his own way the moment he walks through the door at the club's Carrington training complex.

That does not mean that van Gaal will either be unaware of or indifferent to local culture and customs. After initially considering his current Dutch World Cup coaching assistant Patrick Kluivert for the number two position at Manchester, he instead handed the job to United hero Ryan Giggs. It would have been unwise to have dispensed with the Welshman's services. Giggs provides a link with the past and is someone bringing in-depth experience with the inner workings of the club. Van Gaal explained that he commonly retains a coach from the previous regime: 'When I go to a new club, I always want to keep one coach from the existing staff, and that person [at Bayern] was Herman Gerland, who is still working under Pep Guardiola. I wanted to know who was coming through the youth system – and he was the man who said to me, "Müller, Badstuber and Alaba. These are the players." So I let them train with the first team, I observed them – and then I decided where they were going to play. Also, Badstuber was originally a left back and I put him as a left central defender.' Giggs showed his interest in advancing young talent when he gave first-team débuts to United youngsters James Wilson and Tom Lawrence in his penultimate game as interim coach. Whether van Gaal agrees with this preference remains to be seen, but there is no doubt that the new head coach is keen to embrace the emerging talent at Old Trafford, and that Giggs will be a huge asset in facilitating that process.

Raymond Verheijen sees van Gaal–Giggs as a win-win combination: 'Ryan Giggs knows the club so well and can give Louis van Gaal all the information he needs to make a good start at the club. He played the game for a very long time and he has worked with one of the best managers in the history of the game, Alex Ferguson; so these are extremely big plusses for Ryan Giggs. Now the question is – will he be able to transfer all that knowledge and experience to other people? The biggest problem for most of these former top players is that they have all the knowledge and experience inside them but they don't have the skills to transfer it to their players. Obviously, it's a guess from a distance, but I think he will have that ability. I make that judgement based on his personality. Van Gaal will benefit from Ryan Giggs, but I think Giggs will benefit even more from Louis van Gaal.'

Dutch newspapers reported a Ryan Giggs sighting in the Netherlands, at Hotel 'Oranje' in the Dutch national team base of Noordwijk. The meeting with Louis van Gaal was smooth and swift, and Giggs returned to England a few hours later. Giggs reportedly was hugely impressed by van Gaal and he accepted the number two role despite ongoing uncertainty over the futures of coaches and close friends Phil Neville, Nicky Butt and Paul Scholes. He said, 'I am thrilled to have the chance to serve as assistant manager. Louis van Gaal is a world-class coach and I know I will learn a lot about coaching from being able to observe and contribute at such close quarters.' In an open letter on the Manchester United website he wrote, 'I would like to take this opportunity to announce my retirement from professional football and embark upon a new and exciting chapter in my life, as assistant manager of Manchester United. I am immensely proud, honoured and fortunate to have represented the biggest club in the world 963 times and Wales 64 times. […] Today is a fantastic day for Manchester United. Louis van Gaal is a great appointment and let me begin by telling you how delighted I am to be working with someone of his calibre. His credentials are second to none and I'm positive the club will thrive under his leadership over the coming years.' Van Gaal's move of keeping on the club's hero is sure to have won the fans over. If in addition to winning prizes he will be able to turn his hugely popular assistant into the future manager of Manchester United, his legacy will be secure.

Others on the van Gaal management team are Marcel Bout and Frans Hoek. Bout is a close associate of van Gaal's and has worked alongside him during his spell with AZ. He joined van Gaal at Bayern Munich the following year as a match analyst. Bout joins as assistant coach at Manchester, specialising in opposition scouting, having previously also worked at Dutch clubs Telstar, FC Volendam and Feyenoord.

Wherever van Gaal has been, Frans Hoek has never been far behind. One of van Gaal's longest-serving and most trusted lieutenants, the former FC Volendam goalkeeper has worked at Ajax, Barcelona and Bayern Munich. He also joined van Gaal as the Holland World Cup 2014 goalkeeping coach. Hoek has written various books on the training methods of goalkeepers. His emphasis on distribution and starting attacks from the back has paid dividends and has been instrumental in the development of goalkeepers such as Victor Baia, Pepe Reina, United legend Edwin van der Sar and Barcelona's Víctor Valdés. Interestingly, Valdés' retirement from the game at Barcelona coincided with van Gaal's appointment at Manchester United. Valdés came through the club's youth system when van Gaal was in charge and said in an open letter published on Barcelona's website, 'Thank you to Louis van Gaal, for showing the courage necessary to gamble on a talent that only he could see. He began building this historic *Barça* side, which I have been privileged to be part of. My heartfelt thanks.'

Physiotherapist Jos van Dijk is another senior member of van Gaal's backroom team who has worked with him in Spain, Germany and Holland, and is trusted with full responsibility for the medical department. Video analyst Max Reckers first worked with van Gaal at AZ Alkmaar. He then followed his boss to Bayern Munich, where he spent the next two years as his chief analyst, a role he has subsequently carried out for the Dutch national team under van Gaal since 2012.

But success at Manchester United will take more than just van Gaal's confidence, know-how, vision and a great backup team. One of Moyes's complaints was that he inherited an ageing squad. Van Gaal will need a large chequebook to overhaul the team. United's seventh-place finish was their worst since the 1989–90 season. In addition, the club is out of European football entirely for the first time in 25 years. This is not only very unpleasant but also costly. Executive vice-chairman Woodward revealed that United would take a hit of more than £30 million as the price of missing out on Champions League football for the first time since 1995–96. Paradoxically, Woodward was able to console stockholders by telling them business otherwise had been brisk, with money in the bank for player acquisition: 'We will be active in the transfer market … the window is upon us and deals are being done.' The fact that there could be as much as £200 million to spend on new players may have been an additional attraction for van Gaal. If most of that money had already been spent the previous year, he might have been less motivated to take on the challenge.

Van Gaal presumably delivered his transfer wish list to Ed Woodward and is letting him get on with it while he is on World Cup business. He needs a new defence and a new midfield for a start. At the back, Nemanja Vidić and Rio Ferdinand have both gone. The two were fixtures in the Manchester central defence for 8 and 12 years respectively. Van Gaal will also need to tackle the quality deficit that has plagued the Manchester United midfield for years. Borussia Dortmund defender Mats Hummels is on the radar, as well as midfielder Marco Reus. Conversely, the name of Bayern Munich's Toni Kroos, who seemed a prospect earlier, was scrapped. Others rumoured to be on that initial wishlist included Southampton defender Luke Shaw, Barcelona midfielder Cesc Fàbregas and Paris St-Germain forward Edinson Cavani. It is no surprise that van Gaal is keen to pursue Bayern Munich's Arjen Robben, although the fleet-footed winger announced he was happy at Bayern. Who is really on the list only Louis van Gaal knows; everyone else will have to wait and see.

Uncertainty is not limited to potential new players, but also those who have been safely ensconced at Manchester United for years. Van Gaal has the well-deserved reputation of a coach who does not respect established positions. Wayne Rooney is one player who may discover that neither reputation nor a £300,000-a-week contract will leave him immune to the new coach's insistence on adhering to his vision of the game. Included in that equation is who will be captain of the first team. Rooney was due to be offered the captaincy by David Moyes before he was sacked, and he has reiterated he would like to have the job under van Gaal. But while Rooney is United's highest-paid player, van Gaal enjoys a close relationship with Robin van Persie, the club's next best-rewarded footballer. He selected him as the Holland captain and the two were seen together at some matches during van Persie's recuperation from a knee injury. Van Gaal chose to experiment with a 3-5-2 formation during Holland's friendly against Ecuador. Traditionally operating a 4-3-3 system, van Gaal was subjected to suggestions that he was overseeing the 'death of total football' by tinkering with a tried and tested formula. Although the end result was a 1–1 draw, van Persie voiced his support for van Gaal's approach after the game: 'I believe in the new system. It provides a lot of opportunities.' Rooney fans may feel that van Persie is unfairly advantaged, since van Persie is the incoming coach's countryman and understands his thinking well. They can rest assured that van Gaal is not the friend of any player, including van Persie. He is the boss and he decides based on merit.

Van Gaal described what he wants in an on-field leader: 'This is more based on characteristics, which are very important for me. I have to admire him because of his personality, his identity. My captains are very professional, but also very ambitious and honest. You can see these qualities in the captains I have chosen. Age is not important. When I moved to Barcelona, Guardiola was 27 years old. Traditionally in Spain, the captains are the eldest players. I wanted to give him responsibility and transfer my philosophy. I have to click with my captains. I told Pep, "You have to be my captain." He said, "No, no." I told him, "I choose the captain and you understand the game the way I understand the game." That's why I made him my captain. You can see what he is now.'

Who is who in the team will be worked out in due course, and it will be worked out by van Gaal and those in his inner circle. Those outside that circle may feel tempted to offer what they believe to be good advice. Take for example the reporter who stated, 'Juan Mata is a number 10, simple as that. Do not ask him to play anywhere else; do not ask him to track back. It is not part of his game. If you are going to have Mata, he has to be the focal point of the side, the playmaker. Unless van Gaal trusts him, he will have no future at the club.' We will have to wait and see about that: Mata may find himself in goal next season, if van Gaal believes that is where he belongs. Advice, no matter how ingenious and well-intentioned it may appear to the advisor, will be ignored by the coach. Those in the media should particularly take note of this, and also how they ought to approach the man in charge in general.

Immediately after van Gaal's appointment was made public, a 'Ten Point Guideline for Interviewing Van Gaal' appeared in the Dutch press, presumably for the benefit of British journalists. Indeed, such interactions have already become testy at times. After the ill-fated expedition to Portugal from which reporters returned empty-handed to the UK, they got a second chance at the Dutch national team training facility at Hoenderloo. Unfortunately, this trial was not much more successful than the previous attempt. One Dutch report of the encounter read, 'A small army of English camera crews charged towards the Veluwe [the nature area in east-central Holland where the national team training camp is based] to tug Louis van Gaal at the sleeve. "Stupid question!" The BBC reporter barely asked his first question on the gravelled path in the forests of Hoenderloo when the Dutch national team coach gives the Englishman a firm reprimand. "Stupid question!" we hear once more, loud and clear. A moment later van Gaal attempts a friendly smile, as if suddenly becoming aware of the running camera. "Sorry, but I think that is a dumb question. Don't you?" The question seemed innocent enough: What does van Gaal know about Manchester United, and what ought to be done at the club. "Manchester United is the biggest club in the world. And then you ask me whether I know about Manchester United? That's strange, isn't it? Of course I know the club well.'" This episode may well be a small foretaste of what lies ahead in media relations.

Van Gaal was given only one task at Old Trafford: 'The intention is that they return to the number one spot in the league as quickly as possible. That is where they usually were under Ferguson. The intention is that this will happen with stars and young players. That is why Manchester United ended up with me.' Van Gaal confessed that he is 'sick and tired' of being limited to national team trainings, without the possibility of shaping players, team and, yes, club football in general. Because that is what van Gaal does best – moulding the game on a daily basis. When he was linked with a role at Liverpool in 2012 following Kenny Dalglish's sacking, he said, 'My fingers are itching. I am full of fire and want to work with players.' He will get his chance at United.

Manchester United most likely will be van Gaal's final job in management. He will want to go out with a bang, knowing that this is how he will be remembered not only in Manchester but in the entire world of football. The flame still burns brightly inside one of football's most competent, creative and colourful figures.

LOUIS VAN GAAL
CURRICULUM VITAE

BORN: 8 August 1958, in Amsterdam

SCHOOLING: Attended ALO, the Academie voor Lichamelijke Opvoeding (Academy of Physical Education), in Amsterdam, 1968–73

CAREER OUTSIDE OF FOOTBALL: Teacher of physical education at the Don Bosco LTS, Lagere Technische School (Lower Technical School), in Amsterdam, 1977–88

CAREER AS PLAYER:
RKSV De Meer-Amsterdam, first team, 1969–71
Ajax, second team, 1971–73
FC Antwerp, 1973–77
Telstar-Velsen, 1977–78
Sparta-Rotterdam, 1978–86
AZ-Alkmaar, 1986–87

CAREER AS COACH:
AZ-Alkmaar, 1986–87, assistant coach
Ajax, 1987–91, assistant coach

Ajax, 1991–97, head coach

Barcelona, 1997–2000, head coach

The Netherlands national team, 2000–2002, head coach

Barcelona, 2002–03, head coach

Ajax, 2003–04, technical director

AZ Alkmaar, 2005–09, head coach

Bayern Munich, 2009–11 head coach

Netherlands national team, 2012–14, head coach

Manchester United, 2014–, manager

ACHIEVEMENTS AS COACH:

Ajax – UEFA Cup 1991–92; KNVB Cup, 1992–93; *Eredivisie* title, 1993–94, 1994–95, 1995–96; Dutch Super Cup 1993–94, 1994–95; UEFA Champions League 1994–95 (and finalists 1995–96); Intercontinental Cup 1995–96; European Super Cup 1995–96

Barcelona – *La Liga* title 1997–98, 1998–99; European Super Cup 1997–98; *Copa del Rey* 1997–98

AZ Alkmaar – *Eredivisie* title, 2008–09

Bayern Munich – *Bundesliga* title 2009–10; *DFB-Pokal* (German Cup) 2009–10; Champions League finalists 2009–10

SPECIAL HONOURS:

Ridder in de orde van Oranje-Nassau (Knight in the Order of Orange-Nassau), 1997

Rinus Michels Award, 2006–07, 2008–09

Netherlands Coach of the Year, 2009

ABOUT THE AUTHOR

Maarten Meijer spent his childhood years in the small town of Zeist in the Netherlands. After completing his school education, he travelled extensively, from Ireland to Turkey, from Finland to Spain. When Europe became a little small, he sailed a yacht across the Atlantic Ocean to the Americas. After touring the Caribbean islands, he landed in the USA. He enrolled at the State University of New York, receiving a bachelor's degree in science and a master's degree in philosophy. In 1982, he met his wife Myra, a New York City native.

In 1991, a taste for new adventure drove the family, which by then included a daughter and a son, to Russia. Maarten taught philosophy in Moscow, and again travelled widely, from Riga and the Crimea in the west to Lake Baikal and Vladivostok in the east. He received his PhD in Russian literature from Moscow State University, writing a dissertation on an old favourite, Leo Tolstoy. In Russia the family befriended Russian Koreans and Korean natives and developed a taste for kimchi and Korean hospitality.

This ultimately inspired a move to Korea in 2000. Maarten taught English at a Seoul university for several years. He is fluent in English, German, Russian, Dutch, and knows survival-French and Korean. He is the author of *What's So Good about Korea, Maarten?* (Korea, 2005), *Guus Hiddink – Going Dutch* (Australia, 2006), *Dick Advocaat – de grote droom van de Kleine Generaal* (Netherlands, 2009), *Education War* (Korea, 2009) and *Guus Hiddink – portret van een supercoach* (Netherlands, 2010). From March 2006 he has taught philosophy and ethics at a private international school in the

Korean mountains, while continuing his activities as an author, a football commentator and a social critic.

Maarten and Myra have a daughter and three sons. The second son was born in Moscow, the third in Seoul.